9|0%

D0856392

International Political Economy Series

General Editor: **Timothy M. Shaw**, Professor and Director, Institute of International Relations, The University of the West Indies, Trinidad & Tobago

Titles include:

Leslie Elliott Armijo (*editor*)
FINANCIAL GLOBALIZATION AND DEMOCRACY IN EMERGING MARKETS

Robert Boardman
THE POLITICAL ECONOMY OF NATURE
Environmental Debates and the Social Sciences

Jörn Brömmelhörster and Wolf-Christian Paes (*editors*)
THE MILITARY AS AN ECONOMIC ACTOR
Soldiers in Business

Gerard Clarke and Michael Jennings (*editor*)
DEVELOPMENT, CIVIL SOCIETY AND FAITH-BASED ORGANIZATIONS
Bridging the Sacred and the Secular

Gordon Crawford
FOREIGN AID AND POLITICAL REFORM
A Comparative Analysis of Democracy Assistance and Political Conditionality

Matt Davies
INTERNATIONAL POLITICAL ECONOMY AND MASS COMMUNICATION IN CHILE
National Intellectuals and Transnational Hegemony

Martin Doornbos
INSTITUTIONALIZING DEVELOPMENT POLICIES AND RESOURCE STRATEGIES IN EASTERN AFRICA AND INDIA
Developing Winners and Losers

Fred P. Gale
THE TROPICAL TIMBER TRADE REGIME

Meric S. Gertler and David A. Wolfe
INNOVATION AND SOCIAL LEARNING
Institutional Adaptation in an Era of Technological Change

Anne Marie Goetz and Rob Jenkins
REINVENTING ACCOUNTABILITY
Making Democracy Work for the Poor

Andrea Goldstein
MULTINATIONAL COMPANIES FROM EMERGING ECONOMIES
Composition, Conceptualization and Direction in the Global Economy

Mary Ann Haley
FREEDOM AND FINANCE
Democratization and Institutional Investors in Developing Countries

Keith M. Henderson and O. P. Dwivedi (*editors*)
BUREAUCRACY AND THE ALTERNATIVES IN WORLD PERSPECTIVES

Jomo K.S. and Shyamala Nagaraj (*editors*)
GLOBALIZATION VERSUS DEVELOPMENT

Angela W. Little
LABOURING TO LEARN
Towards a Political Economy of Plantations, People and Education in Sri Lanka

John Loxley (*editor*)
INTERDEPENDENCE, DISEQUILIBRIUM AND GROWTH
Reflections on the Political Economy of North–South Relations at the Turn of the
Century

Don D. Marshall
CARIBBEAN POLITICAL ECONOMY AT THE CROSSROADS
NAFTA AND REGIONAL DEVELOPMENTALISM

Susan M. McMillan
FOREIGN DIRECT INVESTMENT IN THREE REGIONS OF THE SOUTH AT THE END
OF THE TWENTIETH CENTURY

S. Javed Maswood
THE SOUTH IN INTERNATIONAL ECONOMIC REGIMES
Whose Globalization?

John Minns
THE POLITICS OF DEVELOPMENTALISM
The Midas States of Mexico, South Korea and Taiwan

Philip Nel
THE POLITICS OF ECONOMIC INEQUALITY IN DEVELOPING COUNTRIES

Lars Rudebeck, Olle Törnquist and Virgilio Rojas (*editors*)
DEMOCRATIZATION IN THE THIRD WORLD
Concrete Cases in Comparative and Theoretical Perspective

Benu Schneider (*editor*)
THE ROAD TO INTERNATIONAL FINANCIAL STABILITY
Are Key Financial Standards the Answer?

Howard Stein (*editor*)
ASIAN INDUSTRIALIZATION AND AFRICA
Studies in Policy Alternatives to Structural Adjustment

International Political Economy Series
Series Standing Order ISBN 0–333–71708–2 hardcover
Series Standing Order ISBN 0–333–71110–6 paperback
(*outside North America only*)

You can receive future titles in this series as they are published by placing a standing
order. Please contact your bookseller or, in case of difficulty, write to us at the address
below with your name and address, the title of the series and one of the ISBNs quoted
above.

Customer Services Department, Macmillan Distribution Ltd, Houndmills,
Basingstoke, Hampshire RG21 6XS, England

The Politics of Economic Inequality in Developing Countries

Philip Nel

Department of Politics, University of Otago, New Zealand

First published 2008 by
PALGRAVE MACMILLAN
Houndmills, Basingstoke, Hampshire RG21 6XS and
175 Fifth Avenue, New York, N.Y. 10010
Companies and representatives throughout the world

PALGRAVE MACMILLAN is the global academic imprint of the Palgrave Macmillan division of St. Martin's Press, LLC and of Palgrave Macmillan Ltd. Macmillan® is a registered trademark in the United States, United Kingdom and other countries. Palgrave is a registered trademark in the European Union and other countries.

ISBN-13: 978–0–230–53779–8 hardback
ISBN-10: 0–230–53779–0 hardback

This book is printed on paper suitable for recycling and made from fully managed and sustained forest sources. Logging, pulping and manufacturing processes are expected to conform to the environmental regulations of the country of origin.

A catalogue record for this book is available from the British Library.

A catalog record for this book is available from the Library of Congress.

10 9 8 7 6 5 4 3 2 1
17 16 15 14 13 12 11 10 09 08

Printed and bound in Great Britain by
CPI Antony Rowe, Chippenham and Eastbourne

Contents

List of Figures and Tables

Figures

Tables

Acknowledgements

A number of institutions and people have contributed to making this book possible. It started life as a research project on income inequality in Africa while I was at the University of Stellenbosch, South Africa. Subsequently, the Department of Politics at the University of Otago, New Zealand, provided a most congenial setting and financial means to expand the research focus to include developing countries in general. Most of the research for the book was done during my 2005 Alexander von Humboldt Fellowship at the Institute of Political Science, Tuebingen University, Germany. I benefited from diligent research assistance provided by Alex De Juan at Tuebingen, by Andrea Fromm at the University of Otago, and from discussions on poverty and inequality with students and staff of the University of Otago Research Cluster on Poverty, Inequality, and Development.

The book is dedicated to Dirkie, Marna, and Rudolph.

1
Introduction: Developing Countries and Odious Inequality

This is a book about the determinants and consequences of inter-personal economic inequality in low- and middle-income developing countries.[1] Interpersonal economic inequality refers to the disproportional distribution of wealth and income between individuals/households in a national unit.[2] 'Wealth', as John Stuart Mill suggested, names 'all useful or agreeable things which possess exchangeable value', including assets such as fixed and human capital.[3] 'Income', in turn, can be seen as the flow of returns on the gainful use of the assets that constitute wealth. I treat the distribution of wealth and income as the core determinants of economic inequality, and use the terms 'income/wealth inequality', 'economic inequality', and 'inequality' interchangeably.[4]

The central message of the book is that during the last decades of the twentieth century, within-country economic inequality in developing countries took on the characteristics of being *odious*. This means that economic inequality became incapacitating, impervious, and pervasive, but nevertheless avoidable. These attributes emerged not only on account of differences in *what people had and received*, but also and perhaps more fundamentally on account of big differences in *how people were, and still are treated in the global division of labour*. This makes economic inequality in developing countries an issue that calls for insight into more than the functional dynamics that determine returns to different factors of production. To understand the odiousness of economic inequality we also have to understand how political power, both on the national and the global level, is implicated in the shaping and perpetuation of structures of privilege and neglect.

1

This book explains how it came about that economic inequality in developing countries took on the attributes of odiousness, and what the consequences were/are for the countries in question. To do this, it engages with the methodology of reaching generalizations that are theoretically persuasive and empirically sound. To overcome the many data limitations that plague studies of inequality in developing countries, this book relies on a recent comprehensive and consistent dataset of estimated household inequality. The unit of analysis is the country-year, and the empirical analysis covers the period 1960 to 1999. While these pages have little to contribute to our understanding of the inequality dynamics in specific countries, they do contribute to a number of general debates about the place and role of developing countries in the global political economy during an era of great historical significance. This period not only witnessed the arrival of a large number of newly independent developing countries on the world stage, but also the re-emergence of the utopian belief that economic openness and the resultant globalization of the world economy represents an unmitigated boon for all concerned, including the poor and marginalized in developing countries.

The conceptual tool through which this book explores the politics of economic inequality in developing countries is the notion of *odious inequality*. The notion is loosely based on the idea of *radical inequality*, articulated by Thomas Pogge (2002: 198) following a suggestion by Thomas Nagel (1977). Radical economic inequality refers to a skewed distribution of income and wealth that seriously jeopardizes the well-being of those at the worst end of the distribution, and deprives these same people of both the agency and the means to escape from their predicament. I am not convinced that the term 'radical' is descriptively and normatively the right word to use in referring to distributions of this type. In the normative tradition with which I identify, 'radical' is not a term of opprobrium. 'Odious' is a more straightforward if somewhat old-fashioned term. Its usefulness stems from the fact that it resonates well with contemporary debates about social justice within and between states. In campaigns to secure debt relief for poor and heavily indebted countries, the notion of 'odious debt' has played a significant role. Odious debt, in the words of Jonathan Shafter (2007: 49), 'is sovereign debt incurred by a government lacking popular consent, utilized for no legitimate public purpose'. Dating back to the 1898 peace negotiations following the

Spanish–American War when the question was raised whether Cuba and the United States of America would be held responsible for debt incurred by Cuba's Spanish colonial masters, the principle that people cannot be held responsible for sovereign debts fraudulently incurred in their names had been mooted. The principle has recently been resurrected in the Jubilee 2000 campaign on debt cancellation, as it is argued that it is not fair that current and future generations in poor countries should be held responsible for debilitating debt arrangements entered into by unaccountable and illegitimate leaders, who often incurred these debts in the name of their nations to further their own personal financial, military, and political goals (Kremer and Jayachandran, 2003). Not passing judgement on the legal and moral desirability of whether these considerations provide sufficient reasons to cancel debts incurred in an odious manner, I wish to explore the conceptual analogy between the nature of economic inequality in developing countries and such fraudulently incurred sovereign debts.

As is the case with odious debts, inequality in developing countries *incapacitates* 'innocents', that is, people who through no fault of their own find themselves at the bottom of a highly skewed distribution of income and wealth. Due to the debilitating burdens imposed by the requirements of debt servicing, many of the heavily indebted poor countries have to slash their already meagre social, health, and education budgets, with disastrous consequences not only for their most vulnerable population cohorts but for society as a whole. Income and wealth inequality in developing countries, as we shall see, in a similar fashion incapacitates those who are already the most vulnerable in these societies. Secondly, the notion of odious debt conveys a sense of the *imperviousness* of the situation in which the victims of such debt find themselves. There are no viable courses of action available to the suffering populations on their own steam to grow or work themselves out of the predicament caused by odious debts. Similarly, again as we shall see, inequality in many developing countries is structured in such a way that it is nigh impossible for those at the extreme left-hand tail of the distribution to escape from the hardships that the distribution imposes on them. The empirical literature shows that persistent inequality imposes poverty traps on successive generations of the same households, and that it is normally beyond the means of these households to improve their lot by relying only on their own ingenuity and devices. Thirdly, the burdens imposed by the massive amounts of fraudulently incurred debt affect not only one dimension of life in the indebted societies, but *pervades* the social, economic, political, and private domains. What makes these debts particularly odious, therefore, is not only the depth of its effects on people, but also the extent of these effects. In an analogous fashion, economic inequality pervades much of public and private life in developing countries, with wide-ranging consequences for the growth and development potential of these societies. Inequality eats away at the social cohesion of these societies, which leads to chronic crime, corruption, and conflict, and undermines the conditions for political robustness, which in turn feeds back into worsening economic inequality. Finally, debts of the sort that the Jubilee 2000 campaign is so concerned about are reprehensible because their very existence points to a dereliction of duty on the part of those who have the power and the ability to prevent the debts from being incurred in the first place. While it is impossible for the innocent victims of these debts to lift themselves out of their predicament, as we have seen, it is in the power of the international society of states to prevent the granting of sovereign credit to illegitimate state rulers who exploit 'the borrowing privilege' in the name of their citizens (Pogge, 2001). The privately managed institutions of sovereign debt ratings do help to constrain unaccountable leaders from continued access to 'cheap money', but the international credit regime is nevertheless very weak when it comes to preventing odious debts from being incurred in the first place despite the fact that there are practical steps that can be taken at relatively low cost to do just that (Kremer and Jayachandran, 2003). In an analogous fashion, the excesses of inequality in developing countries point to a contradiction: While the means exist to avoid the worse aspects of inequality, these steps are neglected, both by the national leaderships of developing countries and by the rule-makers of the international society of states. Economic inequality in developing countries is odious because it is *avoidable* but nevertheless tolerated.

I have no reason to imply that it is only in developing countries that inequality of wealth and income takes on odious proportions. Recent work by Brian Barry on what he calls 'the pathologies of inequality' in high-income countries also traces the particular (re-)emergence of odious inequality in the United States of America and the United Kingdom (Barry, 2005).[5] But there are important differences between developing countries and the high-income countries of the Organization for Economic Cooperation and Development (OECD) when it comes to their respective institutional capacities to address economic inequality. For one, developing countries face a number of fiscal weaknesses that high-income countries do not (see below). More significantly, though, high-income OECD countries, as a rule, have developed the means to effect the institutional separation of the distribution of political rights and competencies from 'the overall system of inequality in society', which is a structural pre-condition for the development of robust and responsive democracies (Rueschemeyer *et al.*, 1992: 41). Developing countries, to different degrees of course, have failed to do so. One must be careful not to idealize the features of political regimes in high-income democracies, given the all too obvious threat of the corrupting influence of wealth on politics in these countries. However, because of the *institutional* insulation of the political sphere from social inequalities in high-income OECD democracies, the latter are relatively more successful than developing countries in limiting and reversing this corrupting influence. In the majority of cases, high-income OECD countries are able to institute and sustain ambitious programmes of redistribution through social spending in order to offset the effects of economic inequality (Lindert, 2004). In contrast, developing countries are char-acterized by a chronic positive correlation between the concentration of wealth and income on the one hand, and the concentration of political power on the other. The result is that even with the intro-duction of all the trappings of electoral democracy, decisive political power is not vested in the median voter, as is shown in Chapter 4. Redistributive policies, to the extent that they are instituted by polit-ical leaders in developing countries, are targeted at groups that share in the privilege of the concentration of political power and thus feed into the stabilization of patterns of authoritarian neo-patrimonialism and populism (Azam, 2001; De Ferranti *et al.*, 2004: Chapter 5). These regressive tendencies are exacerbated by the effects that flow from the place and role of developing countries in the 'open' global divi-sion of labour that has characterized the past three decades. These effects at worst entrench political rule by privileged elites on behalf of their transnational class allies, and at best restrict the capacity of progressive forces to push for fiscal reform aimed at enhanced social spending.[6] On all accounts, an era of deepening economic open-ness in which capital is more mobile than labour is not conducive to institutionalizing the separation of political competencies from the distribution of economic resources, as is all too obvious from the incomplete democratization that has characterized the political history of developing countries in recent years (Epstein *et al.*, 2006).

There are thus many reasons why we should single out developing countries for dedicated analytical attention in our attempt to understand the politics of odious economic inequality. Note, however, that the list of attributes of odious inequality mentioned above does not include a reference to the magnitude of the distributional disproportion as a determining characteristic. What makes a specific distribution of wealth and income odious is not the degree of concentration of these economic resources *per se*. An excessive degree of concentration of wealth and income may contribute to the odiousness of a specific distribution, but it is not the degree of concentration that we should be concerned about in the first place. While it is indeed the case that economic inequality in developing countries on average is much worse than in their high-income counterparts, it is not this fact as such that makes inequality odious in the former group of countries, nor does this fact taken on its own provide sufficient reason to treat developing countries as a distinct analytical category. To illustrate the point that the odiousness of a distribution does not primarily depend on the extent that it is skewed, consider what would happen if a billionaire should relocate to the modest neighbourhood in which I live in Dunedin, New Zealand. Of course the distribution of wealth and income in my neighbourhood will become much more skewed than it was before, and perhaps more skewed than in any other suburb in Dunedin. Would that make the inequality in my neighbourhood odious? Not necessarily. To qualify for this dubious honour, a specific distribution must be shown to be (a) *incapacitating* towards those at the lower end of the distribution in terms of commonly accepted standards of well-being; (b) *impervious*, that is, must make it impossible for the worst off to improve their lot through their own initiatives; (c) *pervasive* in terms of affecting a range of dimensions of human existence; and (d) must be shown to be *avoidable*. It is unlikely that the larger disproportionality of wealth and income which resulted with the relocation of the billionaire to my neighbourhood would necessarily imply that anyone is incapacitated in the sense of either a drastic and debilitating worsening of well-being or in terms of anyone being prevented to formulate and pursue whatever goals they deem to be important. In fact, the billionaire's relocation may build capacity and enlarge well-being in the neighbourhood, rather than destroy these values: For one, property values of all the residential properties in the area are likely to receive a boost, multiplying the financial assets of property owners. The fact that property values in a specific neighbourhood have increased may make it more expensive than before for prospective buyers to move into that suburb, or may push up the price that existing tenants have to pay for rental property. But as long as there are opportunities open to potential buyers to find housing of similar quality in other areas of Dunedin, as long as the occupancy rights of existing tenants are protected, and as long as there are no structural constraints on the ability of anyone in the neighbourhood to enhance their income over their lifetime so that they can eventually afford to buy expensive housing in suburbs where billionaires also want to live, the particular distribution caused by the migration of the billionaire into my neighbourhood is not incapacitating, although it is very skewed. In addition, the large degree of inequality in this example cannot be regarded as unfair/unjust, at least in terms of the well-known maximin principle of distributive justice formulated by Rawls (1971: 302): With the upward surge in property prices, the worst-off property owners in the neighbourhood are now as well off as they could possibly be.

Inequality becomes incapacitating, though, when it has the consequence of limiting or cancelling the opportunities and/or capabilities of those who find themselves at the lower end of the distribution. This is the case in most developing countries. There, income distribution is not only highly skewed, but this skewness is positively and significantly correlated with extreme forms of incapacitating deprivation. According to World Bank figures, the 20 per cent richest households in developing countries during the 1990s earned on average between 15 and 16 times more than the 20 per cent poorest households, a ratio that is three times as high as the mean for high-income countries.[7] The top 20–bottom 20 income ratio for developing countries is positively correlated, at a statistically significant level, with poverty headcount levels especially in rural areas, where the incapacitating effects of odious inequality are most evident.[8] We shall see that this positive correlation also captures a causal connection. In the words of William Easterly, 'Inequality *does* cause underdevelopment' (Easterly, 2002; italics in original).

It is important to grasp that the poor suffer deprivations not only because they earn very little, but also because they earn so much less than the rich. Relative income distribution matters. For one, the high degree of income and wealth concentrations in developing countries is closely bound to market failures that harm the poor more than any other group. One example of this, to which we shall return in Chapter 5, is that the provision of credit in developing countries is highly skewed against the poor, not only because they have no assets to secure loans, but also and perhaps predominantly because the formal providers of credit face overwhelming incentives to lend to the excessively securitized wealthy, and no incentives at all to lend to the asset-less poor who can provide no security. The result is that the poor are driven into the eager arms of the providers of what is euphemistically known as 'informal credit', but which amounts to nothing more than blatant exploitation of the vulnerability of the poor for which the victims themselves bear no responsibility.

The incapacitating effects of odious inequality are matters of life and death. In India, for example, 70 per cent of the population of more than one billion people depend on agriculture for their livelihoods. Of these 700 million rural dwellers almost 40 per cent are small-scale farmers, who farm parcels of land that on average are smaller than 0.2 hectares. In 2003, the last year for which we have reliable statistics, some 17,000 of these small-scale Indian farmers committed suicide. As is the case with social disasters of this magnitude, there are many factors behind the despair of these men: Repeated low crops due to unfavourable climatic conditions, increased competition on global markets pushing down the price of their crops; rising prices of inputs such as seeds, due to the biotechnological revolution sweeping Indian agriculture. But at the core of the malaise lies the inability of small-scale farmers to gain access to credit, that mainstay of successful agriculture in most of the advanced countries of the world: Credit to tie them and their families over for another poor season; to pay for those pest-resistant but expensive seeds peddled so successfully in India by major international pharmaceutical companies; and to get their children to school and keep them there. The formal credit market has failed these farmers spectacularly, largely because of the absence of sufficient collateral that farmers can bring to the negotiating table. Into this breach has stepped the 'informal credit market', run by moneylenders who put the squeeze on their clients when they fail to repay capital and interest on time. According to one study, 86 per cent of Indian small-scale farmers who commit suicide are heavily indebted.[9] It is considerations such as these that bring a development economist such as Debraj Ray to define economic inequality not simply as the dispersal in the distribution of wealth and income, but rather as '. . . the fundamental disparity that permits one individual certain material choices, while denying another individual those very same choices' (1998: 170). I am not sure that this definition applies to all unequal distributions of wealth and income, but it surely does to economic inequality in developing countries, which is why the adjective 'odious' is so appropriate to describe it. Odious inequality systematically favours some while simultaneously denying others, thus determining who lives and who dies, when, and under which circumstances.

The concentration of income and wealth in developing countries constitutes a form of odious inequality also because of its imperviousness. While it has been possible for some individuals among the worse-off in these societies to improve their relative and absolute positions in the distribution through a mixture of good fortune and appropriate effort, the extreme disproportions of income and wealth make it extremely difficult or impossible for the overwhelming majority of the poor in developing countries to improve their lot. Again, this is not simply due to the fact that they have so little to start with, their absolute deprivation, but because the concentration of income and wealth in hands other than their own means that they are radically disfavoured when it comes to generating collective action resources to shape public decision making that could alter the initial distribution. As Barry argues, 'an opportunity to do or obtain something exists for me if there is some course of action lying within my power such that it will lead, if I choose to take it, to my doing or obtaining the thing in question' (2005: 20). For households on the wrong end of the income and wealth distribution in developing countries, the courses of action that allow others to grow their way out of misery by using public resources to improve their stock of human capital through universal and quality education, for instance, are simply not available.

The last observation points also to the pervasiveness that characterizes odious inequality. Income and wealth are, in the words of John Rawls, primary social goods,[10] which means that major disproportions in the way in which these primary goods are distributed are bound to affect other social dimensions of our existence including, as authors as diverse as Adam Smith and Anne Phillips argue, the more intangible but perhaps most important dimension related to the recognition of our human worth by others and by ourselves.[11] More tangibly, the ease with which the concentration of income and wealth translates into the maldistribution of collective action resources such as political power and influence, and of the ability to exercise political rights, is blatantly obvious to the observer with even a cursory familiarity with politics in developing countries. Above, we noted that one of the main reasons why robust democracy is such a scarce commodity in the developing world is the inability of polities there to institutionalize the separation of social inequality and political equality. The failure to separate the distribution of economic resources from the distribution of political power and privileges constitutes one example of what Walzer would call *tyranny*, to be contrasted with complex inequality which observes the integrity and specificity of distributional patterns in different spheres of life (1983). In the context of odious inequality, income and wealth are not *only* economic resources. The inequalities that people in developing countries experience in terms of having differentiated access to preventive and palliative health, to safe, secure, and stable social and natural environments, and to the benefits that flow from the equity of legal protection, property rights, and from education and higher culture are all determined in one way or another by the distribution of income and wealth.[12]

This brings us to the last attribute of odious inequality which, analogous to the notion of odious debt, refers to a contradiction between what can be done and what in effect is done to reverse inequality and to mitigate its effects. To be deemed odious, inequality in developing countries must be shown to be *avoidable*, in a sense of the word that is implied when we say that it is possible to take steps to mitigate the effects of existing odious debts, and to prevent them from being incurred again in the future. Naturally, by exploring this analogy between odious debts and odious inequality I do not want to suggest that it is possible to 'prevent', in any strong sense of the word, economic inequality from occurring in developing countries. The determinants of economic inequality are many, as we shall see in Chapter 2, but a central role is played by economic modernization and industrialization which increases the rewards for skills-based factors more than for other factors of production. As most of the high-income OECD countries also experienced in the early phases of their modernization, rising inequality is to some extent inevitable. But as the experience of these OECD countries also indicate, there are steps that can be taken not only to contain this inevitable rise but also eventually to turn the rising tide around, giving rise to the inverted U-curve hypothesis famously formulated by Simon Kuznets some 50 years ago (1955, 1963). Kuznets points out that rising inequality was eventually turned around by a number of specific political steps taken by the early modernizers of Western Europe and its offshoots in North America and Australasia, and in Japan:

> It is scarcely an accident that legal equality, political equality, and finally economic equality were the successive goals of modern society. And more specifically, the legislative decisions – with respect to education and health services, inheritance and income taxation, social security, full employment, and economic relief either to whole groups (e.g. in farming) or to individuals – can be viewed as manifestations of the general decision to minimize economic inequalities by equalizing as much as possible economic opportunity and compensating for failures that could be debited to defects in the economic and social structures, not to the voluntary action of individuals. (1963: 66)[13]

When I claim that inequality in developing countries is avoidable, I am referring therefore to the potential that exists for these countries to emulate the example of high-income OECD countries to use legislative and other political means to contain the forces of inequality unleashed by economic modernization. Of course, it is not easy for developing countries to emulate these early welfare states. Two sets of constraints stand out: Firstly, lower income developing countries face serious fiscal and other policy constraints. Secondly, there are a number of global systemic factors that also deserve attention.

With reference to the first, developing countries notoriously have low revenue-to-GDP ratios – which reflect the poor extractive capacity of the state, the growing number of people who earn income in the informal sector and therefore pay no formal tax, widespread tax evasion, and the predominance of indirect taxes. These fiscal

weaknesses obviously place restrictions on the ability of developing countries to use the expenditure side of the budget to improve
social spending, a situation that is often made worse by the lack of
state capacity to target and implement health, education, and other
social spending programmes (Chu *et al.*, 2004; Harberger, 1998). However, these fiscal and policy weaknesses are too often exploited to
hide failures on the part of political leadership in developing countries. This becomes obvious when one compares the redistributive
lacunae in the majority of developing countries with the relative success that a handful of countries recently have had with policies to
generate and more equitably distribute human capital, through the
widespread provision of secondary education and the guaranteeing
of general access to preventive and palliative health care. Countries
as diverse in terms of income levels as Sri Lanka, Seychelles, and
Costa Rica, and the Indian state of Kerala all face fiscal constraints
to a larger or lesser degree, but this has not prevented them from
effecting a deconcentration of human capital assets amongst their
population that bodes well for curtailing the forces of economic
inequality over the medium to long term. In addition, countries such
as Argentina, Brazil, Mexico, South Africa, and the Indian states of
Kerala and West Bengal have embarked on programmes of redis-
tributing land and extending security of tenure – both rural and
urban.[14] As Bowles (2006) emphasizes, the broad development of
human assets and the redistribution of fixed assets such as land
not only improve the well-being of those who before were most
incapacitated by inequality, but also bring with it efficiency gains
that raise the welfare of a society as a whole, and thus effectively address the 'leaky buckets' syndrome of redistributive social
transfers (such as income supplements, unemployment benefits, and
non-contributory pensions) to which Arthur Okun drew attention
(1975).

   What contributes to the odiousness of inequality in many developing countries, therefore, is the all too obvious shirking of political responsibility on the part of their leaderships to emulate these
examples of progressive state-led asset redistribution. Chapter 4 will
look in more detail at the political factors that determine this
momentous, even criminal, instance of neglect, but it suffices here to
emphasize that there is a glaring discrepancy between the intensity
with which the negligent leaders of developing countries campaign

for the redistribution of resources from the rich to the poorer countries of the world, and their nonchalant attitude to the redistributive challenges within their countries. Blame is due, however, not only to these leaders. There are also factors that contribute directly to the relative inability of developing countries to avoid the harsher dimensions of odious inequality, but which are not under the sovereign control of the leaders and peoples of developing countries. These factors include the effects of the package of macroeconomic stabilization and liberalization policies that international rule-makers, such as the Treasury Departments of the major donor countries and the multilateral financial institutions, persuaded developing countries during the 1980s and 1990s to implement. While these policies, collectively referred to as the 'Washington Consensus' or 'neo-liberalism',[15] have not been an unmitigated disaster *tout court*, recent studies show that the effects of trade, capital, and labour market liberalization in particular have contributed to rising levels of inequality in many developing countries by worsening the income position of the poorest sectors of the population.[16] As Lance Taylor shows, the inflow of capital that followed capital account liberalization in particular has worsened functional income distribution by weakening the position of unskilled labour, thus offsetting whatever benefits the easing of trade restrictions according to standard trade theory should have had for unskilled labour (2004). An ever-increasing open global economy also undercuts the abilities of governments to tax or alter the returns to factors of production that are transnationally mobile, such as investment capital increasingly became during the last decades of the previous century. In view of these and other effects of the Washington Consensus, it is clear that the rule-makers of the international society of states, and all of us who do not oppose them, also bear responsibility for making the avoidable *unavoidable*, and thus contributing to the odiousness of economic inequality in developing countries. This imposes a negative duty on the international society of states, I would argue, to desist from supporting practices and norms that undercut the ability of developing countries to deal effectively with the problem of odious inequality. But the citizens of the major donors of official development assistance (ODA) also face a positive duty, namely to use whatever financial and technical means at our disposal to encourage and support efforts at asset redistribution such as those pioneered by the developing countries mentioned above.

The foregoing discussion of the various attributes of odious inequality in developing countries underlines the fact that a major precondition for being able to mitigate the extent and effects of this inequality depends on our ability to appreciate the *political* dimensions of this extreme form of economic inequality. We noted that the disproportionality of the distribution of wealth and inequality in developing countries not only incapacitates the poor in terms of reducing their potential to lead long and fulfilling lives, but also curtails their capabilities to engage in collective public action to change the preconditions for the incapacitating and impervious nature of odious inequality. We also saw how economic inequality in developing countries can pervade all domains of life, including the political. Finally, it was noted that the odiousness of economic inequality in developing countries is driven home by the absence of concerted national and international political action to ameliorate inequality and its worst consequences. These considerations justify the need for a book such as the present, which sets itself the task of exploring *the politics of economic inequality* in developing countries.

The phrase 'the politics of economic inequality' refers to two distinct analytical projects, though, and my purpose in this book is to do justice to both. To understand the difference between these two projects we should turn to the distinction that Iris Marion Young makes between two perspectives on distribution, one focusing on the nature and implications of specific distributions, and the other interrogating the social-structural conditions that give rise to the distributions in the first place.[17] In the first perspective, what Young calls 'the distributional paradigm', we are concerned about the nature and implications of specific distributional patterns considering, for instance, questions about its fairness and the effects that it has on the people involved. In the distributional paradigm, Forst (2007: 260) suggests, we ask, *What do people have?* In pursuing this question, we explore the relational politics and justice of inequality. But there is also a second, and in certain respects a more fundamental way of interrogating inequality, one that Young clearly favours. In this perspective we ask about the social-structural conditions of inequality, what Rawls calls the 'basic structure' and 'background social framework' that underpins the distribution of primary social goods in a society (Young, 2006: 91). Here, the focus falls on the power of social structures to determine the place, function, and worth of actors, be they nations, classes, or individuals.

The basic structures that are relevant in the case of economic inequality are embedded in the ways in which we organize and legitimate economic production and distribution on a national and global level. The structures of the mode of production (to use another rather old-fashioned term) define specific and differentiated roles, rights, and privileges for different nations and different groups of individuals within nations, and thus constitute specific configurations of *how people are treated* (Forst, 2007: 260). How people are treated ultimately determines what they get, and hence it is crucial to focus also on the structural features of the national and global division of labour in the latter part of the twentieth century, if we want to understand what happened to the distribution of income and wealth in developing countries during that period.

The development of new theoretical and analytical approaches dealing with distributional questions, spearheaded by Anthony Atkinson, Francois Bourguignon, Amartya Sen, and others, and the emergence of more comprehensive sets of cross-sectional and time-series data on income distribution, over the past decade have generated a remarkable boom in the literature on economic inequality.[18] The existing literature on economic inequality is nevertheless understocked when it comes to the general study of the politics of inequality in developing countries.[19] One reason for this is that studies of inequality in developing countries have largely been the exclusive domain of students of 'the economics of inequality', to use a phrase popularized by one of the foundation texts in income-distribution studies (Atkinson, 1983). The 'economics-of-inequality' tradition is rich in terms of developing parsimonious and testable explanations for trends in both the functional and inter-personal distribution of income, and the chapters of this book extensively rely on these contributions to trace and explain the evolution of inequality in developing countries.[20] However, the broader questions that this book raises – about how national political patterns and the structural power dimensions inherent in the global division of labour influence economic inequality, and how these in turn are affected by inequality – are seldom asked.[21]

The broader political perspective of this book is reflected in the sequence and contents of the chapters that follow this introduction. Chapter 2 develops an inclusive and integrated framework of analysis that helps us to explain why economic inequality in developing countries takes on such odious dimensions. Distinguishing between background and more proximate factors, and between 'outside-in' and 'inside-out' determinants of inequality, this chapter looks at how the specific mode of incorporation into the global capitalist division of labour on the basis of the initial endowments of factors of production shaped, and still shapes the formation of economic, political, and social institutions in developing countries. Against this background, the processes of economic modernization under specific global macroeconomic conditions, of household formation, and of the evolution of public policy capacity determine the relative returns that holders of different factors of production and their households receive, thus setting the trajectories of the evolution of inequality. In Chapter 3, the attention shifts to the evolution of inequality in developing countries over the period 1500 to 1999. The purposes of this chapter are, firstly, to record and use a variety of empirical data sources that have become available recently to trace the evolution of inequality levels in developing countries and, secondly, to use this rich, but largely unexplored data sources to test the empirical adequacy of the framework of analysis that is developed in Chapter 2. In view of contemporary debates about the effect of globalization on income inequality, Chapter 3 pays special attention to what we know empirically about inequality trends during the two recent periods of deep globalization, one at the end of the nineteenth century, and a second at the end of the twentieth century. While there is enough evidence to point to a general worsening of inequality in developing countries during these episodes of globalization, the relationship between economic openness and inequality is mediated by a range of determinants, especially the distribution of factors of production in individual developing countries, and the quality of their leadership and public policies. Given the importance of domestic policy regimes in determining how developing countries manage their inequality levels under the conditions created by their place and role in the global division of labour, Chapter 4 investigates the inequality effects that experiments in democratization over the last decades of the twentieth century have had in developing countries. The literature on comparative political economy is pretty unanimous in popularizing the hypothesis that democratization enables those whose income falls below the mean to shape public policies progressively. This hypothesis fares well in accounting for what happened in the Western democracies with the extension of political power to the median income earner. New sources of detailed time-series data about income distribution trends allow us to test this hypothesis in the context of developing countries. It turns out that this hypothesis is not a good guide to the dynamics of public policy making under conditions of democratization in developing countries, and that there are a number of specific political features in the overwhelming majority of developing countries that inhibit the poor voter to institute redistributive public policies to favour her and her children. Chapter 5 returns to the concerns raised in this introductory chapter about the odiousness of inequality in developing countries. Chapter 5 develops a number of hypotheses concerning the adverse effects of income inequality on the social, political, and economic well-being of societies, and tests them by using the best available data on inequality levels and trends in developing countries. The evidence generated in Chapter 5 confirms that the odious dimensions of inequality in developing societies deserve deeper and more sustained policy attention than it is currently receiving. A final chapter considers the implications of the preceding for current debates about economic inequality. This chapter concludes by suggesting a number of broad policy considerations that deserve the attention of policy-makers both on the national and the international level.

A note on data sources and country groupings

For the purposes of this book, developing countries are defined as low- and middle-income countries in terms of the World Bank's classification, that is, countries that by the end of the 1990s had a per capita income of up to US$10,065, excluding the economies in transition.[22] The latter includes countries that during the 1980s and 1990s underwent transitions from a socialist to a capitalist economic system, including the People's Republic of China. In the pages that follow reference is also made to a group of high-income countries, which include both the high-income members of the OECD and a small group of non-OECD countries, including a number of oil-rich sheikdoms.[23] While some of the chapters that follow contrast the inequality experiences of developing, transition, and high-income countries where the context demands such a distinction, most of the empirical analyses employed use information on all three groups of countries combined to cater for maximum data variability and robustness of the findings.

The biggest challenge facing students of inequality in developing countries is the question of securing reliable time-series data that capture or approximate economic inequality and how it changes over time. As noted, economic inequality is used here to refer to the disproportionate distribution of both wealth and income. Given the general absence of good quality time-series data on the distribution of wealth, most commentators on economic inequality follow the convention of using more readily available data on income distribution as an approximation for economic inequality in general. There is widespread agreement that wealth everywhere is more unequally distributed than income, and that whatever conclusions we reach about the latter would therefore apply also to the former.[24] The problem is, however, that it is notoriously difficult to find data on income inequality in developing countries that are consistently measured across time and across countries to allow for comparative and time-sensitive analyses.

Major advances were made in the 1990s by World Bank officials and their collaborators, and by researchers at the United Nations University World Institute of Development Economics Research (UNU-WIDER),[25] to collect and systematize the available data on income distribution that were available from a variety of historical and contemporary national household surveys. Despite the conceptual and methodological sophistication that went into the construction of these secondary datasets, questions remain about how reliable they are when employed in cross-national comparison and analysis, as they are based on surveys that use different concepts of 'income' (expenditure versus income proper; net versus gross), and that sometimes use the individual and sometimes the household as the unit of analysis. These inconsistencies are well known, and the compilers have introduced quality criteria and adjustment techniques that help the researcher to compensate for some of the inconsistencies. However, unaccounted-for inconsistencies and implausible observations remain, as Galbraith and Kum (2005) show, which raises doubts about the usefulness of these data sources for cross-country time-series analyses.[26] Significantly, the datasets based on the Deininger and Squire template cover developing countries sporadically and infrequently, and contain relatively few sizeable sequences of consistent data on individual developing countries.

Considerations such as these brought James K. Galbraith and his team at the University of Texas Inequality Project (UTIP) to look for ways in which one could construct a more consistent dataset with better coverage of developing countries and with longer sequences of time-series data for individual countries. They start with the credible assumptions that wages are core components of income, and that the wage differential across industries is a fundamental constituent and corollary of inter-personal and inter-household income inequality. Using wage data from the annual Industrial Statistics database of the United Nations Industrial Development Organization (UNIDO), they calculate the dispersion of manufacturing pay across industrial sectors, producing a dataset of just under 3200 observations across a sample of 156 countries, and covering the period 1963 to 1999.[27] Information from these observations is then combined with information from high quality–income inequality observations available in the Deininger and Squire dataset, plus information on the manufacturing employment share to population,[28] to calculate what Galbraith and Kum call the Estimated Household Income Inequality (EHII) dataset, in which the Gini index (0–100) is used as the summary inequality measure. All estimates are adjusted to gross household income taking into consideration income from all sources, and determining household income size before taxes are deducted and/or transfers received. The EHII dataset, although not perfect,[29] is by far the most consistent dataset on within-country inequality, and has the best coverage of developing countries of any existing inequality dataset.

Based on the availability of a range of socio-economic and political data that are used in the empirical investigations in this book, a sample of 147 countries with a total of 3052 country-year observations is constructed from the EHII dataset. Of these, 37 are high-income countries, 21 transition economies, and 89 developing countries. The developing countries are divided into six different geographic regions, namely sub-Saharan Africa (SSA) with 37 countries, the Middle East and North Africa (MENA) with 11, Latin America and the Caribbean (LAC) with 25, South Asia (SASIA) comprising of 7 states, Southeast and East Asia (SEASIA) with 5, and OCEANIA with 4 island states. Appendix A contains a list of the sample countries, while Table 3.4 in Chapter 3, p. 79 lists the regional groupings of developing countries.

This book uses the EHII data extensively in the analyses of inequality trends during the last four decades of the twentieth century, and in the empirical tests of specific hypotheses pertaining to the determinants and consequences of economic inequality during that same period. The longer time frame employed in Chapter 3 implies that we also have to use for data on within-country inequality, or reasonable approximations of it, from periods preceding 1960. The sources and composition of these data, plus all other socio-economic and political data used in this book, are discussed in the relevant endnotes. Naturally, the coverage of inequality in developing countries is sketchier in the earlier periods than what is provided for in the EHII data, but the earlier inequality data are also measured consistently enough to facilitate cross-country comparisons.

2
Explaining Odious Inequality

Odious inequality is by no means restricted to developing countries only, but during the second half of the twentieth century it became endemic to the group of low- and middle-income countries that we are focusing upon. What is it about these countries, their histories, place in the global order, and their political and economic systems that precipitated this socio-economic disaster? This chapter uses the theoretical literature on income distribution and the global division of labour to show that the level and nature of economic inequality in developing countries is a function of a number of historical and contemporary economic and political factors, namely initial factor endowments coupled with the process whereby most of the developing states were incorporated into the world capitalist system as vulnerable economic units, the processes of household formation and economic modernization, and the nature of governance within such countries. In Chapter 3, we shall turn to the empirical record concerning five centuries of inequality in developing countries in order to test the expectations and hypotheses generated by this chapter.

The challenge that we face is to arrive at an integrated understanding of the determinants of odious inequality that can complement and augment the fragmented explanations that dominate the literature on the economics of inequality. In looking for an integrated explanation we should not lose sight of the fact that national political units form part of an international division of labour, and that 'being poor' in global terms is not only a reflection of the level of economic output in a state, but also implies a high degree of vulnerability of this state in its interaction with the world system; a vulnerability that does not necessarily affect all citizens and residents equally or in the same way. Our integrated explanation must therefore focus on the fact that 'being poor' is a reflection, at least partly, of a set of power relationships, both between and within countries. Power is itself a multi-dimensional phenomenon, entailing not only disproportionate abilities to affect outcomes in one-on-one relationships, but also the ability to shape the structural conditions under which actors consider and exercise choices. Hence, in pursuing an integrated explanation for the close negative correlation between national per capita GDP level and odious income and wealth inequality, care should be taken not to emulate the example of many economics-based discussions of income distribution which ignore the dimensions of transnational power relations for the sake of cultivating parsimonious explanations (Campano and Salvatore, 2006; Chakravorty, 2006; Champernowne and Cowell, 1998; Fields, 2001; Ray, 1998).

The literature on economic inequality has not been miserly when it comes to possible explanations for why economic inequality arises to start with, why it persists at odious levels over time, and what can lead to changes in its trends. Given the abundance of explanatory factors one can easily slip into a simple adumbration of one factor after another and thus end up with a complex, lumpy, and unyielding model. Instead, this section aims at identifying the minimum of factors that can help us to tackle the *explanandum* and explain the most variance in the data at our disposal. Apart from the required level of parsimony, three further criteria also determine the construction of the model presented in this section. The first is that the model must be empirically testable, which implies that we must identify possible empirical indicators for the explanatory variables that we introduce, and that we have to find appropriate measures for these indicators. Inequality research is notorious for its empirical challenges, and the data restrictions when we deal with developing countries are well known. Nevertheless, and despite the data constraints, our explanatory model must be able to stand up to standard empirical tests.

Secondly, our explanation must be sensitive to the nature of the data that we have at our disposal. Chapter 1 indicated that the EHII income inequality dataset used in this book estimates overall gross household income, that is before-tax and before-redistributive transfer income that is derived from all sources. Furthermore, in the construction of the dataset, information on wage (pay) income plays a very important part. The nature of the information contained in the data has two implications. Firstly, the fact that wage information is so crucial implies that we have to focus on those aspects that determine the relative value of wages earned by different strata of the labour force, in particular the relative rewards which holders of certain factors of production, say skilled labour, receive in comparison to unskilled labour. The differential between skilled and unskilled labour is a crucial determinant of income inequality in developing countries. The very notion of 'a developing economy' implies an economy in which the ratio of unskilled workers to skilled labour is high, where there is a small stock of physical capital, a small gross national product, a high return on human capital, and a corresponding big difference in the wages accruing to skilled compared to unskilled labour (Ljungqvist, 1993). This feeds directly into the second implication flowing from our dataset. The pre-tax, pre-transfer nature of the data means that we can focus only on those aspects of social spending that can be shown to have a direct effect on pre-tax, pre-transfer income. As defined by Lindert (2004: 6–7), *social spending* refers to (a) public spending on education, plus (b) *social transfers* proper which include basic assistance and unemployment compensation, publicly funded pensions, public health provision, and housing subsidies. Two of these dimensions of social spending, namely public spending on education and on preventive and palliative health care, have a direct bearing on human capabilities, in particular the capabilities necessary to lead a long and productive life, and are thus of direct relevance to the analysis of how income-earning opportunities over lifetimes are distributed. As a consequence, our explanatory framework must include a focus on social spending on public education and health, that is, the use that public authorities can make of revenue to establish and fund universal or near universal public education for its citizens in an effort to redistribute productive skills and earning capacity, and to provide publicly funded health care so that the majority of citizens can put their respective earning capacities to good use. Public education and health provision in developing countries are not necessarily progressively redistributive, as it may be structured in such a way to benefit members of the urban elite more than say the children of poor rural dwellers. Nevertheless, the wide dissemination of educational opportunities and preventive health care are crucial policy dimensions of the tale that this chapter wants to tell, exactly because of the high rate of return on human capital that is such a distinguishing feature of developing countries.

The final criterion that our model must meet is that the explanatory factors considered must reflect both an 'inside-out' and an 'outside-in' mode of analysis. It makes a difference whether we restrict ourselves to understanding economic inequality as only the result of a set of national, natural, institutional, and policy idiosyncrasies (what can be called the 'inside-out' mode of analysis). Instead, the approach followed here is one that complements this inside-out analytical mode with an 'outside-in' focus. By that I mean an analytical approach that makes room explicitly for the vulnerabilities that result from the specific way in which an economy was/is being incorporated into the structures of the world capitalist system with its specific norms and institutions, and how these vulnerabilities shape the domestic institutions and decisions that affect the distribution of wealth and income within that economy.

The outline of an explanatory framework that meets all of the requirements set out above is sketched in Figure 2.1. The model on which it is based makes use of simplifying assumptions given our purpose to arrive at a general and parsimonious explanation of why certain countries are more unequal than others. Nevertheless, the model aims at being 'inclusive' in that it tries to accommodate not only economic factors, but also the political and social context within which inequality develops and stabilizes. Importantly, the model makes provision not only for the effect of domestic factors ('inside-out' determinants), but also for the effects of the role and position of a state in the world economic system. The explanatory framework assumes the presence of feedback loops and circular causality, although all of these dynamics are not necessarily graphically depicted. As indicated, the main focus of the explanatory story that follows is the 89 states that constitute the group of developing countries in our sample.

The model captured in Figure 2.1 is based on the assumption that at any point in time the gross income of the typical individual is shaped by four determinants: Firstly, by the *factor endowment profile* of his/her society, that is, the total amounts of the various factors of production available in the national unit to which he/she belongs; secondly, by the *share* that this individual's household has of the

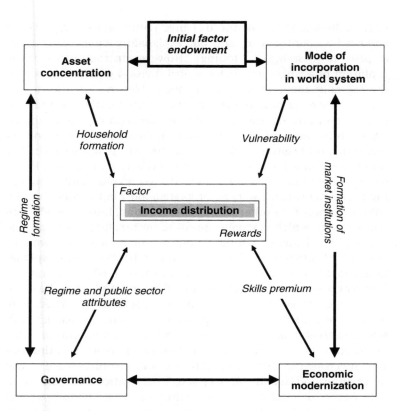

Figure 2.1   The determinants of inequality in developing countries

total amount of different factors of production; thirdly, by the relative *returns* received by the different factors; and fourthly, by the *size
of his/her household*. These determinants are interrelated and subject
to processes that determine why some factors of production are more
'rewarding' (that is, have higher returns) than other factors, and why
some members of society have access to more of the rewarding factors
of production than others do.

The crucial 'deep' *structural* determinant of eventual economic
inequality is *initial factor endowment*, that is, the relative share that
a national unit has of factors of production such as land, capital,
skilled labour, and unskilled labour. These factors of production can

be thought of as the economic 'blessings' nature and geography have endowed a country with, and our explanatory model gives pride of place to these initial 'blessings'. However, in the history of the evolution of a single, integrated global division of labour based on the capitalist mode of production, these 'blessings' in the case of a whole range of developing countries turned out to be the root of persistent poverty and inequality as merchant capitalism toured the earth in search of those specific combinations of initial endowments that could ensure high profit and low cost to those who had or could gain control over them. Specific configurations of such initial factor endowments determine how the geographic units containing these endowments were incorporated, most of the time through colonial conquest or other forms of exploitation, into the world capitalist system which gradually spread to eventually incorporate the whole globe. Different configurations of initial factor endowments determined different modes of conquest, settlement, and exploitation, and the creation of differentiated institutions which determined how assets would be concentrated in that unit and what the dominant mode of economic exchange was going to be. Assets here refer to wealth which, as we explained in Chapter 1, includes both fixed capital and human capabilities, and how they are concentrated or disseminated in society is a function of the type of institutions that are created in that society. Three sets of institutions are crucial in creating and stabilizing access to and control over the available factors of production: the institution of the household, the institutions of the market (through which land, labour, and capital are commodified), and the institutions of political power and governance.

As the top left-hand corner of Figure 2.1 indicates, the pattern of asset ownership (which was shaped by initial factor endowments and the mode of incorporation into the global system) shapes the size of households, which in turn shapes decisions about fertility and other investment in human capital which, as we shall see, have a direct bearing on income distribution. The concentration of assets, on the other hand, both reflects and stabilizes a specific concentration of public power which is institutionalized on the political level in the formation of a specific political regime and sets of governance policies. A political regime is the set of norms, rules, and practices that determine the distribution of political rights between actors in a polity, how these rights can be exercised, and what this means for the exercise of control over institutions of power such as the state (Przeworski *et al.*, 2000: 18; Sanders, 1981: 51–63). Regime and governance politics, in particular the degree to which popular sovereignty is institutionalized, the rule of law is observed, and how successful public authorities are in spreading the benefits of education evenly throughout society, are crucial non-market forces shaping factor rewards and income distribution.

Captured on the right-hand side is the process through which the institutions of the market are created. Again, as in the case of the other two sets of institutions, the precise nature of the market institutions depends on the mode of incorporation into the global capitalist division of labour. 'The market' refers to the set of practices and norms that determine the mode of economic production (distribution and consumption included) in a society, and determine what is produced, how, by whom, and for whom. Crucially, the institutions of the labour market determine how labour will be commodified and regulated, while the institutions determining ownership of land favour those with access to capital and credit. The characteristics of the institutions of the market, against the background of the role of a geographic unit in the global division of labour, plus policies pursued by the authorities determine how and when economic modernization takes place. Economic modernization in broad terms imply that the marginal returns on capital and skilled labour increase relative to that of land, and that skill dissemination takes place to meet the increased demand for skilled labour. This determines the specific rewards that will accrue to holders of specific factors of production, and would hence affect how much income accrue to different holders of different factors of production.

Factor rewards, and hence income earnings, are affected not only through the operation of the domestic market institutions, but also directly through the conditions flowing from the mode of incorporation of the relevant jurisdiction in the global division of labour. These conditions can create and/or exacerbate attributes of economic vulnerability that an economic unit faces within the global system (upper right-hand corner of the diagram in Figure 2.1).[1] Economic vulnerability refers to the relative inability of a unit to adjust to external shocks and/or negative externalities not of its own making. Shocks may come in the form of increases in interest rates in the jurisdictions that control the denominator of the debt held by a vulnerable country, financial instability that results from capital flight, and/or adverse terms of trade as global demand for the dominant export products fall. Negative externalities are costs that flow from market transactions but which are not reflected in the transaction prices, and include adverse effects of environmental degradation, the costs of trading in an open global system dominated by a few huge producers and markets, and failing firms and increases in formal sector unemployment that result from increased international trade competition, amongst others. Both shocks and negative externalities affect factor rewards directly through their effects on employment, but also through their indirect effects on the political regime and the quality of governance. This vulnerability is exacerbated by the 'power fact' that developing economies are rule-takers rather than rule-makers in the global political economy – which again reflect the conditions under which they were originally incorporated into the global system. In general, the macroeconomic norms and rules established by the rule-makers have, in certain periods of world history over the past two centuries, conspired to exacerbate the vulnerability of the low- and middle-income rule-takers. Economic vulnerability can be a feature not only of an economy as a whole, but also of specific groups within the economy. Put differently, the way in which an economy is embedded into the structural whole of the global economy can affect certain groups in a society more adversely than others. At bottom, this vulnerability is shaped by the nature of the factor endowments held by different groups in society, with unskilled labour typically being the most vulnerable in a relatively open world economy, despite what standard trade theory would have us believe (see below). In turn, the specific mode of incorporation into the world economic system of a developing society can favour the economic and political opportunities of other holders of factors of production, such as the holders of capital, land, and skilled labour, who often form the political elite in developing countries.

The above is but a brief sketch of the processes that Figure 2.1 portrays schematically. We now have to unpack the various dimensions of these processes in greater detail, and see to what extent the data at our disposal can help us to put flesh on these bare bones of an explanation. We begin by looking at the top half of the diagram, and

then move on to discuss the phenomenon of economic modernization and its effects on income distribution, The final section returns
to the left lower corner, namely the effects of the political regime and
governance matters.

Background conditions: Factor endowments and incorporation into the global division of labour

Historically speaking, the inequality trajectories of many developing
countries were set by a combination of (a) their initial factor endowments, (b) the mode of their incorporation into the global capitalist
system, and by (c) the concentration of power and influence within
these societies as a result of the features of (a) and (b). While (b) and (c)
have some intuitive appeal as explanatory factors, it is only recently
that attention has shifted to the 'accident' of geography as a source
of explanation for economic development and in particular inequality. Purely on a logical level, as Spilimbergo *et al.* (1999) argue, land
and capital have no upper limits and thus an economy with large
endowments in one or both of these two factors have the potential
for higher inequality than an economy in which skilled labour, which
has an upper limit, is the dominant factor. Economies such as those in
Latin America and the Caribbean, in South Asia, and in sub-Saharan
Africa as a rule are relatively better endowed with land and natural
resources than with skills, and it should thus come as no surprise
that these regions have the highest levels of inequality in the world.
In contrast, the highly industrialized OECD members and countries
in Southeast and East Asia tend to have more capital and skills than
other regions, but less land and natural resources. As in other aspects
of economic development, the 'curse of natural resources' (Gylfason,
2001; Sachs and Warner, 2001) is a significant negative factor also
with respect to economic equality.

But geography can only explain so much, hence the need to focus
on how specific institutional developments introduced by European
colonialism combined with initial factor endowments to promote economic divergence within developing societies and between them and
the colonizing states.[2] In Chapter 3, we shall see how the geographical
location, soils, and climate of Brazil and some Caribbean islands, for
instance, gave them an advantage in sugar and other large-plantation

cheap-labour crop production, and how this advantage was intensively exploited by European colonizers through the securing of
abundant supplies of cheap labour through the importation of slaves
and/or the subjugation of the indigenous people. This predatory
colonization was cemented by the introduction of institutions of
property ownership, labour regulation, and health and education
provision that favoured Europeans and the settler communities to
the detriment of slave labour and the indigenous population (Engerman and Sokoloff, 2005). Similar patterns of predatory colonialism
repeated itself later in parts of Africa and Asia, although the initial
endowment of factors of production differed from locale to locale.
Nevertheless, everywhere the colonial masters institutionalized practices that favoured the settlers and their local allies, and discriminated
against the indigenous populations and imported slaves. As a result,
levels of economic inequality worsened dramatically in those countries where relatively small numbers of Europeans settled, attracted
primarily by the extractive potential of mineral and other resource
abundance, and where they (and their local allies) formed a relatively
well-educated and well-endowed minority amongst a large and poorly
endowed native population. Areas which escaped the disruption of
European colonialism, and where indigenous social and political institutions survived well into the twentieth century, such as East Asia, had
lower inequality levels to start with and maintained these relative low
levels up to today.

Initial factor endowments and the colonial mode of incorporation
into the world capitalist system not only set the tracks for the development of economic inequality in developing countries. It also determined to a large degree the *role* that these countries came to play within
the vertical structured division of labour which characterizes the capitalist world system. The notion of 'role within the global division
of labour' allows us to differentiate, for instance, between national
economies that are predominantly exporters of primary goods, those
that 'specialize' in cheap labour, and those that provide more skilled
inputs to the global economy. It also suggests that it makes a difference whether an economy is a net creditor or a net debtor, and
what kind of credit it depends upon (Haggard and Kaufman, 1992;
Shambaugh, 2004; Stallings, 1992). As Van Rossem has shown, there
is very little reason to accept the strong claim made by world-system
analysts that the development prospects of countries can be predicted

in detail on the basis of their structural role in the global division of labour (1996). Agency, that is, the developmental decisions made by actors within these countries, also determines developmental outcomes and perhaps even more than structure. However, it cannot be doubted that the degree to which a national unit is economically vulnerable, in the sense discussed above, is dependent on its role in the global division of labour. This role is a function of how this unit was originally incorporated into the global system, but it is also something that is constantly being reproduced in terms of the ongoing mode of interaction with the global economy.

The structural role of a national unit not only determines its relative economic vulnerability. It also has an effect on the options and relative abilities of various domestic actors to pursue their interests. The 'outside-in' perspective reminds us of the fact that national economies and national decision-makers are embedded in broader global trends, practices, and norms which constitute material and ideational structures that in their own right shape the choices and options of national actors. That does not mean that one should necessarily think of these structures only as constraints on what decision-makers can or want to do. Many critics of globalization have used a structural metaphor to suggest that the interaction patterns and accompanying norms of globalization either compel actors in developing countries to do certain things or prevent them from doing other. Without ignoring the coercive power that is prevalent in the interstices of global structures and that is available to the promoters of globalization, it is useful to also think about the ways in which global forces enable local actors to explore options for achieving their goals in ways that would not be possible in the absence of these external forces. One example of this is the effect that the global structural role of a national economy has on the likelihood of the emergence of specific political regime within its borders. For instance, it is exactly the opportunities that globalization and liberalization of financial markets in the era 1985–1999 created for elites in the developing countries to relocate their wealth which have made them more willing to reconsider their previous opposition to democratization (Boix, 2003). Whether democracy does emerge, and in what form, is eventually dependent on more than just the structural role of the relevant national economy. Agency decides the process through which the balance of power within a society is shifted to enable the politically excluded classes/groups to stake their political claims and to eventually effect redistribution of economic resources and/or opportunities (Rueschemeyer, Stephens and Stephens, 1992: Chapter 3). However, any explanation that ignores the opportunities created by the outside-in structural factors run the risk of being not only incomplete, but would fail to see how it itself may be contributing to the very processes that it wants to understand.

Thinking along those lines it seems to be important to consider how the shift in global policy norms to supply-side measures that characterized the last decades of the twentieth century had enabled local ruling elites to exercise options that stabilized and extended their wealth, income, and influence, and that of their supporters. This 'outside-in' enabling dynamic was accompanied by normative processes of discrediting alternative policy measures, especially those that would amount to an extension of the fledgling welfare state in developing countries, or the maintenance of social safety nets in transition economies that stemmed from their socialist pasts. This dynamic continues to shape distributional patterns and processes in societies which have been condemned by their mode of incorporation to be rule-takers in world affairs. The long-term processes of asset concentration, economic modernization and regime formation are embedded in global markets and the dynamics of global governance which set the normative framework in which, for instance, one pattern of asset concentration may be regarded as more appropriate or more acceptable than another, in which one set of market features is favoured, and/or in which one form of democratization is promoted at the cost of others. Over the past two centuries, that is, over the period that 'global governance' has emerged as a macropolitical reality (Murphy, 1994), there have been a number of distinct rule-making phases, beginning with an era of expansion and liberalization of markets led by Britain in the 1800s, followed by a period of more cautious regulation of global and domestic markets, eventually to be replaced by a deliberately cultivated process of renewed globalization in the late twentieth century, which aims at increasing the openness of all national economies to global markets. As a rule, the period following the First World War, which saw a careful balancing of the desiderata of unencumbered international trade, regulation of the transnational flow of capital, and the provisions of the welfare state, was characterized by declining levels of inequality in a large number of states in the world, including some developing countries. In contrast, during eras in which economic openness reigned supreme, inequality worsened in those parts of the world that we refer to as the periphery, today's developing countries.

Economic openness refers to the ease with which goods and services and factors of production can flow in and out of an economy (Anderson, 2005). Over the past 200 years the world economy has experienced different phases of openness, but the most recent phase stands out due to the extent of easing that took place as well as the range of economies affected by it. This recent episode of widespread and deep easing, starting in the 1970s, is also remarkable for the fact that it is accompanied by a set of globally disseminated macroeconomic norms that, single-mindedly elevates openness to a goal in itself. Very little consideration is given to the downside of openness, and in particular the effect that it has on vulnerable societies. Most importantly, this dogged and single-minded prescriptive commitment to openness deliberately ignores the historical record of how the advanced industrial countries secured their national development. These high-income economies secured balanced industrial growth in eras in which state protection of politically and economically sensitive sectors was the norm, import tariffs and non-tariff trade barriers were high, and capital mobility was the exception rather than the norm. In contrast, during the later part of the previous century developing countries were increasingly being advised to face up to the icy winds of global competition and capital mobility, and were discouraged to use fiscal means to offer protection to their fledgling sectors and vulnerable citizens. In the absence of beneficial countervailing forces, such as income compensation or programmes of general skills enhancement, openness is bound to increase inequality and this is indeed what transpired during the most recent period of market utopianism.

Historically speaking, then, the combination of three factors – initial factor endowment, vulnerability due to the specificity of incorporation into the world capitalist system, and global macroeconomic norms that are impervious to the developmental needs of norm takers – constitute the background conditions which set the tracks for the evolution of income and wealth distribution in developing countries. While this combination of inside-out and outside-in factors can take us quite far in explaining the differences in historical inequality patterns between sets of countries, there is more to the story of high

inequality in developing countries. There are also a number of proximate determinants of income and wealth distribution that deserve
our attention: The effect of economic modernization, the nature of
household formation, and the impact of political regime and modes
of governance.

Proximate causes (I): Economic modernization and household formation

The diagram in Figure 2.1 identifies economic modernization as an
important dynamic factor through which the features of the market
impinge on the levels of income inequality in a society. As defined
above, economic modernization refers to a process of sectoral differentiation through which the 'modern' urban-based manufacturing
and service sectors increase their share of value added to the GDP of
an economy, while the relative share of the 'traditional' rural-based
agricultural sector declines. Economic modernization is reflected in
an increase of the marginal returns on capital and skilled labour relative to that of land, which feeds into an increased demand for skill
dissemination in a society through the appropriate education of a differentiated labour force. A national unit has consolidated its economic
modernization if it sustains the relatively wide dissemination of skills
through a system of public and private education.

The process of economic modernization is, as a rule, associated with
increasing levels of inequality.[3] The increased factor rewards enjoyed
by skilled labour and capital under conditions of economic modernization widen the income differential in a society. To illustrate why
this is the case, let's assume that an economically active population
is divided between an 'advanced' (modern) and a 'backward' (traditional) sector. Overall income inequality within that population will
depend on the relative size of the two sectors, the difference between
the mean incomes enjoyed in the two sectors, and the way in which
income is distributed within each of these sectors. The modern sector is characterized by a premium on skills and thus by higher factor
rewards for skilled labour. This implies a larger degree of income differentials in the modern sector, and also that the mean income in the
modern sector is higher than in the traditional sector. Modernization
leads to more people being sucked into the relatively more unequal
modern sector. A larger section of the population is thus subjected to

the inequality exacerbating effects of the modern sector, which combined with the widening of the divergence of mean incomes between the two sectors aggregate to increased overall income inequality. In addition, the returns on capital are enhanced in the modern sector with its higher levels of total factor productivity, which means that the returns received by the holders of capital relative to the income of the holders of other factors of production also surge upwards. Rents on land can get left behind in the process, except if agricultural production is also rapidly modernized. Overall, then, economic modernization leads to worsening income inequality. This worsening should taper off, however, when the modern sector becomes the dominant sector. The fewer the number of people left in the traditional sector, the lesser is the effect of the mean income differential between the two sectors. In addition, sustained modernization leads to the wider dissemination of skills throughout the modern sector, and the income differential among labour thus also declines. The residual level of inequality to be found in economically modernized or fully industrialized societies is largely driven by (a) the remaining differences between relatively skilled and highly skilled labour, and (b) the different returns received by labour compared to the holders of capital and land.

The implication of this brief summary is that one of the main intra-economic reasons why developing countries are so much more unequal than high-income industrialized nations is that economic modernization in the latter is further advanced than in the former. Some 50 years ago, Simon Kuznets argued in a series of publications that there comes a turning point in the evolution of economic modernization beyond which inequality starts to decline, after having increased up to that point (1955, 1963). Kuznets based his argument on a cross-sectional comparison of only a limited number of countries for which reliable data were available then. This data suggested, he concluded, that inequality tends to decline in mature economies with higher mean incomes, leading to the conclusion that the relationship between economic modernization (measured in per capita income) and income inequality would trace the pattern of an inverted U-curve. Inequality declines in more mature economies because of, amongst other things, the increasing number of salaried employers relative to the number of independent entrepreneurs on the one hand and unskilled workers on the other, plus the declining share of property rent as a source of household income. In addition, he argued,

> if the differentials between the A [agriculture] and the non-A sectors in product loom large, we should expect the range of the resulting differentials to become narrower as the result and accompaniment of the mere decline in the share of the labor force in the A-sector – the usual 'industrialisation concomitant' of modern economic growth. (Kuznets, 1963: 65)

Kuznets' analysis of the relationship between economic modernization and inequality has been the focus of a number of both supportive and quite critical studies over the past few decades (Anand and Kanbur, 1993; Ray, 1998: 199–207), the general outcome of which has been to challenge the empirical accuracy of the generalization that this relationship traces an inverted U-shape over time. One specific concern that has been raised, amongst others, is that the recent history of income inequality in the countries that make up our sample indicates that while there is some evidence of an inverted U-shape in the cross-sectional data, there is also evidence that advanced economic modernization is associated with rising and not declining inequality.[4] Many of the highly industrialized OECD countries experienced rising inequality after 1970, as did many developing countries. To explain this, the economic modernization argument of Kuznets must be supplemented with a focus on the systemic effects of economic openness on inequality levels, both in high-income and developing countries.[5]

Nevertheless, when we control for the effects of economic openness and the effects of global macroeconomic norms that have accompanied the most recent phases of economic openness, there still seems to be much of value in a Kuznetian perspective on the reasons why modernizing societies tend towards higher levels of inequality. If correctly balanced with the 'outside-in' explanations offered here, and if we take due note of the fact that initial levels of inequality may be a crucial determinant in how modernization affects subsequent inequality levels, the story told by Kuznets must be part of any answer to the question why poor countries tend to be so highly unequal. The developing countries that we are looking at all experienced significant modernization in the second half of the twentieth century.

By the beginning of the 1960s, industry's contribution to GDP in the developing countries was about two-thirds of what industry in high-income societies contributed to GDP, but by the end of the century this had shot up to more than 90 per cent. Part of the reason for this changing ratio is that industrial output's share of GDP in high-income countries shrank compared to other sectors. Nevertheless, compared to the first half of the century there was a major shift since the 1960s in economic activity in developing societies to the industrial sector which, as we saw, places a premium on skills and therefore tend to widen income differentials compared to more traditional sectors. In some cases, such as that of India, this industrial growth and the resultant modernization came after decades and even centuries of deindustrialization caused by one-sided colonial trade agreements. Naturally, the pattern of sectoral change differed from region to region. The shift to industry was quite pronounced in the cases of sub-Saharan Africa (SSA), South Asia (SASIA), and Southeast Asia (SEASIA), and continued to grow throughout the last decades of the twentieth century. However, in the cases of the Middle East and North Africa (MENA) and Latin America and the Caribbean (LAC) the GDP share of the industrial sector shrank since the 1970s, partly due to the rapid expansion of the (highly unequal) service sector in the MENA, but also due to deindustrialization that took place under conditions of trade openness particularly in Latin American states.

To the extent that modernization took place in the developing world during the twentieth century, it did raise the premium on skilled labour and hence richly rewarded the holders of this factor of production. This set in motion the processes of income divergence that Kuznets singled out. However, there is more to the story if we want to make clear why some late-industrializers nevertheless managed to *lower* their income inequality, despite undergoing processes of rapid modernization. Societies in the developing world that managed to reduce inequality over the last 50-odd years (Hong Kong, Singapore, South Korea, Taiwan) have all done so through measures that rapidly equalized the distribution of human capital assets among the population, thus setting in motion a virtuous cycle of rising skill demand and supply. In some cases, such as in Taiwan, the rapid rise in general education levels was complemented by policies of land redistribution that further contributed to the lowering of income and wealth inequality. Generalized education under conditions of modernity creates a virtuous circle: As more educated people enter the workforce this stimulates technological innovation that encourages industry to create more skilled jobs, thus creating bigger incentives among the population to make use of opportunities for educational advancement (Checci, 2004: 107). However, as Checci also shows, it is too simplistic to assume that a linear relationship exists between the mean educational advancement and the reduction of inequality. In fact, educational advancement only mitigates income distribution if two further conditions are met, namely if the initial level of educational attainment is sufficiently low, and second, if the mean educational attainment of a population is raised sufficiently rapidly. In addition, we should note that the countries that increased their average levels of educational attainment rapidly from a low base, have all done so under international conditions of relative economic *closedness*, that is, most of their education reform was already in place before the onset of the current phase of generalized economic openness (globalization) that began in the 1970s. Hence, when the arrival of globalization unleashed opportunities for international trade and foreign direct investment (FDI), these countries had already laid the foundations for their populations to draw generally on the welfare-increasing benefits of economic openness. In contrast, educational opportunities expanded very slowly in SSA, MENA, and LAC during the 1950s and 1960s, and human capital thus remained highly concentrated. The eventual arrival of economic openness in these regions also increased the returns on skilled labour, but only a small labour elite could benefit and economic inequality consequently worsened. Data compiled by Barro and Lee (2000) confirm these contradictory trends: Generalized educational attainment (which is best measured as the number of years spent at school by females 25 years and older) on average improved by 31 per cent from 1960 to 1970 in developing countries as a whole. In East and Southeast Asia the level of attainment was twice the average, while in SSA, MENA, and LAC educational achievement by females improved only by 12, 20, and 8 per cent respectively. The bottom line is that inequality can be mitigated under conditions of modernization and economic openness if educational achievements are increased at a rapid rate. One of the key explanations for the continued (and in some cases, increasing) high levels of income inequality in the majority of developing countries is the failure of these countries to reduce educational inequalities rapidly enough. While access to primary and secondary schooling has steadily increased in nearly all developing countries during the second half of the twentieth century, in most cases progress was very slow and very often excluded large cohorts of female children.

Finally, the distribution of educational achievement in a country is a function not only of the provision of public education, but also of investment choices that flow from the typical pattern of household formation in a country. These investment choices can, under conditions of credit market failure, undermine the building-up of the stock of human capital. As suggested above when we summarized the model captured by Figure 2.1, household formation in general is an important dimension of the broader process that determines the typical individual's income level. This level will depend on the overall income in the household, and how that income is shared. Factors that play a role here is of course whether the household has a predominantly wage income or a predominantly non-wage income. Secondly, specific relations within the household may determine that certain individuals, for instance women, get less than others. Typically, levels of income inequality *within* households in modernizing societies are quite high. Thirdly, the size of the average household is important, with higher levels of inequality being associated with more children per mean household. However, what interests us here in particular is that households in developing countries invest in larger numbers of children in order to increase the household's earning potential, and to provide security to the older generations, but that they normally underinvest in the education of the children. This underinvestment is particularly acute where the concentration of assets denies the poorest households access to credit which could be used to further the education of their children (see Chapter 5). High initial levels of inequality thus lead to an underinvestment by assetless households in education and an overinvestment in children, which in turn feeds into further increases to the level of inequality.

Proximate causes (II): Politics and policies

As emphasized in Chapter 1, inequality in developing countries is determined also by a number of specific political factors. The explanatory model depicted in Figure 2.1 suggests that the shape that the concentration of assets, income, and power eventually takes on in a society is mediated by the establishment of domestic institutions. In the preceding paragraphs we looked at the features of the economic and education institutions. Our attention now turns to how the attributes of political institutions, and the conditions under which they function, can shape inequality levels. The features of the domestic political institutions in developing countries are crucial, we expect, to whether and how these countries deal with the historical legacies and contemporary economic determinants of inequality.

Which features of domestic political institutions are important? The first and most obvious candidate is the nature of the political regime, that is the basic framework in terms of which power and political obligations are distributed in a society. It has become customary to distinguish between democratic regimes on the one hand and autocracies (respectively, authoritarian regimes) on the other. Given the experience of the industrialized capitalist countries, it seems reasonable to expect that voters use the equitable distribution of political power in democracies to introduce income-equalizing state policies, such as state-funded universal education and public health care. Does this mean that democracies are more expropriative, and therefore less unequal, than autocracies?[6] The second feature of domestic politics that is relevant to the study of income inequality is the vexed question of political stability. The reasonable assumption is that more stable political units have a better chance of instituting the medium- to longer-term policy measures that are necessary to reduce income inequality, such as educational reform. 'Political stability', however, is a vague and loaded term and one should be careful when using it. Its usage here does not have the purpose to imply that a political unit that experiences no change at all is preferable to one that does. Stasis should not be equated with stability. Instead, the term 'political instability' is used here to refer to a situation in which either or both of (a) political violence, involving death and destruction of property, and (b) major change to the political regime occurs. Conversely, we regard a political unit as 'stable' if there is durability in the reigning regime type, and if political conflict is resolved through non-violent means.[7] Thirdly, it can be argued that the quality of the public institutions in a society is important for securing property rights which in turn create a favourable climate for investment and job creation. Quality public institutions also effectively penetrate society to generate the revenue that is necessary to fund redistributive programmes, such as public education. Are the odious levels of inequality in developing countries related, perhaps, to institutional failures in the public sectors in these societies?

There are many reasons why we would expect democracies to be better than autocracies at reducing economic inequality. Popular sovereignty, the hallmark of democracy, enables those who find themselves in lower socio-economic positions the opportunities to use state resources to improve their relative income. In the useful phrase coined by Lane and Ersson (2003: 2), democracy is 'a political regime where the will of the people *ex ante* becomes the law of the country...*ex post.*' As Rueschemeyer *et al.* comment, 'democracy, then, is a rather counterintuitive state of affairs, one in which the disadvantaged many have, as citizens, a real voice in the collective decision making of politics' (1992: 41). On *a priori* grounds, therefore, we can reasonably expect that democracies would be more intolerant of high levels of inequality, given the opportunity for effective 'voice' that it accords to citizens whose income falls below the mean income. This theoretical expectation has been formalized in the median-voter hypothesis (MVH) which assumes that the median income earner is the decisive voter, and that her choice of party will favour policies that aim at narrowing the gap between the mean and median income.

When we look in Chapter 4 at the effect of the political dynamics of democratization on inequality in developing societies, we shall have ample opportunity to put the MVH to the test in the context of the dynamics of regime change. For the time being, our focus is on the more static question: 'Which regime type fares best when it comes to mitigating inequality, democracy or autocracy?' The available evidence surprisingly suggests that the influence of regime type on inequality is relatively weak. To the extent that there is an effect, it would seem that democracies fare better than autocracies, but only marginally so. Regime type is important, though, not so much with respect to the distinction between democracies and autocracies,

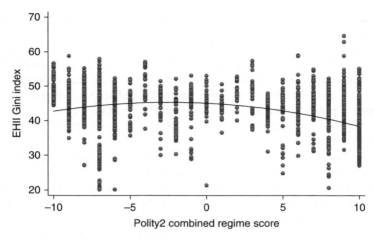

Figure 2.2   The relationship between regime type and income inequality in 147 countries, 1960–1999
Sources: Estimated Household Income Inequality Gini index score derived from UTIP (Galbraith and Kum, 2005).
Polity2 data from POLITY IV dataset (Marshall and Jaggers, 2002).

but with respect to the difference between consistent and inconsistent regimes. To illustrate this, Figure 2.2 uses observations for all 147 countries in our EHII inequality dataset and traces an inverted U-curve relationship between regime type, measured in terms of the Polity2 combined regime score used in the POLITY IV dataset, and our measure of income inequality.[8] Note that the slope of the quadratic prediction is relatively flat, and that income inequality is at it lowest at both ends of the Polity2 distribution, where we would find the most consistent manifestations of democracy and autocracy. Consistent democracies seem to have a slight edge over autocracies, but not by much. How do we account then for the fact that some autocracies at least seem just as intolerant to high levels of inequality as we would expect democracies to be? One answer is that authoritarian leaders face the need to legitimate their rule, and sometime single out high-profile distributional inequities for concerted policy attention in their pursuit of populist legitimacy (Wintrobe, 1998). Another answer is that authoritarian corporatist arrangements between the state and important sectors of the business and working class have proven quite successful recipes for societal transformation. As was the case with the original welfare state – Germany under Bismarck – some of the recent examples of successful state-led income and asset redistribution policies are associated, at least in their origins, with such authoritarian corporatist arrangements (South Korea, Taiwan, and Malaysia).

The regimes that are least successful at dealing with inequality, as Figure 2.2 suggests, are the broad category of 'mixed', 'inconsistent', or 'partial' regime types that are neither 'full' democracies nor 'full' autocracies. Recent episodes at democratization in developing countries have generated a large number of inconsistent regimes in which elections have become common, but where the state to a more or lesser degree remains captive to self-perpetuating elite groups who occupy executive positions and from whose ranks leaders are exclusively selected. In some inconsistent regimes democratic tendencies may outweigh autocratic tendencies, while in others the mix may be reversed.[9] An example of an inconsistent regime in which democratic tendencies outweigh the authoritarian would be the Philippines in the post-Marcos era. The result of the transition after 1986 was a regime in which there was more toleration of opposition politics and regular elections, but where recruitment for leadership positions continued to be restricted to the allies of those in power, and where inadequate checks on the misuse of executive power continued. There can also be inconsistent regimes in which autocratic tendencies dominate. In Uganda for instance, a classic case of an inconsistent autocracy, the National Resistance Movement under the leadership of President Yoweri Museveni between 1986 and 2005 instituted a 'non-party' political regime, which tolerated the existence of political parties, but forbade them to field candidates and partake in elections as parties (Kannyo, 2004). Recent work by Reich (2002), Epstein *et al.* (2006), Gates *et al.* (2006) and Merkel (2005) emphasizes that inconsistent regimes are the most common, but least understood regime type in developing countries, and that the inconsistent features of these regimes account for a wide range of political and social-economic problems that these countries face.

What exactly is it about inconsistent regimes, whether partial democracies or partial autocracies, that explain their poor performance in terms of dealing effectively with economic inequality? Two related explanations present themselves: Firstly, inconsistent regimes are less durable than consistent regimes. Looking at the survival rates over two centuries (1800–2000) among a comprehensive sample of political regimes, Gates *et al.* (2006) find that democracies survive up to four times as long as inconsistent regimes, while the survival rate for autocracies is up to two times that of inconsistent regimes. Low survival rates create volatility in public policies and impose short-term perspectives on policy-makers, which in turn undermines the capacity of the public authorities to devise and implement redistributive policies aimed at generalizing education opportunities and thus equalizing income. Redistributive policies fare best in stable political regimes, independently of whether the regimes are democracies or not. An empirical illustration of the close relationship between regime consistency, stability, and the effect of egalitarian policies is the statistically highly significant negative correlations in our dataset between the POLITY IV regime durability measure, a measure of the consistency of the regime type based on the Polity2 score,[10] and our measure of income inequality.[11]

Inconsistent regimes are twice as likely as consistent regimes to experience violent civil conflict.[12] Conflicts in developing societies have many causes and consequences (Conteh-Morgan, 2004; Eckstein, 1980; Hegre and Sambanis, 2006). However, some of the major civil conflicts in the low- to middle-income societies over the past century were about basic institutional choices: Whether a political regime should be inclusive or exclusive, democratic or authoritarian, and according to which social conception of the good should it be orientated? While we will have an opportunity later to consider the evidence relating high levels of income and wealth inequality to the eruption of conflict in the form of political dissent and opposition, it should be noted here that the evidence incontrovertibly shows that persistent and deep societal conflict worsens economic inequality, as well as other socio-economic indicators (Collier *et al.*, 2002). Pervasive social and political conflict, especially when it takes on violent forms, clearly affects the capacity of states to deal with a whole range of social issues, including the demanding challenges of addressing inequality through instituting and/or maintaining wide-reach public education programmes and other redistributive measures. The inequality-increasing impact of violent civil conflict is confirmed by regressing our measure of income inequality against lagged data registering the onset of civil war, and controlling for the potential effect of the nature of the political regime (also at $t-1$).[13] The incidence of a violent civil conflict at $t-1$, we find, increases the level of inequality by up to 2.5 Gini index points at t. The mechanism through which this occurs involves the adverse affect that violent conflict has on income-earning opportunities for poorer households in the economic contraction that follows violent conflict. The outbreak of violent conflict, our data show, reduces the subsequent five-year average growth in GDP (weighted for PPP) by up to four percentage points.[14] Such contractions affect the poor much more than the wealthy. The wealthy always find ways of protecting or moving their wealth in conflict conditions and thus experience fewer losses in the short to medium term, but these options of diverting the effects of civil war are usually not open to the poor, who are the first to lose employment and other income-generating opportunities in times of violent civil conflict.

The second reason why inconsistent regimes are less successful than their consistent counterparts in dealing with odious inequality has to do with deficiencies in the quality of the public sector in the former. The widespread practice of state capture by exclusive elites so typical of inconsistent regimes undermines the quality of the public sector, on which the successful implementation of policies aimed at mitigating income and wealth inequality depends. It comes as no surprise, therefore, that inconsistent regimes register very low scores on estimates of government effectiveness.[15] As noted, increasing the rate at which quality education is provided to more of the population is a tried and tested policy initiative that can be taken to reduce income inequality over the medium to longer term. The ability of a state to initiate, fund, and sustain a programme of widely distributed education opportunities depends on the capacity of the state to collect revenue and to effectively manage public programmes. An efficient, honest, and politically independent bureaucracy is clearly a *sine qua non* for the success of the redistributive welfare state, but so is the ability to penetrate civil society to impose taxes and collect revenue. Inconsistent regimes have pretty lousy public institutions, and are less successful at generating revenue than states with similar per capita income levels but with more consistent regimes. The first is illustrated by the significant negative correlation in our dataset between the measure that indicates the presence of an inconsistent regime and the control of corruption.[16] The data also show that inconsistent regimes fare badly when it comes to generating revenue.[17] It is the quality, and not necessarily the size, of the public sector that matters. Recent research suggests that the relative size of the public sector can be a source of and not an antidote against inequality. Lee, for instance, finds that if we hold the level of economic development and democracy constant, a bloated public sector is associated with increased levels of inequality, fuelled by the rewards' differential between the public and the private sectors (2005). This applies especially to developing countries, for a variety of reasons: Firstly, the state sector in postcolonial societies tends to monopolize resources in the national economy, leaving relatively little on which to base a vibrant private sector. Secondly, the postcolonial state uses its direct and indirect financial and fiscal resources to instigate state-led industrialization strategies that favour some industries more than others, leading to skill and reward differentials among industries and between urban and rural areas. Thirdly, neo-patrimonial rule in the many autocratic and partial democratic regimes among the developing countries dish out high-paying civil service employment as a ready source of patronage, widening the income gap between the public sector and the private sector with its many informal agriculture, manufacturing, and service jobs. One of the results of these three features of the postcolonial state is that inequality levels are correlated *positively* with public sector size in our dataset, when public sector size is measured as the size of government consumption expressed as a share of total consumption, or as central government expenditure as a percentage of GDP.[18] That does not mean that a smaller state is necessarily better, though. In his study of the effect of public sector size on inequality levels, Lee finds that the positive correlation between public sector size and inequality is reversed the more consistent the level of democracy becomes (Lee, 2005: 174). Consistency and quality matter more than size, but democratic consistency combined with a sizeable and competent state seems to be the best institutional mix to combat inequality effectively. Institutional failures, both as far as the quality of democracy and the capacity of the state are concerned, thus emerge as prominent proximate determinants of the high levels of inequality commonly encountered in developing countries.

Conclusions

This chapter attempted to explain the prevalence of odious inequality among developing countries. The causal processes involved are many and some of these processes have more proximate effects than other. The relative income of households, we saw, are determined by their share of the nationally endowed factors of production, and by the relative returns received by specific factors. Historical patterns of colonial conquest, which can be distinguished according to the initial national endowments of factors of production in the colonized areas, and the introduction of market and political institutions to buttress specific patterns of conquest and settlement, cemented in place highly skewed distributions of wealth and income, economic vulnerability, and fertility rates in the developing world that continued well beyond the end of political colonialism. With the global arrival of economic modernity in the nineteenth century, the group of colonially dominated countries already had high levels of within-country inequality.

Poorer countries are more unequal than high-income countries, therefore, firstly because of how colonialism exploited the initial factor endowments of the former and in many cases introduced economic, political, and social institutions that created and sustained high levels of income and asset inequality. These modes of incorporation into the world economic system established a dual pattern of vulnerability: On the one hand, national units were condemned to specific roles in the global division of labour that continued well beyond the dates of their political independence, and which make them less capable than higher-income countries with their diversified and integrated economies to deal with the challenges and benefits of global economic openness. On the other hand, the creation and sustaining of high levels of economic inequality go hand in hand with the concentration of power and influence in these societies, which enables certain groups to use the national unit's role within the world economy to enhance their own relative wealth and income position versus the poor and vulnerable. The relative intra-state positions of power and wealth can be influenced by structural changes in the global economy such as increased openness, for instance. Contrary to standard economic theory, though, an efficiency enhancing structural change such as openness may actually worsen and not improve the degree of economic inequality in a country, should the relevant state not be able to reduce the rent-seeking activities of the already powerful and rich, and/or to provide support for those vulnerable groups whose livelihood may come under threat from transnational competition. Local agency, and not only the structural role *per se*, thus continues to be an important part of the tale of high economic inequality.

Economic modernization heightens the acuteness of inequality by placing a premium on skilled labour, which remains a scarce commodity in developing countries. The inequality-increasing tendency of economic modernization is exacerbated by increased economic openness, especially under conditions in which national governments are discouraged by the formulators of global macroeconomic norms to engage in redistributive programmes that are intended to reduce levels of national or sub-national vulnerability. Economic openness, especially as far as the easing of the conditions under which trade takes place are concerned, increases the potential of low-income earners to improve their situation, but only if they are provided systematically with the skills to make use of the favourable conditions for enhanced productivity that trade openness encourages. For a variety of reasons, which have to do with both internally and externally imposed constraints, many developing countries – particularly in sub-Saharan Africa, parts of Latin America, and the Middle East and North Africa – have failed to introduce systematic programmes aimed at rapidly increasing skill levels among their populations. Externally, debt burdens and budget restrictions imposed by international funders from the 1980s onwards undermined the capacity of public authorities in these regions to emulate the rapid education advances achieved in East and Southeast Asia in an earlier period during which a more enabling international normative climate reigned. Internally, violent civil conflict and other forms of political instability, the degeneration of the quality of the public sector, and the diversion of revenue into avenues other than rapid skills dissemination meant that the majority of the citizens were not given the opportunity to improve their holdings of the national share of the rewarding factors of production. The evidence reviewed above suggests that the nature of the political regime on its own is less of a determining factor than regime consistency and regime durability, two factors which in turn affect the ability of political authorities to introduce and sustain the publicly funded programmes through which economic opportunities can be broadly disseminated in society. Nevertheless, there is also evidence that an enduring and consistent regime, with a relatively corruption-free and well-funded public sector and with policies in place to improve the education opportunities of all its citizens, is better placed than inconsistent regimes to deal with the inequality-increasing effects of economic vulnerability.

In developing this multivariate explanation of the determinants of high inequality levels in developing countries, we tried to give due weight to both internal and external factors. But the variety of the factors that we had to deal with, coupled with the complexity of the interactions between these various factors, forced us to skim over the empirical evidence that is available to show what exactly happened to inequality in the developing countries during and after their forceful incorporation into the global capitalist division of labour. The purpose of the next chapter is to retrace the historical steps briefly and superficially traversed in this chapter, but now armed with the theoretical explanatory insights developed in the current chapter, and to see how far these insights can take us in developing a fuller understanding of the historical processes that condemned the developing countries to their current levels of odious inequality.

3
The Evolution of Economic Inequality in the Periphery, 1500–1999

Chapter 2 looked at the reasons why developing low- and middle-income countries – here referred to as 'the periphery' – are prone to odious inequality. We proposed an explanatory framework that emphasizes a combination of transnational 'outside-in' and national 'inside-out' factors that determine who owns which factors of production and shape the relative returns earned on different factors. Aiming at a general theoretical explanation, Chapter 2 had to take a synchronic look at inequality in developing countries, riding somewhat roughshod over the long historical processes that shaped the ownership of and returns on labour, land, and capital. The aim of the current chapter is to take an in-depth look at the record that can help us to understand the historical detail of the inequality-generating mechanisms that our theoretical overview identified as important.

Where this chapter then differs from the rest of the book is that it deliberately stretches the time focus to well before the last four decades of the twentieth century, which is the era for which we have consistent quality inequality data for a broad band of developing countries, and which forms the focus of the theoretical and empirical analyses in this book. Stretching the time horizon in inequality studies is fraught with empirical difficulties, as we have very little systematic and consistently gathered information on inequality levels in the developing periphery before the middle of the twentieth century. Many of the peripheral countries that we are interested in were still under colonial control well into the second half of the twentieth century, and the colonial authorities were generally averse to collecting data that would reveal the inequities brought about or exacerbated by their rule. Very few of the peripheral countries that achieved independence before 1960 collected anything resembling national data on income and wealth inequality either. As a result, we have to rely on empirical approximations of income distribution in developing countries before 1960. Most of these approximations have been developed during the past decade as part of the recent spurt of interest in inequality and how it affects economic and human development in the periphery. Thanks to the careful collection and reconstruction of the limited available evidence by economists such as Bourguignon and Morrison (2002) and by Williamson (1997, 1998, 2002, and 2006), we can develop a pretty good idea of the general contours of inequality in the periphery over the last two centuries, and can even take some educated guesses about the levels of inequality in these countries before 1800. However, there is very little detailed information available about the inequality profiles of individual countries, and the reader is well advised to regard the historical material reviewed here as provisional and in need of further explication and refinement. The lack of detailed country-specific data also implies that this chapter follows the practice of the previous chapter in making rather sweeping generalizations about the inequality conditions of regional groupings of peripheral countries, knowing full well that the experiences of adjacent countries are likely to differ markedly. Nevertheless, historical analyses of the type that this chapter attempts have no other choice but to operate within the confines of the available data.

We shall look at the evolution of inequality not only in what today would be regarded as low- and middle-income developing countries in Africa, Latin America, South and Southeast Asia, but also in countries such as China, Japan, and Korea which up until the twentieth century were very much part of the periphery of the capitalist world economy. While some effort will be spent on analyzing the quality data that we have for the period from 1960 to 1999, it is important to also look at what we know about inequality levels within developing countries stretching back to the start of the modern world economy. The start of the modern world economy can be traced back to the emergence of merchant capitalism, which was set in motion with the European voyages of discoveries in the late fifteenth century. Following economic historians such as Immanuel Wallerstein (1979) and Angus Maddison (2003, 2005), the year 1500 can be taken as a convenient date to mark the birth of the capitalist world economic system. This ever-expanding system is based on the commodification of factors of production, and on an uneven vertical and geographical division of labour, all held together by the market as the sole arbiter of exchange value. Taking the story of inequality back to the birth of the modern capitalist world system, and taking the world system as our unit of analysis, enables us to trace in some more detail the processes through which what we today call 'developing countries' became incorporated into the world system as 'peripheral' units in the first place. As suggested in Chapter 2, the roots of modern economic inequality within these countries can be related to these processes of incorporation, the effects of which today are still widely observable in the developing periphery. A further reason for taking an extended time frame is that it also allows us to learn important lessons about the contours of inequality within developing countries from an era in which the world economy displayed similar features to those encountered in the later half of the twentieth century. In this respect, it is quite important to look in detail at the emergence of an era of extensive economic openness during the nineteenth century. It is now well understood that the prospects of the world economy in the mid-1800s were quite similar to those of the 1960s: What lay before was an era of time- and space-shrinking technological innovation, coupled with major demographic shifts and the promotion of economic openness in the form of reductions on the mobility of goods, capital, and people (Lindert and Williamson, 2003). How did economic inequality within the periphery change in response to these forces of globalization, both then and now? Are there any historical lessons to learn from such a comparison? To answer these questions, it is important to contrast inequality trends in the periphery with the inequality patterns in the core. The core are countries which engaged in overseas expansion, in which industrial development arrived first, and whose economic progress over the period under review was based on the privileged position that they occupied in a division of labour for which these industrialized countries determined the norms and wrote the rules.

It is convenient for our discussion to distinguish four periods in the world economic history of inequality since 1500. The first period stretches over three centuries from the beginning of merchant capitalism to just before the industrial revolution in Western Europe and its offshoots (North America, Australia, New Zealand) and involved the initiation and spread of predatory colonialism, first in Latin America, and later into parts of Asia and Africa. As we shall see, many of the contours of subsequent inequality within these regions of the world have their origins in how predatory colonialism sought to exploit the initial endowments of factors of production in these areas, and in the institutions created by the colonial settlers to safeguard their privileged positions. A second period stretches over a century from 1820 to 1914 and witnessed the industrial 'take-off' in Western Europe and its offshoots, the gaining of independence by Latin American countries, and the 'opening' of Asia – in particular Japan, China, Korea, and Siam (Thailand) – to 'Western' capitalism. Falling transport costs and technological innovations in communication during this period led to the *belle époque* of expanding global cross-border trade, and the unprecedented mobility of labour and finance. The latter parts of this period have many similarities with our more recent experience of globalization, and it is not inappropriate to refer to this as the era of globalization 'Mark I'. A third period stretches from 1914 to the 1960s, and was characterized at first by a wholesale rejection of economic openness, but then after the Second World War with a carefully constructed gradual return to economic openness balanced, in some countries at least, with domestic policy compromises aimed at protecting national populations from the effects of openness. Aptly called an era of 'embedded liberalism' by John Ruggie (1983), the post-Second World War period was characterized by attempts to balance national welfare considerations and concerns about macroeconomic stability with the efficiency-enhancing effects of relatively open transnational markets in goods and services. During this same period, the political landscape in Africa, in South Asia, and in Southeast Asia was fundamentally altered as colonial dominions achieved independence on a grand scale. Finally, our attention will turn to the period 1970–1999, a period that can best be described as globalization 'Mark II', and for which we have considerable and good quality data. This period was characterized by a rapid and calamitous reversal of the national and global compromises of 'embedded liberalism', resulting in significant increases in within-country inequality levels for the majority of countries in the world. The effects of increasing inequality during this latter period were less disastrous for countries with well-entrenched programmes of social spending for the sake of equity. However, most developing countries, for a variety of reasons, failed or were denied the opportunity to establish such programmes in the preceding era, and were thus ill-prepared for the iniquitous economic, social, and political effects that globalization 'Mark II' brought in its wake.

The arrival of merchant capitalism in the periphery, 1500–1820

During the first three centuries of the modern world economy, Western Europe and its offshoots were able to double their mean economic output, measured as GDP per capita, the highest rate of expansion anywhere in the world during that period (Maddison, 2003). As Patrick O'Brien (2006) in his overview of the global economic history of European expansion overseas shows, much disagreement exists among economic historians about the exact contribution that predatory Western European colonial expansion into the Americas, Asia, and Africa made towards this spectacular growth. From our viewpoint, however, there can be little doubt that it was the modalities of this expansion that contributed significantly to the rapid deterioration of economic inequality in the periphery. These 'modalities' included the initial endowments of the factors of production (land and natural resources, capital, and labour) in these colonial regions, but also the institutions of property and political rights, and the institutions of the reproduction of cheap labour that predatory colonial expansion systematically brought to the periphery.

Predatory Spanish, Portuguese, and British colonialism brought growth to Latin America and the Caribbean (LAC), but at a cost. Maddison (2003) calculates that GDP per capita in Latin America grew by an annual average compound rate of 0.14 per cent between 1500 and 1820, the second highest growth rate of any region after that of Western Europe and its offshoots. One of the many costs that the LAC had to bear for this growth in economic output was a significant increase in the level of economic inequality, though. Recent historical research has emphasized how specific institutional developments introduced by European colonialism combined with initial factor endowments to promote economic divergence within peripheral countries (and of course also between them and the colonizing states).[1] The geographical location, soils, and climate of Brazil and some Caribbean islands, for instance, gave them advantages in sugar and other large-plantation cheap-labour crop production. These advantages were intensively exploited by European colonizers by using cheap labour in the form of imported slaves and/or through the subjugation of the indigenous people, and through the establishment of legal and social institutions that sanctioned the concentration of land ownership and legitimated slavery. Elsewhere, in the Spanish colonies of Latin America, European settlement led to a concentration of land and mineral ownership rights in the hands of a small elite, while the native population were either decimated by the diseases brought by the Europeans, or if they survived found themselves disenfranchised and devoid of assets. In these societies huge wealth and income inequalities arrived with European settlement, as relatively small numbers of asset- and capability-endowed Europeans settled among relatively large numbers of disempowered indigenous populations and imported slaves. Engerman and Sokoloff (2005) point out that subsequent institutional developments in the domains of land, education, and political rights and privileges tended to entrench and deepen this divergence in economic opportunities and outcomes. Levels of economic inequality worsened dramatically in those countries where relatively small numbers of Europeans settled, attracted primarily by the extractive potential of mineral and other resource abundance, and where they (and their local allies) formed a relatively well-educated and well-endowed minority amongst a large and poorly endowed native population. This pattern was repeated, albeit later than in Latin America, in resource-rich African countries where sizeable European settler communities sprung up during the eighteenth and nineteenth centuries. The introduction of relatively capital-rich settlers amongst sizeable native populations, whose wealth was tied up in communal land and cattle, also set the inequality train in motion there. The colonial masters colluded with the newly arrived settlers to develop property and labour-market institutions that would secure a constant stock of cheap, pliable, and politically emaciated labour. This was most dramatically illustrated in South Africa after the discovery of diamonds (1867) and gold (1886) when land ownership and land occupation amongst black natives were drastically curtailed, and political resistance was forcefully suppressed to secure a ready supply of labour for the labour-intensive gold mining industry (Terreblanche, 2002).

In contrast to these inequality-generating settlement patterns in resource-rich and populous countries of Latin America, different initial factor endowments attracted large-scale settlement of

European small farmers and labourers to North America, Australia and New Zealand, all places where the native population was relatively small in numbers in comparison with the number of European settlers. This fact, plus the different institutional arrangements preferred by these settlers, meant that these Western Europe offshoots had lower initial levels of asset, capability, and income inequality, although slavery (in the case of the United States) and near-genocide (in the case of Australia) worsened the relative economic distribution considerably over time. Areas which escaped the disruption of European colonialism, and where indigenous social and political institutions survived well into the twentieth century, such as East Asia, had low inequality levels to start with.

As a consequence of these different patterns of initial endowments and colonial settlement, Latin America by 1820 on average had the highest levels of within-country economic inequality of the five regions into which Table 3.1 divides the world. In Table 3.1, inequality is measured per region as the ratio of the combined income of the richest 20 per cent of the population to the combined income of the poorest 40 per cent, and is based on historical data for 33 countries and groups of countries reconstructed by Bourguignon and Morrisson (2002). The high average level of inequality in Latin America by 1820 was driven primarily by inequality in Brazil, Peru, Colombia, Bolivia, and Mexico, the countries most affected by the importation

Table 3.1   Ratio of income of richest 20 per cent compared to income of poorest 40 per cent per region, 1820–1970

Region	1820	1870	1890	1910	1929	1950	1960	1970
Africa	3.92	3.92	3.92	3.92	4.13	4.54	4.54	4.63
Asia	3.49	3.56	3.62	3.72	3.82	3.34	3.30	3.30
Japan, Korea, and Taiwan	3.20	3.20	3.20	3.20	3.29	2.51	2.12	2.22
Latin America	5.65	5.65	5.65	5.65	5.65	5.52	5.65	5.81
Western Europe and offshoots	3.60	3.97	4.05	4.01	3.41	2.78	2.76	2.64

Source: Based on data used in Bourguignon and Morrisson (2002). The data on income distribution cover 15 countries with high quality data and 18 regional country-groupings with similar per capita GDP levels.

of inequality in the form of predatory settlement. By 1820, Brazil was the second most unequal territory in the world after South Africa, where stark inequality arrived during the eighteenth and early nineteenth century as well-endowed European settlers embarked on a systematic land grab, undermining the communal, non-cash economic basis of the large native population (Terreblanche, 2002). In contrast to these patterns of inequality inducement through European settlement, other parts of the periphery namely Asia, East Asia and Africa (South Africa excluded) on average had much lower levels of inequality.

The period 1500 to 1820 thus saw the emergence of two significant inequality contours affecting the periphery. The one was the growth divergence that took place between Western Europe and its offshoots on the one hand, and the peripheral world on the other. One indication of this was that the ratio of mean output (GDP per capita) between Western Europe (plus its offshoots) and the periphery increased by 68 per cent over this period. The second important contour that emerged was the increase in and stabilization of economic inequality within LAC and southern Africa in particular at levels that exceeded the worst forms of inequality that could be found anywhere else in the world. These two contours continued to worsen in subsequent eras of the evolution of the world economy, as a result primarily of the arrival of economic modernization in the form of the industrial revolution.

Industrial revolution and globalization 'Mark I', 1820–1914

The era of industrial take-off in Western Europe and its offshoots from 1820 onwards worsened patterns of inequality *between* countries significantly as average income levels diverged dramatically. This trend is captured in the line in Figure 3.1 that traces the development of *between-country* inequality summarized over 33 countries and country-groups, weighted for purchasing power and population size. Those countries that first exploited the opportunities provided by economic diversification and market expansion, plus the technological revolution that characterized the industrial revolution, saw their per capita income levels soar ahead of the 'backward' periphery. This pattern of 'big time' divergence (Pritchett, 1997) between countries continues up

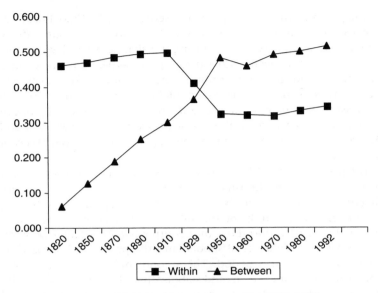

Figure 3.1   Within- and between-country inequality, 1820–1992

Note: Theil statistic is used as inequality measure (y-axis).
Source: Based on data used in Bourguignon and Morrisson (2002). The data on income distribution cover 15 countries with high quality data and 18 regional country-groupings with similar per capita GDP levels.

until our day. Industrialization, accompanied by the commodification of land, labour, and capital on a grand scale, enabled Western Europe to double its output between 1820 and 1913, while during the same period unprecedented expansive growth made for an almost fivefold increase in GDP per capita in its offshoots, particularly in the USA. The ratio of per capita GDP in the West compared to the rest of the world increased from 1.9 to 1 in 1820, to 3.2 to 1 in 1870, and 4.3 to 1 in 1913. Although the number of rapid industrializers increased during the late nineteenth and into the twentieth century, as Germany, Japan, and other Asian nations followed suit, the 'spread' between the West and Japan on the one hand and the rest of the world on the other continued to expand right up to the end of the twentieth century, when the West (and Japan) was almost seven times as wealthy as 'the Rest' in GDP per capita (Maddison, 2003).

But the numbers on which Figure 3.1 is based also reveal that the increasing divergence between countries triggered by the industrial take-off coincided with a deepening of within-country inequality in the industrially advanced (core) countries as well as in the periphery, although within-country inequality worsened at a slower rate than that of between-country divergence. Rapid industrialization is associated with rising within-country inequality as economic modernization encourages skilled wage earners to explore higher income positions in the manufacturing sector, leaving behind earners in the primary sector and also outstripping the incomes of low-skilled workers in the modern sector. In addition, the returns on investment capital tend to outpace land rents during an era of industrial modernization, driving within-country inequality even higher. In the USA, for instance, the income ratio between the richest 20 per cent and the poorest 40 per cent shot up from 3.51 to 1 in 1820, to 4.95 in 1890 (Bourguignon and Morrisson, 2002). In the Scandinavian countries this ratio increased from 3.4 to 4.3 over the same period, and the UK also experienced a steady increase in inequality of wealth and income up until the extensions of the franchise between 1867 and 1884 – followed by the Redistribution Act of 1885 (Lindert, 2000: 168).

Industrial take-off in the advanced economies was complemented by the expansion of trade following the repeal of the Corn Laws in Britain in 1846, and the spectacular drop in transport costs during the second half of the nineteenth century. Not all European countries followed the example of Britain in pursuing open trade, though. France, Germany, Italy, Portugal, and Spain instituted protectionist measures from 1860 onwards – but there was nevertheless an unprecedented net surge in global foreign trade between 1850 and 1913. The 'globalization action' was not restricted to what O'Rourke and Williamson (1999) call the Transatlantic Economy, which also included Latin America and the Caribbean and parts of Africa. In Asia, China and Siam (Thailand) agreed to lower trade barriers in 1842 and 1855, while autarkic Japan and Korea were compelled to open their markets in 1858 and 1876 respectively. India and Indonesia at that time had little choice but to follow the 'free trade' lead of their colonial masters (Lindert and Williamson, 2003).

What was the effect of increased trade during the 1800s on within-country inequality patterns? According to standard trade theory, increased trade openness should allow individual countries to use their abundant factors of production more intensively, which should raise the returns on these factors of production and reward their holders disproportional to the returns received by holders of scarce factors of production. Initial relative endowments of the factors of production (land, labour, capital) and the determinants of the relative returns on them are important parts of the story behind the contours of inequality, as we saw in Chapter 2. One of the implications of this is that in the absence of distributional data appropriate for summary measures of inequality – such as the Gini coefficient/index, the Thiel statistic, or the ratio measure used in Table 3.1 – we would be justified in using data on relative factor returns as a substitute approximation of income inequality. The regional inequality averages reported in Table 3.1, and the summary measures on which they are based, obscure considerable variations within the regions and over time, and have to be complemented if we want to trace the distributional effects of trade openness within specific countries. To reveal the effect of trade on factor returns, Williamson (1997, 2002, 2006) suggests that we use information on the value of the wage for a day's work by an unskilled labourer (w) compared to the mean of farm rents (r) per acre. This gives us a measure of how many days of labour by an unskilled landless wage labourer would be required to pay the rent on an acre of agricultural land owned by a landlord. As a relative factor price it helps us to determine the distributional effects of trade in an era in which agricultural production was an important part of total economic output, and in which income and wealth was significantly determined by ownership of land.

Not surprisingly, relative trade openness during globalization 'Mark I' favoured landowners in the land-abundant European offshoots (Australia and North America) more than it did labour. These land-abundant regions consequently experienced an increase in inequality, reflected in a wage to farm rent (w/r) ratio that decreased by as much as 69 per cent in the case of Australia and the USA combined during the period 1880–1914. In contrast, relative land-scarce and labour-abundant Western European countries experienced a decline in inequality as wages grew relative to land rents (Williamson, 2002). This pattern of growing inequality in land-rich and declining inequality in labour-rich countries was made more pronounced by the large immigration of unskilled labour from the latter to the former (Lindert and Williamson, 2003: 242–5).

What did all of this mean for inequality within developing countries? To answer this question, we must take note not only of effects of trade, though, but also of the effects of the process of deindustrialization that beset many developing countries during this era. We begin with the effects of trade. We have data for the period 1870–1914 only for a small number of countries/areas, namely Argentina, Uruguay, Burma, Siam, Egypt, and the Punjab, all economies with an original abundant endowment of land (Williamson, 2002: 73). We can nevertheless assume that this sample is largely representative of the developing world at that stage (with the exception of East Asia), in view of what we know of the mix of factor endowments in the periphery in general. Despite the prevalence of high levels of trade protectionism in independent peripheral countries – which was fuelled partially by a desire to generate revenue for cash-strapped governments and partially by a desire to offset the effects of deindustrialization (see below) – these countries/areas were all exposed to increased trade during the latter part of the nineteenth century (Williamson, 2006: 110–43). The per capita value of Argentina's exports, for instance, increased by a factor of 8 between 1830 and 1870 (Prados de la Escosura, 2006: 490), while rice exports from Burma and Siam, and cotton exports from Egypt also grew substantially during this era. In sub-Saharan Africa, external commodity trade grew some 160 per cent between 1897 and 1913 (Munro, 1976: 178). The effects in all these countries with an original abundant endowment of natural resources, including land, were in line with what standard trade theory would predict: Wages fell relative to land rents, albeit at different rates, with the result that inequality increased significantly in all of these land-rich countries/areas (Williamson, 2002). The easing of trade, especially during the period known as the *belle époque* (1870–1914) contributed to a general increase in income inequality in the developing periphery. One exception was in the labour-abundant countries of East Asia (Korea and Taiwan) where the easing of trade improved the wage/rent ratio (Lindert and Williamson, 2003: 239–40).

In essential respects, then, standard trade theory is a good guide at helping us understand what happened with inequality in the developing periphery during this era. Note should be taken of a second major contributing factor to rising income inequality in most of the periphery, though. The easing of trade during the nineteenth century was accompanied by large-scale deindustrialization in the capital-starved and low skill-based countries of the periphery. Industries located in the periphery produced more than two-thirds of the world's manufactures in 1750; by 1913 that figure had declined to 8 per cent, at most (Bairoch, 1995: 91). India in particular was heavily hit after 1813 by the influx of British manufactured goods when the East India Company's trade monopoly was abolished: The result was that India's share of world industrial output spectacularly declined from a level of 25 per cent in 1750 to 2 per cent in 1900 (Clingingsmith and Williamson, 2005).[2] In Latin America, trade also had a major depressing impact on local industries. Independence, which was completed between 1808 and 1825, broke exclusive trade relations with Spain and Portugal, and better quality and cheaper goods were more readily imported from the rest of Europe and from North America. This further delayed post-independence industrialization, despite the fact that decolonization lifted some of the heavy fiscal burdens that Latin American countries carried during the colonial era (Prados de la Escosura, 2006). According to the figures constructed by Maddison (2003), deindustrialization meant that GDP per capita contracted in Latin America during the second half of the 1800s. Some deindustrialization also took place in Africa during the 1800s, but from a much lower base than in India or Latin America (Bairoch, 1995).

One way of measuring the inequality impact of such episodes of deindustrialization, and also of industrial change in general, is to look at the changes over time in the unskilled wage rate relative to GDP per capita. Trends in this ratio tell us how much the wage of the typical unskilled worker near the bottom of the income range gains on/falls behind the mean income in a country. A declining ratio indicates a situation of worsening inequality. Table 3.2 reports the data on the wage/GDP per capita ratio that we have for a selection of developing countries in Asia and Latin America for the period 1870–1939. In all cases inequality worsened during the latter part of the nineteenth century up until the outbreak of the First World War, a period of increased economic openness in the global economy. Given the history of deindustrialization in parts of Asia and much of Latin America, and hence the creation of unemployed surplus industrial labour which drove the wages of the typical unskilled worker down, it is not surprising to find that the wage ratio generally declined in these two regions, with India, Siam (Thailand),

Table 3.2 Ratio of mean unskilled wage to GDP per capita, selected countries, 1870–1939

Period	Argentina	Brazil SE	Brazil NE	Colombia	Cuba	Mexico	Uruguay	Japan	Burma	India	Indonesia	Korea	Philippines	Taiwan	Siam Thailand
1870–1874	1.6947							1.4016		2.1486	1.5218				1.9264
1875–1879	1.3286							1.2644		1.7803	1.5550				1.7828
1880–1884	1.4769					1.1881	1.9047	1.2106		2.0345	1.5882				1.9002
1885–1889	1.5663					1.0899	2.2004	1.1526		2.0515	1.6214				1.7687
1890–1894	1.5191					1.0387	2.2555	0.8749		1.7892	1.6031				1.3852
1895–1899	1.4428					0.0503	1.6946	1.0058		1.5953	1.5074				0.8261
1900–1904	1.4570	1.2209	1.5325			0.9702	1.3658	0.9981	1.7407	1.4692	1.3885		1.2781	1.2883	0.8968
1905–1909	1.0500	1.1529	1.4431		1.2108	0.8633	1.0966	0.9794	1.6477	1.2094	1.1887		1.0525	1.1818	0.6968
1910–1914	1.0433	1.0318	1.1451	1.3317	0.9924	0.7738	1.0759	1.0123	1.0404	1.0369	1.0221	1.0231	0.9811	0.9377	0.9116
1915–1919	0.9230	0.7899	0.6751	1.5811	0.9329	0.2982	0.8981	0.8824	0.6210	0.9666	0.8276	0.8667	1.2483	0.7985	0.8963
1920–1924	1.1298	0.6280	0.5383	1.9191	1.2210	0.3615	1.1346	0.9955		1.3295	0.7020	1.3046	1.8559	1.1512	1.0046
1925–1929	1.2440	0.5912	0.5361	2.2206	1.4785	0.4613	1.1785	0.8927		1.4189	0.6964	1.0986	1.2785	1.0175	0.8913
1930–1934	1.4144	0.5760	0.3652	3.0818	1.5704	0.6903	1.4745	0.9896		2.4310	1.0620	1.0060	1.4769	1.0943	1.5066
1935–1939	1.3032			2.0995	1.4853	0.5129	1.2918	0.4103		2.2626	0.9750	0.9168	1.4729	0.8174	1.3449

Sources: Based on Williamson (1997, 1998, 2002, 2006) and Lindert and Williamson (2003).

Argentina, and Uruguay affected significantly. Note, however, that the ratio can be expected to decline also when mean income rises while the unskilled wage is left unaffected. As we saw in Chapter 2, economic modernization in the form of increased industrialization raises the premium on skilled labour, and thus shifts the mean income upwards. This factor explains why the figures in Table 3.2 show that Japan also experienced rising levels of inequality, while we know that this increase could not have been due to the effects of deindustrialization as in the case of most of the other countries of Asia represented in Table 3.2. During the second half of the nineteenth century, Japan experienced a period of rapid industrialization and growth following the Meiji Revolution which aimed at modernizing Japanese society. As Japanese GDP per capita during the late nineteenth and early twentieth century soared by an average compound rate of 1.5 per cent per year (Maddison, 2003), it outpaced the rate of growth of the wages of the typical unskilled labourer. The result was a steady increase in income inequality that continued to climb right up to the outbreak of the First World War (Tachibanaki, 2005: 71).

During the long nineteenth century, therefore, income inequality worsened in most parts of the developing world. Although there is still much that we do not know about the extent of income and wealth inequality in developing countries before the second half of the twentieth century, the available evidence suggests that increased economic openness during the nineteenth century worsened inequality in the periphery by favouring land rents in countries with abundant land resources, and depressed wages of unskilled labour in labour-rich countries by exacerbating patterns of deindustrialization. It was only in the relatively human-capital-rich countries (Japan, Korea, Taiwan – the latter two then still part of the periphery) that increased trade had a positive effect on the wage/rent ratio, but rapid economic modernization in Japan offset these equalizing tendencies (Tachibanaki, 2005: 70–71). In general, economic openness during the era of globalization 'Mark I' was all but favourable to developing countries as far as their descent into odious inequality was concerned. A similar tendency would play itself out during the era of globalization 'Mark II', as we shall see below. However, after the First World War it took a while for the world economy to reach the levels of economic openness that it recorded during the *belle époque* years.

Economic openness reversed, then 'embedded', 1914–1970

Autarky

The significance of the reversal of economic openness after 1914 should not be underestimated, but one must also be careful not to attribute inequality trends between the two world wars only to the effects of the autarkic policy measures. The First World War sounded the death knell of globalization 'Mark I', and thus also for the rentiers of open trade and high finance. After the war, many advanced countries, but also a significant part of the independent developing periphery retreated behind the autarkic walls of national protectionism which came in the form of trade barriers, restrictive immigration policies, and the near-complete segmentation of financial markets (Lindert and Williamson, 2003: 230). The value of trade as a percentage of world GDP dropped from 22 per cent in 1913 to 9 per cent in 1938 as tariffs and transport costs went up (Estevadeordal, Frantz, and Taylor, 2002). Transnational capital mobility also declined sharply. Taylor finds that the average size of capital flows in the pre-First World war era for a group of countries that included both developed and developing countries was often as high as 4 to 5 per cent of national income. International capital flows declined significantly in the decades immediately following the war, though, and in the late 1930s constituted less than one-and-a-half per cent of national income (Taylor, 1996).

In the industrialized core capitalist countries of Western Europe and its offshoots, the retreat behind autarkic protective walls coincided with a decline in the income ratio of the richest 20 per cent compared to the poorest 40 per cent of the population, as Table 3.1 illustrates, and hence an easing of income inequality. Work done by Thomas Piketty and others on the evolution of top incomes in the industrialized world shows that the institution of autarky was only one of the factors that reduced top incomes (Atkinson and Piketty, 2006). Piketty and his colleagues use tax data for different income brackets, including information on the corresponding number of tax payers for each income bracket, their income earned, and their tax liabilities to trace the fate of top income earners during this period and beyond (Piketty and Saez, 2006). While this methodology does not cater for tax evasion, the data generated are the best estimations of inequality that we have for a large group of core countries before the advent of household surveys. Piketty and Saez (2006) attribute the epochal decline in inequality in the US, Western Europe and its offshoots (and eventually also in Japan) during this era to the severe shocks incurred by capital owners during the major economic contraction that occurred in the late 1920s and early 1930s, followed by the major destruction of assets that took place during the Second World War. To illustrate the robustness of this explanation, they point to the fact that inequality in Switzerland did not decline, because top earners there were spared the shocks brought about by high inflation, physical destruction, and bankruptcies. It seems, therefore, that the reduction of inequality in the industrialized core countries is attributable less to the inefficiency effects of autarky than to that of the destruction of assets brought about by the depression and the outbreak of a major war. In the developing countries autarky also seems to have had only a small effect, although there is so much variation in the levels of measures taken in different regions and countries that it is impossible to generalize. As we noticed above, many independent countries of the periphery – predominantly in Latin America – already had high levels of trade protection tariffs well before 1914 in attempts to reverse the scourge of deindustrialization and to generate state revenue. However, this does not mean that there was no anti-globalization backlash in Latin America after 1914. Williamson (2006: 111) presents evidence of a continued secular increase in the unweighted average of tariffs for the Latin American region as a whole, and the result was to reduce the returns on abundant factors, in particular land. If we use the inequality proxy employed by Lindert and Williamson (2003) which captures the ratio of the average unskilled wage to GDP, there is evidence that inequality improved somewhat in Argentina, Colombia and Uruguay during these years, but that was not a general trend in the region as inequality increased in Brazil and Mexico. Overall, inequality in Latin America changed little during this period (see Table 3.1, and De Ferranti *et al.*, 2004).

In contrast to the independent periphery in Latin America, the majority of peripheral countries in Asia and Africa were still dependent colonies. The dependent periphery continued to suffer unequal trade and commercial treaties which favoured the colonial masters and thus restricted the use of local protective policy measures. As there was little change in the external policy regimes of the dependent periphery after

1914, the inequality-inducing dynamics that we noticed with respect to era preceding the First World War continued to take their toll. Trade with the external world still favoured land/resource rents in the land/resource abundant countries of Africa and Asia, which benefited the settler or colonial landowners at the expense of the indigenous unskilled labour force, while the processes of deindustrialization in labour-abundant dependent areas continued to weaken the income share of unskilled labour. The result was that inequality levels continued to climb in Africa and Asia during the period before and in the case of Africa also immediately after the Second World War, as Table 3.1 illustrates.

Embedded liberalism

The decades that followed the Second World War tell a tale of rapid worldwide economic growth and divergence of incomes between countries, combined with a continuation of the declining inequality levels in the core capitalist countries of the world. We noted that inequality levels in the core industrial countries declined during this era, as the earning potential of top income earners was rapidly eroded by the joint effects of economic contraction and the physical destruction of property. In contrast, the widespread equalization of income that took place in core industrial states after 1945 coincided not with economic decline, but with spectacular economic expansion. Considering what we know about the determinants of income inequality, and in particular that periods of rapid expansion often go hand in hand with increases in inequality, we have to look outside the strictly economic sphere for an explanation of the coincidence of high growth and lower inequality in the period 1945 to 1970. This explanation lies in the combination of two factors. The first factor is the institutional innovation introduced in the polities of the core capitalist industrial countries that is today known as the welfare state. As used here, this term refers to government regulation over industrial and labour market policies, plus the introduction of progressive taxation and the use of the revenue by public authorities to finance social spending on basic income assistance, unemployment compensation, public non-contributory pensions, public health, housing subsidies, and on universally available free or subsidized education. Lindert suggests that we should distinguish between social transfers (all of the above, except the provision of education) and social spending, and notes that before the First World War, progressive taxation and the use of social revenue for social transfers was extremely limited and largely restricted to a few welfare innovators in northern Europe. However, median spending on social transfers as a percentage of GDP in the core countries increased from 0.69 in 1910 to 10.41 in 1960 (Lindert, 2004: 12–13). He attributes the rise of the welfare state to a mix of factors, including the granting of 'political voice' through universal franchise to significant portions of the population who did not have it before, the relative aging of the population which increased the demand for pensions and public health spending, and changing conceptions of social justice, especially in the Roman Catholic Church after WW II. The second factor of significance is the emergence during and after WW II of a set of international norms and institutions that not only tolerated but actively encouraged the establishment of social welfare provisions by national governments to protect their citizens from the nasty shocks and disruption that economic openness brings with it.

The significant growth of the welfare state in North America, Western Europe and its offshoots, and in parts of Asia was not accompanied by the inefficiencies that some contemporary economic thinking typically would predict. In fact, exactly the opposite applied. Following a period of only modest growth between 1913 and 1950, per capita GDP in Western Europe more than doubled between 1950 and 1973, constituting an unprecedented annual compound growth rate of 4.05 per cent. Comparable growth in the Western offshoots in the same period was 2.5 per cent, a growth rate never before and since then achieved. The most spectacular growth occurred in Japan, where GDP per capita increased tenfold with an average annual compound growth rate of 8.06 per cent between 1950 and 1973 (Maddison, 2003: 263), on the back of the restoration of democracy, significant welfare reforms, and a policy of equalizing blue and white collar wages (Tachibanaki, 2005: 58–62). There were many reasons for this exceptional growth in the core capitalist countries, but at the core of it lies the wide range of socio-political compromises that a number of core nations and their constituent classes and political groups achieved from the mid-1930s onwards, laying the groundwork for the expansion of the world economy after WW II (Frieden, 2006: 279). One of the crucial domestic compromises

that contributed directly to the spurt of productivity and innovation after 1945 was the significant investment made by the core
capitalist countries in education and social transfers to assist the
poor. Lindert shows how the specific mix of public transfer policies
in these countries, plus their extensive investment in public education raised productivity levels well beyond what would have been
possible without these redistributive policies (Lindert, 2004: 32–3,
227–63). The post-war international compromises reflected in the
embedded liberalism of the Bretton Woods arrangements, through
which national autonomy and robustness was balanced with the promotion of closer international economic 'association' (Ruggie, 1983:
18) through transnational markets, provided a stable and supportive context for the domestic search for the middle ground in which
parties from both the left and the right participated (Frieden, 2006).
The prudent policies of state-led redistribution, embedded as it was in
a protective international normative framework that valued national
development and societal robustness, laid the groundwork for the
most exceptional period of economic expansion in the history of
the industrialized countries. At the same time, it presided over a significant decrease in economic inequality within the core countries.
Between 1929 and 1970 economic inequality in East Asia (Japan,
Taiwan, South Korea) declined by a third, while inequality in Western Europe and its offshoots declined by 20 per cent during the same
period (see Table 3.1).

The post-WW II years heralded an era of major political and economic transformation for many countries in the developing periphery
as well. Political independence from the colonial motherlands for
many coincided with increased export earnings that resulted from
a boom in global demand for commodities. In Asia, economic output doubled between 1950 and 1973. In Africa and Latin America
growth was more modest, but nevertheless reached average annual
compound growth rates of two and two-and-a-half per cent respectively (Maddison, 2003). However, as Table 3.1 makes clear, only Asia
experienced a marginal decline in income inequality between 1929
and 1970, mainly due to land and education reform. Inequality in
Africa continued to rise, as income earnings from the global commodity boom tended to favour the holders of these abundant factors
of production and not low-skilled labour. In addition, political independence and the creation of a new indigenous managerial and civil

service class further widened the income gap between urban and rural areas. Latin America also continued on its steady-state high-inequality path, despite the widespread rise to power of egalitarian political and social movements. In Bolivia, Colombia, Cuba, Mexico, Nicaragua, and Peru, amongst others, such movements effectively challenged the hegemonic hold of land rentiers and their political allies. However, the potential equalizing effects of these political and social changes were not supported by the appropriate egalitarian educational and industrial policies. As De Ferranti and his co-authors note, the educational systems of Latin America after WW II continued to perform poorly compared with those of North America (and of East and Southeast Asia, we might add) in terms of the dissemination of skills throughout society. Combined with the hard-to-break patterns of social exclusion and marginalization of poorer sections of the population that endemically characterize much of Latin America, low-quality education did not help to ensure upward mobility for low-income earners. Persistent imperfections in the credit market in Latin American countries, combined with inward looking industrial policies that undervalued investment in human capital, also prevented the emergence of the low-inequality high-growth patterns that characterized successful late-developers in East Asia, for instance (De Ferranti *et al.*, 2004: 121).

Africa experienced a major export boom following the Second World War as reconstruction, consumer demand fuelled by rapid economic expansion worldwide, and stockpiling just before and during the Korean war created a demand for its agricultural produce, minerals, and other natural resources. Munro calculates that sub-Saharan Africa's total external trade grew by more than 500 per cent between 1945 and 1960 (current prices, not corrected for inflation), which even outstrips the spectacular growth in African external trade during the *belle époque* (Munro, 1976: 178). While real incomes improved after 1945, especially in the agricultural sector, not everyone shared in the returns created by the export boom, and inequality continued to worsen. As before, colonial ownership structures ensured that the bulk of the returns of this commodity boom went into the coffers of the colonial administrations and the 'imported' owners of the commodity sources. Many new jobs were created in the extraction and other primary industries, which further increased the migration from the rural areas – notoriously neglected by colonial administrations – to the cities and towns. But the wages accruing to these jobs were kept arti-ficially low in the presence of a huge surplus labour force, and in the absence of collective bargaining institutions. In South Africa – admit-tedly an extreme case but nevertheless important given the fact that South Africa contributed the most of all countries to total sub-Saharan external trade – the real incomes of European settlers increased by a staggering 46 per cent between 1949 and 1955, while the incomes of blacks stagnated (Munro, 1976: 197; Terreblanche, 2002: Chapter 9). The dawn of independence for a large number of African states, starting with Ghana in 1957, changed little in the basic factors that had placed Africa on its road of ever-increasing inequality, and in some cases worsened the prospects for the equalization of income and wealth. The transfer of political power to local elites only gradu-ally and haltingly changed patterns of the ownership of the means of production and when it did, it favoured the educated urban African elites who became the main beneficiaries of newly created jobs in the state sector, including the military, and in the import-substituting manufacturing sector that sprang up before and after independence. This led to a marked increase in the real wages earned by urban dwellers, but left much of the rural areas to continue to slide down the income ladder. In the decades after independence, such spatial inequality between urban and rural Africa became a major driving force of overall within-country inequality, in some cases overlapping with ethnic and tribal divisions and thus setting the scene for eventual civil strife.

To summarize: The second third of the twentieth century witnessed a significant decline in inequality levels in many core capitalist coun-tries, and in parts of Asia. The effect of this, and of the introduction of strict egalitarian policies in the Soviet Union and parts of Eastern Europe was that world levels of within-country inequality declined significantly, after creeping upwards for most of the preceding cen-tury (see Figure 3.1). While economic contraction and generalized war in the 1930s and 1940s did much to reduce top incomes and thus reduce inequalities in the core capitalist countries, the most sig-nificant part of this decline was produced by the important advances made in East Asia, Western Europe, North America, Australia, and New Zealand after the Second World War in using tax revenue and state power to deliver social transfers and social investment to broad sectors of the population. These successful national experiments in building the welfare state was made possible and was sustained by a favourable international normative climate, in which the twin goals of economic growth and equity were balanced. In contrast, much of the periphery (with the important exclusion of parts of Asia) experienced an increase in inequality (dependent Africa) or failed to reverse high levels of inequality (Latin America). Colonial and postcolonial authorities in Africa increasingly catered for an urban elite, thus exacerbating the already expanding income and wealth gap between town and country. Governments in Latin America failed to translate larger investments in education into the successful dissemination of quality skills among their populations. Internationally, the spirit of compromise that underpinned the welfare state compromise in the core countries was not transplanted to the periphery. Western governments were primarily concerned to ensure that decolonization would not hinder continued access to the commodities that their fast-growing industries needed and their rapacious consumers demanded, and that the Soviet Union and its allies would be prevented from gaining a foothold in the developing world. The latter consideration brought core countries such as the USA, UK, and France to deliberately undermine left-leaning politicians in developing countries and their proposed redistributive policies, thus exacerbating the problems of both newly independent and older developing countries to get a solid policy grip on income and wealth inequalities. The upshot was that developing countries, outside of small group in East Asia, were ill-prepared to face the distributional onslaught that a new era of globalization soon was to unleash on them.

Economic openness and inequality in the late twentieth century, 1970–1999

The domestic and international compromises that characterized the era of embedded liberalism came under increasing pressure from the 1970s onwards. Globally, under the tutelage of the US Treasury and G-7 led multilateral financial and economic-coordination institutions, macroeconomic norms shifted in favour of pursuing economic openness as a goal in itself, to the detriment of the national welfare component of embedded liberalism. To appreciate the inequality effects of the normative and policy revolution that characterized the last three decades of the twentieth century, we should turn to the collection of consistently generated and broadly representative income inequality data that is available for the period 1963 to 1999 in the University of Texas (UTIP) Estimated Household Income Inequality (EHII) dataset.[3] So far, our analysis of inequality patterns from 1500 to the 1960s had no other choice but to rely on a motley variety of sketchy estimations and approximations of income inequality, represented in Figure 3.1 and in Tables 3.1 and 3.2. As explained in Chapter 1, the EHII dataset is not only the inequality dataset with the best coverage of developing countries available, but also uses an estimation technique that is reliable and consistent across countries, thus allowing us to engage in cross-sectional analysis. Of course, the methodologies behind the construction of the inequality indicators reflected in Figure 3.1 and in Tables 3.1 and 3.2 differ from that used in constructing the EHII dataset, but these differences do not obscure the two central messages that all data sources on developing countries confirm: The first is that inequality steadily increased in the majority of developing countries ever since these countries were incorporated into the expanding capitalist world economy. Secondly, episodes of increased economic openness tend to worsen inequality in developing countries, except in the cases of countries that manage to improve their endowments of human capital resources rapidly and on a broad scale. As we shall see, these conclusions are underlined by the patterns that can be detected in the EHII dataset.

As the within-country inequality trend line in Figure 3.1 indicates, the last third of the twentieth century was characterized by a general increase of within-country inequality in the world. A variety of factors precipitated this aggregate outcome, and these factors worked themselves out in different ways in different groups of countries. What happened in the so-called transition countries during the 1980s and 1990s accounts for a significant portion of the aggregate trend of worsening within-country inequality. The economies that embarked on a transition from the communist to the capitalist mode of production during the last two decades of the previous century, including China, on the whole experienced a calamitous increase in inequality levels during the 1990s in particular, with mean inequality rising by 14 per cent for the decade as a whole (see Table 3.3). The primary explanations that have been offered for these trends in the transition economies are, in the case of China, the big divergence

Table 3.3 Inequality trends in low- and middle-income developing countries and transition economies, 1960–1999

		1960–1964	1965–1969	1970–1974	1975–1979	1980–1984	1985–1989	1990–1994	1995–1999
SSA	EHII Gini	46.526	47.888	47.853	46.573	46.707	47.713	48.648	49.402
	Rate of change		0.259	0.486	-0.925	-0.641	2.384	1.292	2.423
	Relative inequality	1.138	1.126	1.134	1.134	1.124	1.141	1.130	1.131
MENA	EHII Gini	47.474	45.749	43.841	43.810	43.455	41.851	45.506	47.429
	Rate of change		-2.875	-3.281	-1.618	-0.430	-1.309	6.234	3.583
	Relative inequality	1.161	1.076	1.039	1.067	1.046	1.001	1.057	1.086
LAC	EHII Gini	45.555	45.559	45.396	44.049	44.491	45.763	47.631	47.314
	Rate of change		0.251	-1.688	-2.118	0.991	2.840	4.260	0.357
	Relative inequality	1.114	1.071	1.075	1.072	1.071	1.094	1.106	1.083
SASIA	EHII Gini	44.236	45.289	43.880	45.394	45.496	46.647	47.183	46.882
	Rate of change		0.626	3.018	3.512	-0.494	0.396	0.183	-0.288
	Relative inequality	1.082	1.065	1.040	1.105	1.095	1.115	1.096	1.073
SEASIA	EHII Gini	46.216	45.894	46.714	45.989	44.849	46.836	44.531	44.761
	Rate of change		0.706	-1.881	-1.699	-2.499	4.179	-4.976	0.443
	Relative inequality	1.130	1.079	1.107	1.120	1.080	1.120	1.034	1.025
OCEANIA	EHII Gini	48.263	46.601	46.083	43.702	47.188	48.936	46.607	40.667
	Rate of change		2.960	-1.194	-0.876	8.138	3.700	-1.451	-15.326
	Relative inequality	1.180	1.096	1.092	1.064	1.136	1.170	1.082	0.931
TRANS	EHII Gini	28.406	27.451	26.291	26.886	26.969	32.353	37.843	41.903
	Rate of change		-3.376	-3.315	-0.575	0.251	3.418	16.030	12.708
	Relative inequality	0.695	0.645	0.623	0.655	0.649	0.774	0.879	0.959

Source: Own calculations, based on UTIP EHII data (Galbraith and Kum, 2005).

between rural and urban wages which resulted from the economic reforms since 1978 (Blecher, 2005), and the effect of the institution regulating population movement (the *hukou*) which severely inhibits mobility between the rural areas and urban centres (Liu, 2005). In the case of the transition economies of Central and Eastern Europe and Central Asia, a number of factors contributed to the worsening of income inequality, among which were the rapid rise of unemployment as job security was removed in the wake of the capitalist reforms started in the late 1980s; the fall in minimum wage compared to the average wage as wage-setting norms changed in the wake of large-scale privatization; and the rise of the informal sector (Cornia, 2004: 7). To this list we can add the failure of the educational system to help the unemployed to re-school and re-tool; the effect of rapid inflation and macroeconomic instability; and the ability of the relatively well off and politically powerful to capture rent-seeking opportunities at a direct cost to the less influential. Hellman, Jones, and Kaufmann (2003) shows how what they call a 'capture economy' has emerged in many transition countries, where the rapid and unregulated selling-off of state-owned enterprises in the absence of strong regulatory and democratic institutions provided opportunities for public officials and politicians to sell rent- and unequal wealth-generating advantages to private firms.

However, rising mean within-country income inequality for the world as whole cannot be attributed solely to the impact of developments in the transition economies. Both the group of high-income countries and the low- and middle-income developing countries also saw their mean inequality levels increase significantly. In the case of the high-income countries rising inequality set in during the 1980s, while the worsening of inequality in the developing countries was already evident in the 1970s, and in the latter case this increase in inequality took place from an already high and debilitating level for most developing countries. The general increase in inequality in the core capitalist countries, who had organized themselves by then into the Paris-based Organization for Economic Cooperation and Development (OECD), was due to a mix of factors, of which three stand out: Firstly, the rapid technological change that characterized production in advanced industrial countries in the late twentieth century; secondly, the liberalization of foreign economic policies on national and regional levels, which was deemed to be the 'correct' response to the stagflation of the 1970s, and, thirdly, the deepening of cross-border economic integration which resulted from the policy decisions to liberalize external economic relations (Garrett, 2000). Together, the three factors gave rise to the phenomenon of globalization 'Mark II' and brought significant changes to employment and wage policies, and with it to income distribution patterns. Increasing sophistication in the technologies driving high-value production for the international market, combined with the new ease with which capital could relocate to low-wage destinations, threatened the job security of older generations of blue-collar workers, who found it difficult to adjust to the new production and often leaner production techniques. These blue-collar workers, the traditional main beneficiaries of the golden age of social transfer welfare policies, either ended up unemployed or were forced to take lower-salaried positions lower down the technological scale. At the other end of the income-earning scale, high-tech production significantly increased the returns on highly skilled labour and managerial expertise, allowing the top income earners in the English-speaking countries in particular, to claw their way back to the spectacularly high-income levels that they last achieved in the years immediately preceding the Great Depression (Piketty and Saez, 2006).

The details of how within-country inequality worsened in developing countries during this period are captured by Table 3.3, which traces the contours of inequality within the regions[4] that make up the group of low- and middle-income countries in the EHII dataset. The semi-decade mean inequality levels for developing countries and the transition economies are reported, plus information about the rate of change from one semi-decade to the next. A third row under each region compares the regional semi-decade means to the semi-decade mean for the full sample of 147 countries in the dataset, constituting a measure of 'relative inequality'. The ratios in these rows confirm what we know from the analysis in this chapter so far, namely that sub-Saharan Africa (SSA) and Latin America and the Caribbean (LAC) were the regions with the highest mean inequality,[5] followed by South Asia (SASIA), OCEANIA, Southeast and East Asia (SEASIA), the Middle East and North Africa (MENA), and the transition economies in that order. As would be expected the transition economies were the least unequal on average, given their socialist-egalitarian legacies. MENA countries used to be less unequal than other developing countries, but mean inequality in MENA has so drastically worsened since the mid-1980s that one can no longer identify an inequality-mitigating 'Islam effect' (see Gradstein, Milanovic, and Ying, 2001).

The finely calibrated and better representative EHII data in Table 3.3 confirm that inequality in sub-Saharan Africa on average continued to increase into the 1970s. However, the data also reveal episodes of inequality reduction in the region during the late 1970s and 1980s. The country-specific data confirm that this reduction was noticeable in the cases of Benin, Botswana, Ethiopia, Republic of Congo, Kenya, Madagascar, Mauritius, Nigeria, Rwanda, and Tanzania. Changing patterns of land settlement and employment (specifically in the civil service) that favoured the indigenous population probably account for most of these declines. There were some instances of declining inequality in the LAC region during the 1970s as well, but this was not as widespread a phenomenon as in the case of SSA. Notable declines took place in Chile, El Salvador, Haiti, Jamaica, and Uruguay, but the opposite was the case in Argentina, Bolivia, Brazil, Dominican Republic, and Guatemala, with little change in the rest. East Asia and Southeast Asia continued to register significant reductions in inequality during the 1970s, with Malaysia and high-income South Korea and Singapore standing out, and with more modest improvements in Indonesia, the Philippines, and Thailand. With the exception of South Asia, where inequality on average rose significantly in the 1970s, it is possible to speak of the 1970s (and in the case of SSA of the early 1980s also) as something of a golden era in the mitigation of inequality. However, this trend did not become sustainable and inequality again came under significant upward pressure as the effects of the systemic changes that globalization brought about started to kick in from the late 1970s onwards.

Table 3.3 also reveals that inequality on average was significantly worse in the 1980s and 1990s compared to earlier decades for three of the developing regions, namely SSA, MENA, and LAC. In the case of SSA and LAC, inequality worsened on average by three Gini index points since the late 1970s, while MENA's mean inequality shot up by six points from the second half of the 1980s. South Asia also experienced a worsening of inequality between the early 1970s and early 1990s, but there was modest decline in mean inequality in this region in the 1990s taken as a whole. SEASIA and Oceania are the only two regions whose mean inequality levels and relative inequality declined over the last four decades of the twentieth century.[6] The arrival of globalization 'Mark II' in the periphery, in the form of a generalized opening up of the economies by the governments of developing countries, either voluntarily or under pressure, thus clearly took its toll.

Table 3.4 helps us to disaggregate these regional trends. This table summarizes the inequality experiences of all the low- and middle-income countries in our sample over the period 1980 to 1999. The second column lists all the states that experienced an increase in inequality over this period, in a sequence that lists the country which experienced the biggest increase first, down to the country with the smallest increase. The third column contains the names of countries that experienced no increase in inequality between 1980 and 1999, or saw their inequality levels improve. A last column lists the countries for which too few observations are available to discern any trend. Among the countries for which more than one observation exists, only five SSA states, three each in MENA and in LAC, and one among the transition countries did not experience an increase in their inequality levels since 1980. While it is likely that idiosyncratic features of the individual states can explain the specific degree and nature of adverse inequality change, there is also evidence that common features of the policy regimes in and around these states are an important part of the explanation of the fact of worsening inequality. The net effect of these policy changes was the easing of conditions under which national economies interact with one another, hence the use of the term 'economic openness'.

The process of easing the conditions under which national economies interact with one another is determined by technological developments such as cost-cutting advances in transport and electronics, but also by the decisions of governments to reduce tariffs on the flow of goods and services, for instance, and to remove other regulatory barriers. These steps are usually seen as part of a broader process of 'liberalizing' the economy, which aims at lowering transaction costs and reducing inefficiencies. Indicators of 'economic openness' are of two types: One type attempts to approximate the policy process of liberalization by capturing the degree to which taxes on trade have been reduced, or the degree to which restrictions on capital flows have

Table 3.4 Dynamics of income inequality in low- and middle-income countries, 1980–1999

Region	Inequality increased since 1980	No change, or decline since 1980	Too few observations to detect trend
SSA (37)	Mozambique, CAR, Nigeria, Lesotho, Rwanda, Cameroon, Malawi, Congo Republic, Gabon, Tanzania, Senegal, Zimbabwe, Seychelles, Madagascar, Liberia, South Africa, Cote d'Ivoire, Ghana, Botswana, Ethiopia, Zambia, Togo, Gambia, Angola, Somalia	Kenya, Swaziland, Equatorial Guinea, Mauritius, Uganda	*Benin; Burkina Faso; Cape Verde; Mauritania; Namibia; Sierra Leone; Sudan*
MENA (11)	Algeria, Iraq, Iran, Egypt, Syria, Turkey, Oman, Libya	Morocco, Jordan, Tunisia	
LAC (25)	Jamaica, Venezuela, Trinidad, Suriname, Guatemala, Uruguay, Ecuador, El Salvador, Panama, Peru, Argentina, Mexico, Bolivia, Honduras, Barbados, Dom Rep, Brazil, Colombia, Chile	Nicaragua, Haiti, Costa Rica	*Belize; Paraguay; St Vincent*
SASIA (7)	Bangladesh, Pakistan	India, Sri Lanka, Afghanistan, Nepal	*Bhutan*
SEASIA (5)	Philippines	Myanmar, Malaysia, Indonesia, Thailand	
OCEANIA (4)	PNG	Tonga, Fiji	*Samoa*
Transition Countries (21)	Albania, Ukraine, Moldova, Hungary, Bulgaria, Armenia, Poland, Slovak Republic, Yugoslavia, Macedonia, Mongolia, Russia, China (PRC), Croatia, Kyrgyzstan, Czech Republic	Lithuania	*Romania; Azerbaijan; Bosnia; Latvia*

Source: Based on UTIP EHII data (Galbraith and Kum, 2005).

been removed, for instance. We refer to these as indicators of liberaliz-ation. The other type captures the outcomes of a general process of the 'easing' of trade and factor flows between countries, and is what we have in mind when we refer to 'economic openness'. Economic open-ness is partly determined by liberalization policies, but is also affected by technological advances that lower transport and communication costs. Three indicators are often used to capture economic openness: Firstly, the ratio of gross private capital flows to GDP, that is, the sum of the absolute values of direct, portfolio, and other investment inflows and outflows recorded in the balance of payments expressed as a percentage of GDP ('private capital flows'). Secondly, the flow, stock, and/or rate (flow/stock) of foreign direct investment (FDI) rel-ative to GDP (sometimes referred to as 'FDI penetration'), and thirdly, the contribution of the combined value of imports and exports to GDP ('trade openness').

The tale about the changing conditions within their national bor-ders and in the global political economy that compelled countries of the periphery to liberalize their economies from the 1980s onwards is well known. Faced with the double blow of declining income from commodity exports due to economic contraction in the core coun-tries on the one hand, and a blow-out of their debt dues after interest hikes in the USA on the other, developing countries were unable to resist the pressures for policy restructuring that came as condi-tions with aid packages disbursed by multilateral lending institutions. The policy restructuring favoured by lending institutions such as the IMF, the World Bank, and regional multilateral banks was focused on cutting state spending and opening the respective economies to increased trade and foreign investment as efficiency-enhancing mechanisms. Coercive measures used by the multilateral lending institutions and their main backers were complemented by the com-mercial preferences of business elites in the peripheral countries, who found new channels for 'voice' through the democratization pro-cesses that swept through the developing world between the mid 1980s and the mid-1990s. The move towards regionalism in the 1980s and 1990s provided further impetus to reducing traditional barriers to trade and financial flows (Cornia, 2004: 10–23; Frieden, 2006: Chapter 17).

Table 3.5 provides an overview of the degree of openness achieved by developing countries over the last four decades of the twentieth

Table 3.5 Relative economic openness in developing and transition countries, 1960–1999

Region		1960–1964	1965–1969	1970–1974	1975–1979	1980–1984	1985–1989	1990–1994	1995–1999
SSA	PrCapflows			10.554	8.206	7.541	7.439	8.634	16.321
	FDI Stock					15.443	17.803	17.500	23.820
	Trade	54.969	58.105	65.301	74.397	72.051	68.201	72.709	80.976
	Free trade		4.879	4.695	4.890	4.960	5.137	5.895	6.199
MENA	PrCapflows			7.707	6.360	4.158	4.687	8.794	7.124
	FDI Stock					11.029	13.166	14.971	16.494
	Trade	54.327	45.028	57.565	69.850	67.202	55.191	68.020	62.867
	Free trade		4.302	5.653	4.737	4.760	4.961	5.679	6.365
LAC	PrCapflows		4.600	5.996	21.017	18.896	16.815	12.552	15.078
	FDI Stock					9.773	11.926	15.679	22.188
	Trade	48.341	48.908	51.777	60.083	61.967	59.012	61.392	69.255
	Free trade		5.278	5.386	5.111	4.643	5.571	6.908	6.771
SASIA	PrCapflows				1.096	1.739	3.365	5.603	4.380
	FDI Stock					1.734	2.084	2.512	4.456
	Trade	40.661	31.106	24.798	30.598	39.573	40.112	44.468	51.277
	Free trade		2.433	3.430	4.255	4.042	3.829	4.859	5.489
SEASIA	PrCapflows			7.350	6.426	6.515	5.900	11.469	12.846
	FDI Stock					7.256	8.728	11.608	20.205
	Trade	41.081	38.216	41.948	48.890	56.033	56.021	71.922	91.513
	Free trade		4.931	5.303	5.826	5.610	5.761	6.011	6.421

Table 3.5 (Continued)

Region		1960–1964	1965–1969	1970–1974	1975–1979	1980–1984	1985–1989	1990–1994	1995–1999
OCEANIA	*PrCapflows*				5.348	6.932	6.200	9.431	14.509
	FDI Stock					14.474	15.193	19.898	26.028
	Trade	66.640	78.003	91.388	90.715	93.749	94.852	94.317	103.895
	Free trade		5.647	6.065	6.400	6.515	6.375	6.429	6.233

Notes:

PrCapflows = Private capital flows.

FDI Stock = Stock of Foreign Direct Investment as percentage of GDP.

Trade = Sum of value of imports and exports as percentage of GDP.

Free trade = Estimation of degree of economic openness in the trade sector.

Sources: Own calculations, based on economic openness data reported in World Bank *World Development Indicators, 2006 CD-ROM*. Assessments of 'free trade' from Gwartney and Lawson (2004).

century, using three measures of economic openness (private capital flows as percentage of GDP; the stock of FDI as percentage of GDP; and the combined value of exports and imports as a percentage of GDP), and one measure of trade liberalization ('free trade'). The latter is derived from Gwartney and Lawson (2004) and is a 10-point index capturing the extent to which a country reduces taxes on international trade and removes other regulatory trade barriers.

The discussion of inequality trends above has revealed that SSA, MENA, and LAC are the three regions that experienced the most significant worsening of inequality during the era of globalization 'Mark II'. Table 3.5 indicates that worsening inequality coincided, in all three cases, with significant trade liberalization over the same period, and that capital and trade flows also increased steadily in all three cases. Before we conclude, however, that increased openness therefore always worsens inequality, note should be taken of the fact that increased openness can also be associated with lowering of inequality levels, as we see in the case of SEASIA since the 1970s. Clearly, the relationship between openness and liberalization, on the one hand, and inequality trends, on the other hand, is more nuanced than is often believed. Everything seems to hinge on the conditions under which openness and liberalization take place.

From the perspective of standard trade theory, trade openness favours the holders of abundant/cheap factors of production. The Heckscher-Ohlin trade model concludes that under conditions of an open trading system countries will tend to export goods intensive in the factors that they have in abundance, while they will import goods that use factors that are relatively scarce. With the easing of trade that generalized openness brings, domestic prices of goods whose production uses scarce factors will tend to fall as imports drive down local prices, while prices for goods that use abundant factors intensively will rise. Stolper and Samuelson (1941) extended this insight by adding that returns to the holders of factors of production that are intensively used will rise absolutely and disproportionally as prices for those goods rise, while the exact opposite will happen to the holders of scarce factors used in the production of goods whose prices fall (Ray, 1998: 648–652; Reuveny and Li, 2003: 579). All else being equal, then, countries whose advantage lies in the primary and extractive industries would receive returns that favour the holders of land and resources which, given the historical patterns of land ownership in developing countries, would be to the benefit only of a small sector of the population, driving up inequality levels as a result. This mechanism probably accounts for much of the rising inequality trends in SSA, MENA, and in the resource-abundant countries of LAC during the latter part of the twentieth century. But, this can only be part of the explanation of rising inequality because it ignores the fate of manufacturing labour with which quite a few countries, specifically in the LAC region, by the 1970s were relatively well endowed. In view of the predictions of trade theory, one would expect trade openness to generate increased returns for abundant labour in these countries, and hence declining levels of wage inequality. However, it is becoming increasingly clear that standard trade theory is not a reliable guide to predicting the relative income of labour under conditions of openness. To understand why the return on labour declines, rather than increases as trade theory suggests, we have to expand the basic trade model discussed above to include many countries with varying ratios of skilled to unskilled labour. In general, openness in a large n system should raise the relative demand for skilled labour in middle-income developing countries whose supply of skilled relative to unskilled labour is higher than the world average (Anderson, 2005: 1047). In addition, the presence in a relative open world system of large producers and exporters of goods which use unskilled labour intensively may reduce the advantage that smaller latecomers may have in unskilled labour, thus altering the demand-structure in favour of more skilled labour in these societies. If skilled labour is relatively scarce, though, this shifting demand will benefit only a few and overall inequality will thus increase (Wood, 1997). Thus, while East and Southeast Asia in the 1960s and 1970s could benefit maximally from the inequality-reducing effects of its increased trade with the rest of the world – thus confirming standard trade theory – this option was relatively closed for the manufacturing sector in LAC. When countries of this region started to ease trade restrictions in the 1980s, they were confronted with the presence on world markets of large, dominant producers of cheap goods that used unskilled and low-skilled labour intensively, in particular China. This undermined whatever little advantage the manufacturing sector in LAC had in unskilled labour, by increasing relative returns on skilled labour, and thus pushing up wage inequality (Wood, 1997). Robbins (1996) found that the relative demand for skilled labour indeed did increase during episodes of trade liberalization in LAC countries such as Argentina, Costa Rica, Colombia, Chile, Mexico, and Uruguay. Subsequent studies on LAC, reviewed by Anderson (2005: 1056), confirm the finding that the easing of trade in LAC in the 1980s and 1990s favoured skilled labour disproportionally to unskilled labour. Dani Rodrik suggests that trade allows firms in developing countries to replace unskilled labour with cheap imports, thus further countering the inequality-mitigating effects that standard trade theory postulates (Rodrik, 1997).[7]

Increased FDI penetration also played a role in worsening inequality in host developing countries during this era, but again the full story of the effect of FDI is more complex than is often assumed. The negative consequences of FDI for inequality levels in developing low- and middle-income countries are emphasized by a number of studies that are theoretically informed by the world-system approach (Bornschier and Chase-Dunn, 1985). Authors in this tradition argue that expansive globalization is fuelled in particular by the predatory behaviour of transnational capital which aims at incorporating far-flung parts of the world into the global capitalist system. The chosen means of transnational capitalism is FDI by transnational corporations (TNCs). High levels of FDI penetration into low- and middle-income countries, so the argument goes, exacerbate 'dualism' in the economy by creating well-paid jobs in the modern 'international' high-skill sector, but leaving large segments of 'traditional' low-skilled or unskilled workers marginalized. In addition to the technological changes introduced by FDI, the bargaining power of TNCs could deflate revenue earnings and hence the welfare spending of host governments, and could undermine the achievements of organized labour (Rudra, 2002a, 2002b; Rudra and Haggard, 2005). FDI penetration leads to a modernization of certain local sectors which would increase the relative demand for skilled labour, which in turn would lead to higher levels of inequality in developing countries if skills are not widely disseminated. Larger degrees of FDI penetration should, therefore, correlate with higher levels of inequality, despite the neo-liberal article of faith that openness favours unskilled labour.

These expectations have been tested by a large number of studies, notably Kentor (2001) and Beer (1999), and Beer and Boswell (2002) who find a significant positive correlation between FDI penetration and inequality. Tsai (1995), on the other hand, finds that this correlation only holds in certain regions of the world, and not in others. The most sophisticated study to date (Alderson and Nielsen, 1999) partially confirms the theoretical expectations of the world-system perspective, and also finds that the inequality effect of FDI penetration extends across all regions of the developing world. However, their study detects a non-linear relationship between FDI stock per capita and inequality, suggesting that the inequality effect is more concentrated and deeper in countries that rely very heavily on imported investment capital and weaker in countries with a low dependence on FDI. It is relative dependence on foreign investment that determines whether FDI leads to greater income inequality, they conclude (Alderson and Nielsen, 1999: 627). As a rule poorer countries are more dependent on foreign investment than wealthier states, given the relatively low levels of domestic saving in the former. Given the expectation that FDI increases returns on skilled labour, and because the distribution of skills are so skewed in peripheral countries, one would expect FDI to be more positively correlated with rising inequality in the latter than in higher-income countries. To check whether this is indeed the case, Figure 3.2 plots inequality levels against FDI stock/GDP for two groups of countries for which we have data on FDI stocks since 1980. The scatter plot and fitted regression line on the right includes all developing countries in our sample, while the plot on the left includes the transition countries and the high-income countries. Peripheral countries indeed register a strong positive connection between FDI penetration and inequality, while the exact opposite holds in the case of the other category.

Low- and lower-middle income developing countries are clearly more vulnerable to the inequality-increasing effects of economic openness than their richer counterparts. Independent confirmation of this openness-vulnerability thesis is supplied by Milanovic (2002), who finds on the basis of evidence gleaned from household surveys that the inequality-increasing effects of openness and liberalization are much more pronounced in the case of lower income countries. This vulnerability accounts, to a large extent, for the increases in mean

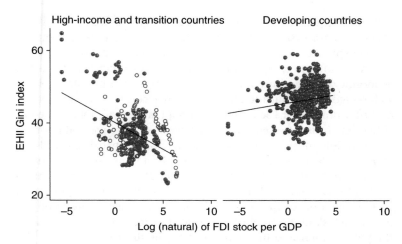

Figure 3.2 The relationship between the stock of FDI/GDP and income inequality in developing and non-developing countries, 1960–1999
$N = 1235$
Notes and Sources:
Estimated Household Income Inequality data from UTIP (Galbraith and Kum, 2005); observations at $t+5$.
Foreign Direct Investment stock as percentage of GDP from UNCTAD (2002); observations at t.

inequality over the last two to three decades of the twentieth century in regions where low- and lower-middle income countries are concentrated, such as SSA, LAC, and MENA.

That does not imply that economic openness is an unmitigated curse for developing countries. As is the case with so many of the other variables we are looking at in explaining why developing countries are more unequal than high-income countries, the dissemination of skills through broad quality education also in this case determines whether a society benefits from economic openness or not. As skills dissemination is positively correlated with per capita income level, we find that middle-income countries with relatively solid educational systems, such as those populating the SEASIA region, share the higher factor rewards that flow from openness more generally, and that openness in those countries is thus associated with declining inequality levels.

Rising inequality is thus not attributable to increased openness *simpliciter*, but at the same time economic openness is an important part of the explanation why the populations of poorer developing countries have not universally shared in the income-enhancing effects that economic openness potentially brings. If a country's population is not well served by its educational system and access to skills remains the exclusive domain of a select few, that population will not share equitably in the fruits of economic efficiency. The challenge that poor and lower middle income countries thus face in a globalizing world is to increase the level and efficiency of its public and private commitment to disseminate quality skills widely and rapidly (Alderson and Nielsen, 1999: 611; Checci, 2004: 105–106). To prescribe to developing countries to open up to the presumed benefits of a globalized economy before such skills dissemination has taken place, is to lead them down the path of increased inequality and all the ills associated with that (see Chapter 5).

The failure of many developing states to provide quality education to a broad segment of society is an important part of the explanation of persistent high levels of economic inequality under conditions of economic modernization. The backlog facing developing countries in terms of disseminating educational opportunities and skills more equitably amongst their population is illustrated by Table 3.6. The table compares public spending on education, equity in educational opportunities, and depth of educational achievement across three groups of countries. The degree to which educational opportunities are equally available for the population as a whole or whether education is the privilege of a few is captured by Thomas, Wang, and Fan (2003) in a dataset which contains a Gini coefficient measure (0–1) of educational inequality. Depth of education refers to how well educated a population on average is, and this can be traced using Barro and Lee's (2000) measure of how many years of schooling the population aged 25 and older on average had received. By the end of the 1990s, developing countries on average were roughly twice as unequal in the provision of education opportunities to their populations compared with the other two country categories, and they had achieved only about half of the educational depth that these two groups of countries had. Notice, however, that public spending by developing countries on education as a share of GDP did not trail that of the other two groups by much, implying that the level of

Table 3.6 Education profile of three groups of countries, 1960–1999

		1960–1964	1965–1969	1970–1974	1975–1979	1980–1984	1985–1989	1990–1994	1995–1999
High income	Education inequality	0.361	0.347	0.358	0.325	0.317	0.297	0.290	0.284
	Education spending	3.172	3.910	4.547	4.932	4.919	4.741	4.898	5.000
	Depth of education	5.760	6.198	6.594	7.109	7.626	8.169	8.664	8.955
Developing countries	Education inequality	0.656	0.637	0.628	0.584	0.560	0.540	0.522	0.504
	Education spending	2.519	3.216	3.609	3.840	4.006	3.781	3.982	4.107
	Depth of education	2.147	2.397	2.596	3.081	3.426	3.845	4.311	4.681
Transition	Education inequality	0.292	0.266	0.305	0.276	0.282	0.245	0.246	0.246
	Education spending	3.550	4.230	1.823	2.448	4.514	4.469	5.356	4.852
	Depth of education	6.518	6.983	6.883	7.317	7.561	8.449	8.774	8.814

Sources: Figures on education inequality (in Gini coefficient) from Thomas *et al.* (2003).
Data on spending of central government on all forms of education (per cent of GDP) from *World Development Indicators 2006* CD-ROM.
'Depth of Education' is from Barro and Lee (2000), and registers number of years spent at school by cohort 25 years and older.

spending is not be the determining factor. We should look at how well the money is spent, and at whom it is targeted.[8] Countries in Southeast and East Asia spend less of their GDP on education than states in SSA, but outcomes in terms of dissemination and quality differ substantially between these regions. Nevertheless, the level of public spending is important: In the regions where income inequality increased since the 1980s, educational spending stagnated or declined in the preceding and concurrent periods. In SSA, educational spending declined from a cross-country mean of 5.3 per cent of GDP in the semi-decade 1980–1984 to a mean of 4.3 per cent over the next 15 years. In LAC, the mean across countries declined from 4.2 per cent for the period 1975–1979 to 3.8 per cent over the next 20 years. MENA also experienced a decline in the average educational spending during the 1990s. Declining public investment in education in SSA, LAC, and MENA is one reason why there have been very slow improvements in the depth of education achieved in these regions compared to mean levels achieved for the sample as a whole. In contrast, East Asia and parts of Southeast Asia invested heavily in widely targeted education, registered significant increases in the depth of educational achievement compared to the mean for the total sample, and also registered decreasing levels of inequality, completing the causal chain.

Domestic policies, specifically those that have to do with the improvement and dissemination of skills, are therefore as important as the external factors of trade and capital openness when considering the causes of the exacerbation of inequality in developing countries during the late twentieth century. The most significant intervening variable that determines the exact nature of the effects of economic openness is the degree to which countries have managed to institute programmes of rapid and equitable skill dissemination. Those countries that have done so before the arrival of globalization 'Mark II' were best prepared to draw the undeniable wealth-increasing benefits of trade and foreign investment, in a way that increased economic opportunities for a broader cross section of society than those who did not. As globalization 'Mark II' intensified during the 1980s and 1990s, increasing the constraints on many poorer developing due to debt hangovers and the fiscal discipline that an open world economy imposed, it became increasingly difficult for them to make up the lost ground. In addition, a significant number of countries were prevented from engaging in the demanding processes of general skills enhancement due to internal leadership failures, violent civil conflict, and in extreme cases, state collapse. As Robert Wade notes, however, the phenomenon of state collapse is not unrelated to the dynamics of globalization propped up by the norms of the neo-liberal economic ideology that came to dominate macroeconomic thinking and policy making in the 1980s and 1990s (Wade, 2005a). This is not to deny that leadership failures also played a significant part in the story of worsening inequality during this period. As we shall see in Chapter 4, the widespread experimentation with democracy in the developing world in the 1980s and 1990s often made matters worse from an inequality perspective, rather than better.[9] State capture by predator elites became a feature of a number of states in the developing world during this era, as a second generation of post-independence state leaders shared less of the commitments to equity and nation building than their immediate predecessors had. The predator state emerged in its most glaring depravity in Zaire under Mobutu (Young and Turner, 1988) and in Bokasa's Central African Republic, but elements of it could be detected also in many other locations on the African continent and in parts of LAC and MENA. Predation by elites who use the state and its resources for personal enrichment and promotion of their kin was tolerated during the Cold War by both sides in the ideological divide, and turned out to be one of the main reasons for the poor quality of public policy and institutions in these states. Elite dominance of political and economic processes is by no means restricted to predator states, but, as we shall see in Chapter 4, is a significant feature of even those developing societies who successfully completed transitions to democracy in the 1980s and 1990s, giving rise to what Karen Renner termed 'exclusionary democracy' (1985), that is, democracy that produces socio-economic benefits that accrue only to an elite group.

Conclusions

We began Chapter 2 with a puzzle: Why is it that lower income countries are so much more prone to inequality than higher-income countries? Now, after having reviewed the theoretical arguments (Chapter 2) and the empirical evidence related to five centuries of inequality (this chapter), we can venture an answer. The reader who has followed the lines of arguments developed in these pages will realize that any simplistic one-variable answer cannot do justice to the question, but that it is nevertheless possible to develop an integrated multi-faceted answer as long as we have clarity on what the *explanandum* entails. What has to be explained is why the gross incomes of households/individuals in developing countries are so dispersed compared to the narrower scope of dispersion of incomes in higher-income countries. We saw that individual gross income is determined primarily by how a country is endowed by factors of production, by the share that the household members have of these endowments, by the returns received on those endowments, and by the size of the household to which the individual belongs. A broad dispersal of individual/household incomes in a country is primarily due to (a) an unequal distribution of ownership of the endowed factors of production, and (b) large differences in the returns on the different factors of production held. As a rule, developing countries are characterized by concentrated ownership of those factors that receive the most lucrative returns in an open global economy. This concentration is not an accident of nature, although the initial 'natural endowments' that individual countries received do play a role. The rich endowment of developing countries with land and natural resources determined that expansionary merchant capitalism from the sixteenth century onwards was constant on the lookout for ways in which to incorporate these regions into the global division of labour on which capitalist expansion depends. This incorporation created clear distinctions between the core and the periphery with attending divisions of power and privilege. The politically subjected periphery was burdened with providing those factors of production that were in relative short supply in the core countries. For the first four centuries of the evolution of the capitalist world economy, this division of labour ensured large returns in the periphery for the owners of land and natural resources. In those peripheral regions where the initial factor endowment favoured large-scale exploitation of the land and natural resources, the colonial authorities and their local allies created institutions of property ownership, political control, labour markets, and patterns of education provision that ensured that ownership of land and resources was concentrated in the hands of the colonial commercial interests and settlers, while the indigenous population was reproduced as a source of pliable, cheap labour. The combined effect of these institutions was to create and sustain large differentials in the returns/income received by property-owners compared to that of the majority of citizens – the owners of unskilled labour power. In countries where the indigenous population was large compared to the number of settlers from abroad, the median income sank massively below the mean income. Peripheral areas which were less richly endowed with land and natural resources, and where returns on labour were relatively high in comparison to land rents, did not escape colonial domination altogether but at least escaped the worst of the inequality-creating effects of colonialism that were focused on gaining control over land and natural resources. By the nineteenth century, patterns of colonial expansion and control determined that relatively land- and resource-rich Latin America and the Caribbean, Africa, South and Southeast Asia would be high-inequality areas, while labour-rich areas in East Asia would have relatively lower income inequality levels.

The arrival of the industrial era and the expansion of the trade in manufactured goods and the flow of investment capital that accompanied it worsened inequality levels in most of the periphery. Due to the unequal dynamics of the political and market institutions in operation in both the independent and dependent periphery, only a small portion of the population benefited from the economic modernization that the industrial era brought. Modernization increased the premium on skilled labour, and thus further increased income differentials which were no longer driven only by the differentiated returns received by landowners and non-landowners in the traditional sectors, but increasingly also by the difference of mean incomes between the traditional and the modern sectors, and by the dispersal of income within the modern sector. This same dynamic played itself out in the rapidly industrializing core countries, but by providing generalized education and income-enhancing social relief from the 1880s onwards, starting with Bismarck's social welfare policies in Germany, the major distributional effects of economic modernization were mitigated over time, to such an extent that by 1950 the core countries had brought income inequality largely under control. The countries of the independent periphery, except in East Asia and gradually also in parts of Southeast Asia, were largely unsuccessful in emulating these inequality-mitigating policies of the core, and where redistributive programmes were launched, the absence of popular sovereignty and effective democratic control over the implementation of state policies meant that the redistribution of assets, including skills, favoured only the landed elite and sections of the urban middle classes, including a small labour aristocracy. The spread and depth of education in Latin America and South Asia continued to lag way behind that of the core countries, while the rapid expansion of education opportunities achieved in East Asia were not matched either. Economic modernization in the dependent periphery of Africa arrived slowly and unevenly, but where it did arrive it further worsened inequality in the absence of any national capacity to take actions to counter the negative distributional effects of modernization.

When globalization 'Mark II' burst onto the scene during the last three decades of the twentieth century, only the core industrialized countries, plus a sprinkling of peripheral countries with well-established education programmes and competent state authorities, were capable of weathering the worsening of inequality that resulted from the global demand for technology- and skills-intensive goods and services, and the redesigning of the global division of labour that now favoured countries with rich endowments of relative cheap, semi-skilled, and skilled labour. Mainstream economic theory predicts that countries with a relatively rich endowment of labour would register declining inequality under conditions of enhanced trade in manufactured goods and increased stocks of FDI, but the empirical record shows that this happened only in peripheral countries that had already invested well in spreading industrial skills broadly among the population in the preceding years, namely Costa Rica in Latin America, Indonesia, Malaysia, South Korea, Singapore, parts of India, and Mauritius and to some extent the south of Uganda in Africa. For the rest, globalization may have brought many other benefits, but the mitigation of high levels of inequality was not one of them. Failure of leadership in many newly independent developing countries in the 1980s and 1990s undermined the capacity of governments to devise and implement strategies to mitigate the negative externalities of globalization 'Mark II', and to exploit its positive externalities. The result was the exacerbation of economic inequality in most parts of the developing world, pushing historically already high levels to the odious heights registered at the end of the second millennium.

4
Democratization to the Rescue?

Domestic politics and policies, the previous two chapters have argued, contribute substantially to the maintenance and exacerbation of odious inequality in developing countries. Does this mean that political reform, and in particular the introduction of democracy, can reverse the historical patterns of increasing inequality? After all, Chapter 3 argued that it was the introduction of universal franchise and responsive government, amongst others, that contributed to the ability of core capitalist countries to put a break on inequality during the heyday of the welfare state.[1] It is commonly assumed that the introduction of democracy into a polity allows the poorer sections of the community to alter the distribution of wealth and income in their favour. The assumption that the acquisition of political power by the once disenfranchised leads to greater economic equity was and is at the core of the political programmes of many working-class based political movements, and also provides one of the motivations for rich owners of immovable wealth in unequal societies to resist democratization vehemently, and as long as possible (Boix, 2003). Understandbly, thus, expectations were high that the eventual widespread arrival of democracy in the developing world during the 1980s and 1990s would empower the poor and previously disenfranchised to mitigate odious inequality and to secure a larger degree of economic equity. Were these expectations justified?

Given the brief comments made in the two previous chapters in this regard, the reader should by now be forewarned that the relationship between regime type and economic inequality is quite complex, particularly in an era of generalized economic openness. We noted that the data for the latter part of the twentieth century suggest that it is the distinction between consistent and inconsistent regime types, rather than the distinction between democracy and autocracy alone, that is important. Economic equity is more likely to be achieved in countries with stable political regimes and effective public policy institutions, and both attributes are associated more with consistent than with inconsistent regime types. Consistent democracies seem to have a slight edge on autocracies when it comes to durability and effectiveness, but these differences are less significant than the distinctions between consistent and inconsistent regimes. This chapter aims at deepening our appreciation of this important finding by considering not only the impact that the nature of a political regime has on distributional outcomes, but also what the effect of *regime change*, and in particular *democratization* is. The chapter thus considers the dynamics of politics, rather than just the statics of regime types and state attributes. The availability of data restricts our analysis to the period 1960 to 1999, but the results produced also have a resonance beyond the turn of the century, with experiments at democratization still continuing in a large variety of low- and middle-income countries.

The last third of the twentieth century witnessed numerous and in some cases repeated regime changes in the developing world, due firstly to the effect of decolonization in Africa and Asia in the 1960s and 1970s, secondly to the tumultuous reshaping of the political landscape in many parts of independent Latin America during these same decades, and thirdly to the worldwide political transformations in the wake of the decline and collapse of alternative ideological programmes to political and economic liberalism during the 1980s and 1990s. The latter two decades in particular witnessed 'a democratic breakthrough without precedent in world history' as Larry Diamond calls it (1999: 24).[2] Despite the prevalence of the phenomenon of regime change in low- and middle-income countries during these decades, very few studies have moved beyond the static focus on regime type and regime duration to also look at how *change* in the type of reigning political regime subsequently affects the distribution of wealth and income in a country.[3] To fill this gap, this chapter proceeds by first defining and operationalizing the concept of regime change before looking at what the empirical record tells us about the distributional effects of regime change. A theoretical framework is developed to help us explain why democratization today is so seldom successful in mitigating odious inequality in developing countries, and is then put to some empirical tests. The general conclusion that emerges is that the introduction of competitive elections based on general franchise is not sufficient for the mitigation of odious inequality in countries with high initial levels of economic inequality, and under global conditions of macroeconomic openness. Instead, there is a high likelihood that electoral democracy and its trappings could exacerbate inequality in the medium to longer term, if special care is not taken to offset the systemic and country-specific factors that propel the machinery of odious inequality.[4]

The dynamics of regime change

As noted in Chapter 2, the term *political regime* refers to the set of norms, rules, and practices that determine the distribution of political rights between actors in a polity, and what this means for the exercise of control over institutions of public power (Przeworski *et al.*, 2000: 18; Sanders, 1981: 51–63). In its broadest meaning, 'regime change' refers to the process in which one regime type is replaced by another. In this chapter we focus on one specific manifestation of regime change, namely *democratization*, that is, the process through which a regime becomes democratic or deepens its democratic nature. As emphasized by the recent and growing literature on 'inconsistent' (also referred to as 'mixed', 'partial', or 'defective') regimes, the political landscape of the developing world is dominated by variations on the democratic theme.[5] These variations reflect different configurations of the elements or attributes that constitute 'consistent democracy', alternatively 'consolidated' or 'full' democracy.[6] Consistent democracies are characterized by a number of essential and interdependent features: Firstly, by formal and substantive *political equality*, that is, the political regime guarantees civil and political liberties, and has done away with formal and informal restrictions on political participation and with privileged political positions for certain groups (such as the military, for example). Secondly, by institutions and procedures that empower citizens to influence public policy decisions decisively. Thirdly, by institutional mechanisms that place effective controls and constraints on the recruitment of and exercise of power by the executive branch of government.[7] In short, consistent democracy is characterized by *popular sovereignty*. Inconsistent democracies, on the other hand, are deficient in at least one but very often more than one of these interdependent features. Typically, inconsistent democracies have the trappings of popular sovereignty such as regular competitive elections based on universal franchise, but are characterized by exclusionary politics in which political participation and equality is constrained, and legislative and executive power is captured by a powerful elite group who cannot be held accountable by the broad citizenry.[8] As Merkel comments,

> For democratic elections to be 'meaningful', not only does the selection process of the governing elite have to be democratically fair, but there also has to be an institutional guarantee that the democratically elected representatives rule by democratic and constitutional principles in the time period between elections. (2005: 37)

In inconsistent democracies, the distribution of political power and influence is thus not adequately insulated from the distribution of economic or other forms of privilege and power (Rueschemeyer, Stephens and Stephens, 1992).

In view of the above, the term 'democratization' has a broader scope than simply as reference to the process through which an autocracy is transformed into a democracy. Democratization can also refer to the transition from an autocracy to an inconsistent democracy, and/or to the transition from an inconsistent democracy to a consistent democracy. This implies a three-way distinction: Democratization can refer to a regime *transformation* from (a) autocracy to democracy, or from (b) autocracy to inconsistent democracy, and to (c) a regime *transition* from an inconsistent democracy to consistent democracy. This three-way distinction contrasts with another set of regime changes, here referred to as *adverse regime change*. This includes adverse transformation (when either a consistent or an inconsistent democracy turns into an autocracy) and adverse transition (which refers to a consistent democracy sliding back into an inconsistent form of democracy).

The table in Appendix B to this book begins our exploration of the effects of regime change on economic inequality during the period

1960 to 1999. It includes all the regime changes in countries for which we have data on both their Polity2 regime score from Marshall and Jaggers (2002), and their Gini index score derived from the Estimated Household Income Inequality (EHII) dataset (Galbraith and Kum, 2005). During the period 1960 to 1999 there were a total of 142 regime changes, of which 86 involved democratization. Seventy-eight regime transformations witnessed the introduction of competitive electoral politics based on universal adult suffrage into previously autocratic societies, while eight were transitions from inconsistent to consistent democracy. Appendix B also reports on incidences of *adverse* regime change: In all but one case inconsistent democracies deteriorated into autocracies, and there was only one example (Malaysia) in which a consistent democracy changed into an inconsistent one. While democratization was by far the most common regime change in the period 1960–1999, very few democratic experiments resulted in the creation of consistent democracies. Among the developing countries, that result was achieved only in the case of Mongolia and Uruguay. On the other hand, adverse regime changes were quite common. By the end of the twentieth century, consistent democracy continued to be an extremely scarce commodity among developing countries.

As we are interested in tracing the effects, if there are any, of the dynamics of regime change on inequality levels, the last two columns of the table in Appendix B list observations of the available EHII Gini index scores for the country experiencing the transition. The first observation is from the year in which the change occurred or was completed (t), and the second at $t+5$. The picture that emerges from comparing these last two columns with the regime change columns is very mixed, though, and no dominant pattern emerges. Both pro-democratic and adverse regime-change incidents are associated with rising *and* with declining inequality. Investigating the relationship between the various categories of regime change and a measure that distinguishes between rising/declining inequality post-regime-change also produces very low and statistically insignificant Pearson's two-tailed correlation scores. Clearly, political change taken on its own is not a good predictor of what will happen subsequently with economic inequality. Could it be that it is the conditions under which democratization takes place, rather than democratization as such, that play the determining role? A fruitful way of answering this question is to turn to an *a priori* investigation of the logic of the hypothesis that democratization should result in a redistribution of economic opportunities, as exemplified in what has come to be known as the median voter hypothesis (MVH).

Why the rabble can't redistribute[9]

The MVH contains the clearest statement of the expectation that democratization should *mutatis mutandis* enable the middle class and their class allies to redistribute income and the opportunities to generate income. The MVH originally became associated with thinking about inequality and redistribution in attempts to find a political-economy explanation for the negative effects that high levels of inequality are said to have on economic growth. It has been argued that higher levels of inequality lead, in democracies at least, to government initiatives to redistribute wealth through progressive tax systems. The logic behind this assumption is that the more a median voter finds his or her income levels to fall below that of the mean income level, the more he/she will favour redistribution (Alesina and Perotti, 1996; Alesina and Rodrik, 1994; Persson and Tabellini, 1994). Progressive taxes in turn are assumed to punish those who invest and save most, and thus serve as disincentives which in turn harm growth prospects. However, the MVH also has a life of its own in the study of comparative politics outside of the study of the effect of inequality on growth (to which we shall return in Chapter 5).[10] It can be used – as in this chapter – to specify and operationalize the mechanism through which democratization could lead to redistribution. The MVH is an extremely parsimonious model of voting outcomes, and deliberately so. It seems more constructive to start with a minimum model and then consider what to add to enable us to understand a phenomenon, rather than to try and grasp the complexity of the phenomenon in one comprehensive swoop. Although the ideas behind the MVH can be traced back to the liberal fears of the nineteenth century that democracies could be more expropriative than oligarchies (Lee, 2003) it was Downs (1957) and especially Meltzer and Richard (1981) that gave current currency to the MVH.[11]

The MVH asks us to imagine, not unrealistically, that a society is composed of members who are differentiated in terms of their individual share of total income. In high-inequality countries the citizenry is rather starkly divided into a rich, powerful elite and a poor mass public who compete with one another.[12] Let us further assume that the median income level is lower than the mean, which is the case in all 'real existing' societies. The regime is a democracy in which all adult citizens have the vote. The government sets the tax rate and can use the revenue earned to promote equality of opportunity through, amongst others, universal quality education. Two parties form and compete for the majority of the votes on the basis of a platform that consists of one item only, namely the desired tax rules that will tax all incomes at a common rate and deliver educational opportunities for everyone. A poorer citizen can be expected to vote for the party whose proposed tax rate will maximize her children's educational opportunities. In contrast, the elite power-holders would want to extend educational opportunities only marginally to favour economic growth, but not to the extent that it threatens their knowledge-based power. The MVH states that the tax rate chosen will coincide with the wishes of the voter whose income equals the median income. From a game-theoretic perspective the two competing political parties can reach a unique Nash equilibrium – that is, an outcome where no player can benefit by changing her strategy while the other player keeps her strategy unchanged – if both parties propose the preferred tax rate of the median voter. The MVH entails two conclusions. Firstly, and assuming that all else remains equal, the introduction of the popular vote should enable the poor mass (those citizens whose income levels fall below the mean) to improve their income share anything up to the level of equality around the mean. Extending the vote to all adult citizens thus empowers the 'rabble to redistribute', implying that democracy may be more expropriative and therefore more equalizing than autocracy. Secondly, higher levels of inequality can be expected to lead to increased incentives on the median voter to favour deeper redistribution, seeing that the higher the level of income inequality the bigger the gap between median and mean (Alesina and Rodrik, 1994; Persson and Tabellini, 1994).

Seen from this perspective, what autocracy with its restrictions on political rights and participation does is, in effect, to censor the distribution of voters on the income ladder, shifting the income position of the influential voter higher than that occupied by the median income earner (Rudra and Haggard, 2005: 1018). The likely result is that the decisive 'voter' in an autocracy (if that is not too much of an oxymoron to consider) is not the median income earner whose income falls below the mean, but someone with a higher income. The result is that purely on logical grounds one can expect autocracies to be less committed to redistribution, although this should not be taken to imply that redistribution can never take place within autocracies.[13] The question is whether there are features of the process of democratization in developing countries, or the conditions under which these regime transitions and transformations take place, that could have a censoring effect similar to that of autocracy. What could possibly happen in the case of democratization that could shift the influential voter higher on the income scale than the median income earner? Following the lead of Shapiro, we propose that these features and conditions can be divided into two sets, namely *demand*- versus *supply-side* factors (2003). Applied to the impact of democratization in developing countries, the demand-side factors that stand out are (a) the possibility that the transition to democracy is incomplete, and (b) the effect that policy trade-offs plus the fear of capital flight may have on the strategic calculations of the influential voter. The ability of the public sector to finance and implement programmes of redistribution to a broad section of the population has rightly been singled out as a necessary supply-side condition. Starting with the demand-side factors first, the next few paragraphs explore these features and conditions in somewhat more detail.

Demand-side: When the median income earner is not the median voter

As noted, the MVH assumes that in a democracy the median income earner is also the median voter, that is, the influential voter. If the influential voter, for whatever reason, finds herself higher than the median position on the income scale, it follows that she would demand a tax rate not of equality, and would generally be less inclined to support redistribution than if she was the median income earner. The inconsistent nature of the democracies that generally emerge from regime change in developing countries is one factor that alters the income position of the influential voter in these countries. In inconsistent democracies, political influence tends to be concentrated in the hands of a narrow band of privileged income earners, and not around the median. If we assume that political influence is a consumption good, then citizens with higher incomes should be able to secure more of it than those lower down the income and wealth ladder (Bassett, Burkett, and Putterman, 1999; Putterman, 1997). The politics of incomplete democratization ensures that decisive influence on policy matters is not vested in the electoral process as such, but in mechanisms that systematically privilege a certain influential group whose income status is well above the mean. This includes mechanisms that guarantee a privileged role to the military, for instance (Pakistan, Turkey, and pre-1994 South Africa). More common is that the electoral trappings of democracy are overlaid by networks of patron–client relationships between the occupiers of the executive positions and specific ethic groups in society. Extreme examples of this continued 'big-man' neo-patrimonial form of rule have come to overshadow many recent democratic experiments in Africa (Bratton and van de Walle, 1997: Chapter 7). These features, which relate to the absence of institutionalized constraints on the power of the executive, the incompleteness of the rule of law, and/or gaps in the range of civil and political rights granted to citizens, all restrict the ability of the median income earner to shape public policy through the ballot. More often than not, the net effect of these features of inconsistent democracy ensures the continued dominance of a politically powerful elite group, who use the electoral process to give legitimacy to their rent-seeking predatory activities. This political elite is also an income and wealth elite, and they use whatever political tools available in the tool chest of partial democracy, including elections, to perpetuate their elite position. Under these circumstances, public policy is devised and implemented to favour the already privileged, to the detriment of the median voter and her class allies.

In addition, the influential voter can only be found amongst the voters who turn up at the election booth (Downs, 1957; Lee and Roemer, 1998: 230 and 238). For the turnout to be achieved that would validate the MVH, broad sections of the population must be incorporated in the formation and reproduction of party politics. Well developed and robust programmatic parties, with the capacity to mobilize voters and to successfully articulate their wishes, is a rare commodity in the developing world, even in countries with relatively long histories of independence such as in Latin America (De Ferranti *et al.*, 2004: 130). Also, poor infrastructure and geographic distance may pose prohibitive costs for the poor median income earner and her class allies even to turn up at the ballot station. In addition, there is evidence that the lack of access to education is an important inhibitor of political participation, a factor which affects those potential voters who earn less than the mean income most.[14]

Confirmation comes in the form of evidence that suggests that judging from the most recent wave of mostly incomplete democratic experiments in developing countries, the median voter and her class allies are not able to affect a narrowing of the income differential in their societies. There are of course many factors that influence inequality trends in a society – see Chapter 2 – but in view of the popular but not very discerning belief that all good things flow from democratization, it is instructive to see what effect democratization actually has on the income share of different groups in a society. One instructive study (Nel, 2005a) uses a measure of the income-share gain or loss experienced by households arranged into income deciles. A distinction is made between the poor (the 20 per cent lowest income earning households), the quintile to which the median income earner belongs (the third income quintile), and the rich (top 20 per cent income earners). The required detailed income distribution data for a number of developing countries and for the last two decades of the twentieth century are available through the World Bank's Global Poverty Monitoring Database, which relies on income and expenditure surveys to determine the income/expenditure of households divided into deciles.[15] The study identifies 36 low- and middle-income countries for which we have income/expenditure distribution data for the mid-1980s and the mid-1990s, a period that straddles a large number of recent democratic experiments in developing countries and which is long enough for redistributive effects to be noticed. The sample countries include eight from sub-Saharan Africa; six from the Middle East and North Africa; 13 from Latin America and the Caribbean; and nine from South Asia, Southeast Asia and the Pacific.[16] The available data allow us to trace what happens to the income share of different income groups over a 10-year period from circa 1985 to circa 1995. Figure 4.1 contains three sets of box plots, reflecting the spread of income-share gains/losses made by (a) the third quintile, (b) the poorest quintile, and (c) the wealthy elite (quintile of highest income earners) following democratization (right-hand box in all three sets), and when no democratization had taken place (left-hand box). Democratization is clearly associated with a general tendency towards income-share losses for the median voter and her poor class allies, while the reverse is true for the share of the wealthy elite. When the income-share gains of the two deciles constituting the top quintile are compared (not shown

(a) What happens to the income share of the quintile to which the median voter belongs?

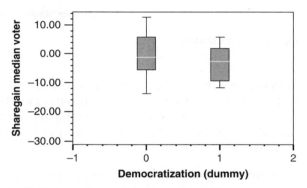

(b) What happens to the income share of the poorest quintile?

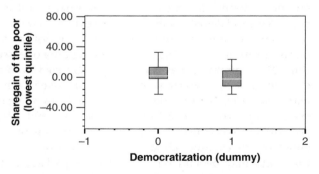

Figure 4.1   Income/expenditure share-gains/losses under conditions of democratization in 36 developing countries, 1985–1999

Note: In all three cases, the right-hand box indicates countries that underwent democratization.

(c) What happens to the income share of the richest quintile?

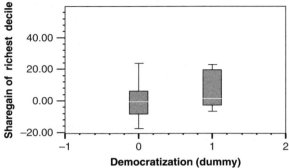

Figure 4.1   (Continued)

in the graphs), it turns out that it is the top decile that registers the highest overall income gain after democratization. One of the effects of inconsistent democratization in developing countries is to shift the influential voter into the ranks of the top 10 per cent of income earners.

Demand-side: Policy trade-offs and the threat of capital flight

The first demand-side factor that we considered above relates to the question whether the median income-earner is indeed the median voter. A second demand-side factor comes into view once we drop one of the core assumptions of the MVH. The logic of the MVH depends on the assumption that the electorate faces only one issue at election time, an assumption that is clearly far removed from the reality of election campaigns where voters are usually asked to choose between party platforms that include a variety of policies, some of which may even imply a trade-off to be made (Roemer, 1998). Party platforms presented to voters usually contain a myriad of issues and the influential voter's eventual choice is determined by trade-offs amongst these and may depend on which party's package deal of issues is most attractive on balance. This may affect her choice of what should be included in the favoured redistributive package, and how redistributive elements such as universal education, public health services, old-age pensions, for instance, should be balanced with policies aimed at promoting economic expansion and creating conditions conducive to investment. The influential voter is likely to be swayed by both immediate and longer-term considerations, and the latter could most likely also include her assessment of which policy platform mix is most conducive to creating the conditions under which her offspring could maximize their economic opportunities. This implies, amongst others, that even when the median income earner is indeed the influential voter, she will not necessarily prefer a tax rate of equality if there is reason to believe that this may harm her or her descendants' future income-earning potential. The history of democratization in advanced countries shows that the rabble hardly ever used the vote to expropriate wealth *tout court*, even if it was possible in terms of the distribution of political power (Lee, 2003), exactly because they rationally would want to avoid instituting policies that could punish them or their descendents at a later time. The demand for equity is thus subject to censoring by the rationality of risk avoidance.

The rational calculations made by the median voter could also be decisively influenced by the epistemic trends in the public debates about macroeconomic policy making and reigning beliefs about the causal effects of specific policy decisions.[17] Clusters of macroeconomic ideas, and the intense ideological struggle for hegemonic status among their proponents do not only shape the choices of decision-makers (Blyth, 2002), but also the decisions made by voters. While the choices made by voters are rational to the extent that they are based on assessments of opportunity and risk, it is likely that the specific understanding of what constitutes opportunity and what risk, and the specific mix of the two, will be shaped by the prevailing ideological 'consensus'.

Most episodes of democratization in the developing countries that we are looking at took place in an era in which a very specific set of macroeconomic beliefs had managed to achieve hegemonic status. A globally organized and deeply entrenched ideological apparatus, favouring the mobility of goods, services, and capital (but not of labour), and which extolled the virtues of fiscal prudence, liberalization of the capital account, of foreign direct investment, and of minimal state regulation of the economy, reigned supreme during the 1980s and 1990s. Using Antonio Gramsci's insights into the ideological component of class rule which is based not only on coercion, but also on the creation of illusionary consensus based on 'common sense'

(1971), authors such as Taylor (2001) and Robinson (1996) show how the macroeconomic consensus of neo-liberalism had come to determine decision making in and around developing countries during the latter part of the twentieth century.[18] Although Taylor and Robinson do not focus on the effects that the hegemony of neo-liberalism had on voter preferences, it is highly likely that this influence was, and perhaps still is, pervasive.

There are two ways in which the ideological impact of neo-liberal beliefs could be decisive: Firstly, if the median voter could be persuaded that the use of fiscal means to redistribute income and wealth would harm, both in the short and longer term, the growth prospects of the society in question, it is highly unlikely that a tax rate of equality would be the preferred choice come election time. As we shall see in Chapter 5, the belief that redistribution is bad for economic growth continues to be one of the most pervasive beliefs in both the academic and popular economic discourse and your run-of-the-mill median voter should not be blamed for internalizing a belief that comes with such impeccable credentials. Secondly, the ideological coherence and persuasiveness of neo-liberalism is self-enforced by the very conditions of economic openness that it propagates. By selling the idea that the liberalization of the capital account is a core dimension of ensuring economic efficiency and eventual growth, the proponents of neo-liberalism not only guarantee that the holders of capital would benefit from the increased returns on mobile capital, but also impose a self-generating check on the desire of the disadvantaged to try and use the vote to significantly alter the distribution of economic opportunities. The more voters in developing countries buy into the idea that capital mobility is good for everyone and under all conditions, the more the voters voluntarily accept restrictions on their ability to redistribute. The bogeyman of capital flight continues to throw its long shadow over the macroeconomic debates in developing countries.

Work done by Boix (2003) and Acemoglu and Robinson (2006) shows that the mobility of capital is indeed an important consideration for elites in highly unequal societies when they have to weigh up the relative costs of continued repression under autocracy versus the potential costs of redistribution. One explanation for the rush of democratization in many repressive autocracies in the latter decades of the twentieth century is that the liberal global regime of relaxing capital controls made elites more inclined to accept democratization, as they could either credibly threaten capital flight and hence restrict the redistributive costs under such a regime or if this tactic proves unsuccessful they could indeed shift their wealth. These options depend on the mobility of the wealth at stake. Should wealth be relatively immobile, for instance when it consists primarily in the form of extensive land owning, or in the form of ownership of country-specific natural resources such as gold or oil, one would expect the wealthy to resist democratization longer than in the case of countries where wealth is more easily transferable to capital that can be moved offshore. As Boix puts it, 'The process of capital liberalization (in a politically fragmented world) fosters the exit option of asset holders that speeds up the introduction of democracy' (2003: 240). But the reverse also holds. The process of capital liberalization undermines the bargaining power of the median voter to effect significant redistribution, as the threat of capital flight holds the process of expropriation to ransom. The demand for redistributive expropriation thus might well be a function of the degree of capital mobility in a world of multiple political jurisdictions.

Supply-side factors

Apart from conditions which could affect the demand for redistribution, the implementation of redistribution driven by popular sovereignty also depends on the ability and capability of public authorities to live up to the demands of the median voter. This means that we have to consider not only the demand-side but also the supply-side of the democracy-redistribution equation.[19] Crucial in this regard is the capacity of the state to collect revenue and to manage effectively redistribution programmes such as a system of public education, basic health provision, social welfare, old-age pensions, and anti-cyclical macroeconomic policy measures to offset the effects of economic contractions or external shocks. We had an opportunity in both Chapters 2 and 3 to review the importance of publicly funded general programmes of education, and noticed that those countries that effectively enhanced the educational opportunities of a broad segment of the population were the most successful in distributing the income windfalls of increased economic interaction with the outside world equitably among their citizens. Here, we consider how democratization affects the ability of public authorities to raise revenue, how this revenue is spent, and who benefits from these spending patterns.

Over the period 1960 to 1999, democratization was not associated with enhanced capacity on the part of states to raise revenue. Instead, there is a statistically significant *negative* correlation between the capacity of states to raise revenue and the incidence of democratization in our sample. The capacity of a state to raise revenue is measured here in terms of what Feng, Kugler, and Zak (2000) call the 'relative political capacity' (RPC) of the state, measured as the ratio of actual government revenue to predicted government revenue.[20] Part of the explanation for this negative correlation lies in the fact that regime changes, even pro-democracy ones, introduce elements of uncertainty and instability to a polity, especially when the transition results in inconsistent democracies which we know are subject to high incidence of political turbulence (Gates *et al.*, 2006), including violent civil conflict (Schatzman, 2005). This explanation must be complemented, though, by looking at how political factors interact with the specific macroeconomic policies implemented by governments under conditions of democratization. Retrogressive fiscal policies, for instance, or the decision to reduce tariffs on imports, would influence the capacity of the state to raise revenue. Figure 4.2 traces how the ability of a state to raise revenue is affected by the political-economic order in that society. For both democracies (right) and non-democracies (left) in the developing world, the implementation of neo-liberal macroeconomic policies is associated with declining capacity to raise revenue. The measure of the extent to which neo-liberal policies are pursued by state authorities is the so-called 'economic freedom' measure developed by the Fraser Institute (Gwartney and Lawson, 2004). A state scores high on this measure if it manages to keep the state sector small, removes obstacles to international trade and capital mobility, respects private property rights, and deregulates the labour and other markets in general. Neo-liberal democracies – that is, exactly the type of political-economic regime that the foreign policies of OECD countries and the multilateral financial institutions have sought to encourage in the developing world – are the least capable of raising the revenue that is indispensable for implementing the type of policies that the median income earner would prefer if she had the decisive vote. The ideological hegemony of neo-liberalism does not only affect the demand for redistribution as we saw above. It also places constraints on the

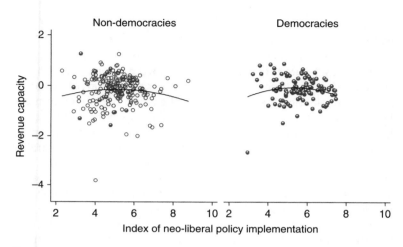

Figure 4.2 Regime type, macroeconomic policies, and the capacity of developing states to raise revenue, 1960–1999

$N = 338$

Notes and Sources:

Revenue capacity data from Feng, Kugler, and Zak (2000); observations at $t+5$.

Index of neo-liberal policy implementation is the 'economic freedom' measure developed by the Fraser Institute (Gwartney and Lawson, 2004); observations at t.

ability of public authorities to supply the means to satisfy whatever net demand for redistribution is created by extending political rights in developing countries.

Let us assume that a developing country democracy does manage to raise sufficient revenue, and that it decides to target education and health spending as two priority social-spending programmes. There is some evidence that this is indeed what many developing countries decided to do in the last decade of the 1990s, following the spurt of democratization episodes in Africa and Latin America in particular.[21] However, studies by Castro-Leal *et al.* (1999) and by Ross (2006) find that it is not the median voter and her class allies amongst the poor who necessarily benefit from such policies, but rather a narrow urban elite. This evidence, combined with what we had learned above about the relative share-gains of the poor and the middle class compared to that of the rich, suggests that whatever social spending there is in developing countries is not well targeted, with the result that its effects are more regressive than progressive in terms of mitigating economic inequality. Ross' study covering the period 1970 to 2000 provides independent corroboration of the general patterns suggested by Figure 4.1, namely that democratization in developing countries does not necessarily benefit the poorer sections of the population. In distinction from our focus on the effects of democratization, Ross concentrates on the effect of the level of democracy (using the Polity2 combined regime scale). His dependent variable is the well-being of the poor, measured in terms of the national infant mortality rate. As the incidence of infant mortality is concentrated in the lowest income quintile, what happens to this rate over time is a good approximation of changes in the well-being of the poor and how well public health policies cater for their interests. He finds that if one controls for income level, population density, economic growth, and the impact of HIV/AIDS, democracy has no perceptible effect on the reduction of infant mortality rates. Infant mortality rates declined in most countries of the world over the second half of the twentieth century, mostly due to the global spread of better preventive and curative medical practices. Democracy's contribution to this decline in developing countries is insignificant, though, equivalent to about a single five-week boost to the declining infant mortality trend over the whole three-decade period 1970 to 2000 (Ross, 2006: 868).

Considering the supply-side factors that may affect the applicability of the redistributive prognosis suggested by the MVH, developing countries as a rule lack the institutional and fiscal means to put redistributive preferences into effect. To the extent that redistribution of income and opportunities does take place, it is often ill-targeted and favours the established elite more than those who are supposed to benefit from it. Such supply-side disfunctionalities combine powerfully with the demand-side constraints mentioned above to suppress whatever potential democratization could hold for the mitigation of odious inequality. The incompleteness of the democratic transitions in many countries, and the political instability that accompanies such transitions, is partly to blame for this. So is the relative incapacity of the bureaucracies that have to devise and implement the necessary social spending programmes. However, some blame must also go to the way in which the ideology and practice of capital mobility has been imposed on developing countries by their transnational creditors, often in collusion with the wealthy and politically powerful elites within the developing countries themselves. It is important to be reminded that successful democratization and redistribution led by the median voter in the high-income OECD model democracies occurred under an international regime of stricter capital controls and more national fiscal autonomy than what late democratizers in developing countries have had to face in recent decades.

A multivariate test

In the previous section we identified a number of important demand- and supply-factors that inhibit the potential of democratization to deliver on its promise of mitigating economic inequality. So far, we have investigated these factors/conditions only one at a time. It is now opportune to consider a multivariate empirical test of the significance of these factors/conditions. By using the full range of potential variation across low-, middle-, and high-income countries, I hope to arrive at a more robust set of answers than would be possible if we concentrate only on the developing countries in our sample. Data constraints limit the sample size to 105 countries.

The model that we want to test is based on the preceding discussion of the MVH, and stipulates that the level of inequality in country j at t is determined by democratization at $t–5$, the institutionalization of a consistent democracy by t, the degree to which controls over capital mobility had been reduced in country j, and the capacity of the state in country j to raise revenue. The unit of analysis is the country-year, and the dependent variable is the five-year moving average of the EHII Gini index score, measured at t. Episodes of democratization are recorded by means of a dummy variable, with zero being equal to no democratization (the reference value). The presence of a consistent democracy at t is indicated by another dummy variable (one equals presence of consistent democracy). As there is a close positive correlation (Pearson's two-tailed $r = 0.7$) between per capita GDP and the presence of consistent democracy, and as per capita GDP also captures a variety of additional factors relevant to economic inequality (see Chapter 2), the latter is used as an alternative to the consistent democracy measure. The measure intended to capture the degree to which capital controls had been removed is supplied by the Fraser Institute's indicator of 'capital mobility'. 'Capital mobility' measures the access of citizens to foreign capital markets and foreign access to domestic capital markets, as well as the degree of freedom enjoyed by citizens to engage in capital-market exchange with foreigners (Gwartney and Lawson, 2004). A higher score indicates more capital mobility. Using sources of inequality data other than the EHII dataset used here, Lee (2005) finds that the ability of states to mitigate the degree of economic inequality is dependent on their capacity to raise revenue, measured as a percentage of GDP, and I consequently also test for this effect.[22] Finally, I include a control variable with four values, each representing one of the last four decades of the twentieth century, starting with the 1960s (= value 1; 4 = 1990s). As we saw in Chapter 3, inequality levels for all country groups tended to increase over the four decades. These decade values are used also to control for potential time-specific omitted variable bias. The continuous control measures are all represented by their five-year moving averages measured at t.

Both random- and fixed-effects estimators are applied to the panel data at our disposal. Fixed-effects models control for the idiosyncrasies of the panel countries used in this study, and thus not only reduce country-specific omitted variable biases, but also help us to determine the effects on the dependent variable of country-specific variation in the explanatory variables over time. Random-effects models, on the other hand, helps us to also understand the cross-sectional dynamics of the panel data (Petersen, 2004). Table 4.1 reports the results of five models run according to the above specifications, three using fixed-effects and two using random-effects estimations.

The results confirm the *a priori* expectations formulated during our discussion of the MVH, including the general point that regime change *per se* is not a significant predictor of subsequent inequality trends. Model 1 confirms that a pro-democracy regime change does not necessarily assist a country to mitigate inequality. In fact, it can contribute to the worsening of inequality if the democratization takes place under conditions of increasing capital mobility and expanding economic openness, and if the country in question is relatively poor. However, the inequality worsening effect of democratization is substantially less if the regime change terminated in a consistent democracy (Model 3), and the effect can be reversed if the relevant state is relatively competent at raising revenue. As Lee (2005) argues, this competency approximates a range of public policy abilities, and we can accordingly conclude that democratizing states which manage to improve their public policy capacities

Table 4.1 Democratization and income inequality, 1960–1999

Estimation model	(1) Fixed effects	(2) Fixed effects	(3) Fixed effects	(4) Random effects	(5) Random effects
Explanatory variables					
Democratization	0.421	−0.006	0.020	0.419	−0.064
	(0.326)	(0.291)	(0.286)	(0.301)	(0.318)
GDP *per capita*	−0.000**	−0.000**		−0.000**	−0.000**
	(0.000)	(0.000)		(0.000)	(0.000)
Decade	0.647**	0.991**	0.785**	0.702**	1.124**
	(0.070)	(0.099)	(0.095)	(0.062)	(0.082)
Capital mobility	0.267**	0.119**	0.145**	0.251**	0.084**
	(0.029)	(0.030)	(0.030)	(0.027)	(0.029)
Revenue		−0.095**	−0.111**		−0.119**
		(0.020)	(0.020)		(0.015)
Consistent democracy			−0.215		
			(0.421)		
Constant	40.683**	41.387**	41.673**	41.061**	42.180**
	(0.179)	(0.380)	(0.385)	(0.579)	(0.536)
Observations	2793	2050	2002	2793	2050
Countries	105	102	102	105	102
R-squared	0.12	0.14	0.13	0.16	0.47

Notes: The dependent variable is the five-year moving average of the EHII Gini index score, measured at *t*.
Robust standard errors in parentheses
** significant at 1%.

are best suited to do something about odious inequality. Model 5, contrasted with Model 4 confirms the importance of controlling for the revenue-raising capacity of states. These empirical results underline the fact that through the latter half of the twentieth century, it became increasingly difficult for poorer countries to do credit to the median voter under the constraints imposed by capital mobility and economic openness. While it is likely that the liberalization of the capital account may unleash other processes that could also contribute to raising subsequent inequality levels, our theoretical discussion gave us reason to believe that increased capital mobility may be associated with increased concerns about the possibility of capital flight, which is bound to undermine the demand for and supply of redistribution through fiscal means. The regression results reported in Table 4.1 confirm this expectation. Again, once we control for the ability of states to raise revenue, the potential of democratization to put brakes on inequality increases.

The evidence reviewed here suggests that the promotion of democratization in developing countries, both from within and from without, should be treated more circumspectly and discerningly. While positive regime transitions and transformations hold many potential benefits, it is clearly a mistake to assume that democratization is in and of itself a *panacea* for all societal ills. Read together with recent findings by Michael Ross (2006) that democracy does very little to improve the conditions under which the poor live, it becomes evident that redistribution and poverty relief are policy outcomes that have to be targeted separately and specifically under conditions of economic openness. Improving the income and wealth share-gain of the middle class and the poor will not simply flow automatically from the extension of the popular vote.

In addition, it is clear that raising the public policy capacity of the state is a major and significant precondition for the mitigation of economic inequality through democratic means. The relative extractive capacity of the state is but one of the attributes of the quality of governance that is needed to ensure that the preferences of the median income earner receive the attention they deserve in a democracy, but it undoubtedly is of crucial importance in the struggle against odious inequality. However, what also emerges clearly is that the overall capacity of states to deal effectively with inequality has become very circumscribed in an era of generalized economic openness. The evidence is pretty overwhelming that analysts and policy advisers should reconsider the general assumption that economic openness, *tout court*, is desirable for all countries and at all times. While there is good reason to believe that trade openness can enhance growth and equity in societies which have achieved a certain level of human capital development, there are also reasons not to impose liberalization of the capital account on societies where democracy is a recent and tender implant. Popular sovereignty can be an antidote to runaway inequality – this much we know from the experience of many high-income OECD countries – but it needs nurturing which has to be accompanied by the careful sequencing of economic reforms.

5
The Consequences of Inequality

Introduction

We come now to a central claim of this book, namely that economic inequality at the levels commonly found in developing countries is a scourge and that an obligation rests on public policy-makers, both nationally and internationally, to do whatever is in their power to reduce it. In the previous chapters we looked at the historical evolution and contemporary attributes of the various mechanisms that cause and exacerbate inequality, and that may prevent communities from distributing assets and income more equitably among their citizens. In this chapter the focus shifts to the *consequences* of inequality. Odious inequality affects not only the poor – although its debilitating effects on the poor should never be underestimated – but a society as a whole can also be devastated by odious inequality.

This chapter will show that the pattern of economic inequality in developing countries is closely related to forms of deprivation that condemn hundred of millions of people to live lives that are 'solitary, poor, nasty, brutish, and short', in Thomas Hobbes' celebrated description of the conditions of life in the anarchic state of nature.[1] While Hobbes had different intentions than ours in using this phrase, it does provide a very useful summary of the consequences of economic inequality and will thus serve quite nicely as the organizing device for the argument in this chapter.[2] Inequality, we shall argue, denies people the capability to act with and through others

117

and thus generates and perpetuates social exclusion ('solitary'). As a result, unequal societies are characterized by a high incidence rate of violent conflict and strife ('brutish'), and by the collapse of institutions of property rights which encourages crime and exposes the lesser-endowed citizens to exploitation and rent-seeking behaviour by the rich and powerful ('nasty'). By undermining both the rate and quality of economic growth, inequality also leaves large sections of a population with inadequate access to the material and spiritual resources that are necessary for a long and fulfilling life ('poor' and 'short').

In short, this chapter shows that inequality holds serious consequences for human well-being in developing countries. Human well-being is a multifaceted concept and differences exist about the most appropriate way of conceptualizing and measuring it.[3] The literature evoked by Amartya Sen (2000a) and Martha Nussbaum's work (2000) suggests that relative well-being depends on a range of diversified capabilities that people must have in order to live healthy, long, and fulfilling lives. Important as it is to consider the full range of these capabilities, and the fact that different individuals would need and desire different configurations of capabilities, there can be no doubt that Hobbes' list of deprivations points towards a core set of capabilities: The capabilities to share in the fruits of social reciprocity and to enjoy security from violence, exploitation, and material deprivation. In what follows, I discuss each of these capabilities in turn, showing how and to what extent economic inequality as measured by the EHII Gini index score impacts on empirical indicators that can be used to approximate each of these capabilities. As elsewhere in this book, the emphasis falls on seeking ways to formulate generalizations that can stand up to empirical tests by identifying cross-sectional trends, rather than on developing detailed insights into the inequality conditions of specific countries. The attention first turns to what can be referred to as the socio-political consequences of inequality. We discuss how inequality contributes to the breakdown of social cohesion, a breakdown exemplified by the phenomena of social exclusion, corruption, crime, and the prevalence of politically inspired violence. In a further section the attention turns to how inequality negatively affects the rate and quality of economic growth, and how this inhibits the abatement and relief of poverty in developing countries.

The socio-political consequences of inequality

A review of the existing literature and the data at hand can lead only to one conclusion: The high level of wealth and income inequality is one of the main reasons for the relative absence of social cohesion in developing societies. Extreme economic inequality not only deprives a large section of the inhabitants of material capabilities to live long and fulfilling lives, but it also deprives *all* the inhabitants of these societies of the social capabilities to live decent lives built on reciprocity and trust. Social cohesion can be defined as an attribute of a society in which decent cooperative reciprocity is institutionalized, reflected in

> [T]he willingness of members of a society to cooperate with each other in order to survive and prosper. Willingness to cooperate means they freely choose to form partnerships and have a reasonable chance of realizing goals, because others are willing to cooperate and share the fruits of their endeavours equitably. (Stanley, 2003: 5)

Before we explore the meaning of social cohesion further, it is worthwhile to pause briefly and consider the implications of the recent return of appreciative notions such as 'social capital', 'trust', 'solidarity', and 'social cohesion', and of the opprobrious term 'social exclusion' to the conceptual inventory of social scientists. On one level the renewed popularity of these terms can be seen as one of the many indicators of an intellectual resistance to the fragmentation and atomization brought about by the normative hegemony of neo-liberal economic thought and practice during the latter decades of the twentieth century. Looked at from the perspective developed by Karl Polanyi in his analysis of the dialectical double movement set in motion by the disembedding of the market from society through the ideological hegemony of what he termed 'market utopianism' (Polanyi, 1945), the current popularity of these 'social' notions is a clear signal of an attempt to re-value those societal bonds that neo-liberal economic policies are accused of having torn asunder. Tracing its pedigree back to late nineteenth century scholars such as Emile Durkheim, the concept of social cohesion, for instance, has taken on the double significance of being the expression of an analytical insight but also of being almost a neo-romantic protest against rampant market utopianism that is perceived to undermine the conditions that make community possible. Similarly, social capital, trust, solidarity, and social exclusion can be seen not only as analytical tools, but also as political protests. But herein lies a danger: In using these terms, we have to be careful not to imply necessary agreement with any of the political projects that lurk behind the popularity that these notions have acquired in recent years. While there is very little good to say on behalf of the atomism and anomie that can be linked to the market utopianism of neo-liberalism in our time, warning lights should go up if this leads us to conceive of the alternative as a society that is highly integrated and cohesive to the extent that the collective goals begin to outweigh the right of individuals to pursue legitimate goals, even if they go against the norm, or in which the creative potential of non-conformist behaviour and conflict are completely smothered by the pursuit of collective action. Collective action is not all it is touted to be by Romantics, as Mancur Olson (1965) rightly pointed out. However, being on our guard against the political projects that lurk behind the recent 'rediscovery of society' does not imply that we should avoid concepts such as social capital, solidarity, social cohesion, and social exclusion altogether. Although they have been invented or re-invented to reveal specific features of the post-industrial societies of North America and Europe in the first place, there is scope to use them also to try and understand the devastating consequences that inordinate levels of economic inequality have had on the well-being of people in developing countries, as long as we strip them of their romantic and homogenizing connotations.

It is best to conceive of social cohesion as an emerging property or attribute of a society in which the pursuit of individual goals and mutual cooperation are kept in balance. The attribute of social cohesion is realized when individuals think of themselves as belonging to and having a recognized place in the society in question, and when they perceive that they have the opportunity to participate in socially accepted institutions and practices as means through which to pursue both individual and collective goals. Social cohesion should be distinguished from *social capital*, a term that has also received considerable attention in recent years. Social capital is not an attribute of a society but rather a resource 'that accrue to an individual or group

by virtue of possessing a durable network of more or less institutionalized relationships of mutual acquaintance and recognition'.[4] This
resource can be used to advance narrower interests as much as it can
be used to promote broader ones, but there is nothing inherently
socially inclusive about social capital. By that I mean that a particular group in society may be able to draw on a ready and well-stocked
supply of social capital within its own ranks, and then use it to promote their narrow group interest with vigour and with much success
to the detriment of the general well-being of society. Oligarchies can
rely on high stock levels of social capital within its own ranks, but
the actions of oligarchs seldom promote social cohesion as defined
above. A society characterized by cohesion is not necessarily one in
which collective goods are preferred over private aims, but rather is
a society in which the pursuit of private gain takes place in a manner that does not prevent others from pursuing their private goals
equally vigorously. Social cohesion depends on a mutual and impli-
cit agreement that everyone has as much right as everyone else to
pursue self-regarding goals, as long as such self-regarding actions are
pursued in a way that does not diminish the capability of anyone
else to do the same. Conceived of in this way, social cohesion reduces
the transaction costs involved in the pursuit of self-regarding action,
and egoistically inclined individuals would thus gain more from living in a society characterized by well-established social cohesion than
from one in which social cohesion is fragile. Social cohesion thus
guarantees the smooth functioning of the market. But as our definition suggests, it also plays a role in the establishment and upkeep
of the public forum, the place where members of a society combine
their efforts and resources to produce the public goods that cannot be secured, or cannot be fully secured by self-regarding action
in the market place, including the public goods of generalized trust
and mutual respect. Social cohesion, in short, is the attribute of a
robust and *decent* society. Often taken for granted, we detect the
importance of social cohesion only in the pathologies that reflect
its absence from or incompleteness in a society, such as instances
of social exclusion, the breakdown of trust due to the prevalence of
crime and corruption, and the resort to violence as a means of conflict
management. These pathologies of the breakdown of social cohesion
are not rooted solely in pernicious wealth and income inequalities,
but economic inequality does provide both incentives and enabling

conditions for these pathologies to emerge and/or to worsen. While we here focus only on developing countries, it is worthwhile to notice that these pathologies have also become widespread in the majority of transition economies and in high-income societies that have seen their inequality levels rise in recent decades, confirming the close association between inequality and the breakdown of social cohesion.

'Solitary': Inequality and social exclusion

The phenomenon of social exclusion is closely related to high or rising levels of inequality. Caution in approaching terms that uncritically celebrate 'society' is advisable especially in view of the specific political uses that have been made of the term 'social exclusion'. This term has become popular in analyses of the rise in Europe of what North Americans would call the 'underclass', that is, individuals and households who, for one reason or another, do not 'fit in' with the going normative expectations of advanced industrial society: The destitute, the uninsured unemployed, lone parents, hooded ghetto kids, and anyone who lives in a society but has managed to escape the panoptical surveillance mechanisms of the modern industrial welfare state. While the notion of 'social exclusion' points towards the existence of 'a problem', its use has not always been clear about the source of the problem and who and what is to blame. In some contexts, as Christine Everingham argues, it has been used to shift the blame onto the destitute themselves: They are destitute because of their failings to acquire the skills of social and economic advancement (Everingham, 2003: 29). In post-Thatcherite Britain the term 'social exclusion' gained credence as an attempt to replace notions of equity through redistribution with the policy of 'including' the destitute in formal employment and to get them 'to improve their relative position through their own efforts', as Jordan puts it (2003: 82). These uses stand in contrast to an earlier use of the concept which placed the 'blame' for exclusion elsewhere. Max Weber, for one, employed the term 'social exclusion' to refer to the strategies of social closure used by the privileged to advance their interests through subordination of the less privileged, today best symbolized by the development of what economists would call 'club goods', such as gated residential areas, private schools, and privatized medical care (Burchardt *et al.*, 2002). Agency is clearly a central concern in defining and operationalizing social exclusion.

Ever since the 1995 UN World Summit for Social Development, considerable time and effort has been spent to make this concept also relevant to the developing world. Often, these applications have latched onto 'social exclusion' as a fashionable concept and have not explicitly considered the conceptual distinctiveness of the term, nor is due consideration always given to what it can contribute to our understanding of deprivation and inequality in the developing world. One important exception in this regard is the *Social Development Paper* that Amartya Sen contributed to the Asian Development Bank (2000b). According to Sen, social exclusion has a place in the conceptual arsenal of the development studies to the extent that it places emphasis on the *relational* dimensions of deprivation/poverty. If poverty equals a situation or end-state of being deprived of the capabilities to pursue activities that a person would have reason to value, then social exclusion can be seen as a relational *process* through which individuals or groups of people can be denied the capability to be recognized as agents in their own right within the broader reciprocal social structure of which we spoke above. Social exclusion, Sen argues, is thus *constitutively* relevant: If you are not recognized as a full-blown member of society in your own right, it is likely that you will be treated – and that you will come to see yourself – as a means to an end, rather as an end in yourself. In this respect social exclusion can be distinguished from the act of voluntary social isolation (Barry, 2002). To be able to choose the option of voluntary 'exit', people have to be first constituted as agents with the capability to choose. At its worst and most basic, social exclusion deprives people of agency and re-constitutes them as choice-less victims whose voices are not heard or *recognized* by others in a society. But social exclusion can also be instrumentally relevant, that is, exclusion can be a causal factor in depriving individuals and groups of the specific capabilities that flow from attaining a reasonable education standard, having access to credit and to employment opportunities, and from having access to the means to influence decision making, to name a few of the most serious capability deprivations in developing countries. The extent of social exclusion in developing countries, due to both deliberate strategies of exclusion used against minority or marginalized ethnic and religious groups, rural women, and

physically and mentally disabled individuals, or due to the unin-
tended consequences of market imperfections, is well documented,
as are the effects that these forms of exclusion have on worsening
poverty levels.[5] What is not so well explored and documented in the
social exclusion literature to date is the effect that vertical economic
inequality has on the manifestations of social exclusion, both in its
constitutive and instrumental variants. One reason for this is that it is
challenging to distinguish clearly between social inequality in general
on the one hand and social exclusion on the other. However, as Brian
Barry has shown, it is possible to conceive of the causal relationship
between the condition of interpersonal income/wealth dispersion and
the process of social exclusion, if we consider how the distribution of
income/wealth inequality affects people's ability to share in the common institutions on which the commonalities of fate that we call
societies are based (2002). Income/wealth is of course only one of the
attributes relevant here, and may not be the most important either.
In the multi-ethnic, multi-lingual, multi-religious, and multi-caste
societies of developing countries the ascriptive attributes of descent,
language, belief, gender, and status play a significant part in determining who's in and who's out and who earns/owns what. Keeping the
degree of horizontal discrimination constant, it is nevertheless possible to discern a distinct effect of income inequality on the degree
to which people are included or excluded from both the market and
public-forum institutions on which social reciprocity and cohesion
depends.

One of the most pernicious exclusionary effects of the concentration of wealth in developing countries is to deny those at the
lower end of the distribution the opportunity to acquire and use
credit and insurance. The role of inequality in credit market exclusion has received considerable attention in the literature that explores
the potential effects of inequality on economic growth (see below),
and cross-sectional and country-specific studies confirm that the relative deprivation of assets slants the credit market in favour of those
who own assets, while it discriminates against the asset poor.[6] This
exclusionary result is well summarized in the words of a poor res-
ident in Ha Tinh, Vietnam: 'While the rich get loans, the poor get
consideration for loans.'[7] One study of six rural villages in Kerala
and Tamil Nadu in India conducted during the 1980s reports that
nearly 60 per cent of available credit went to the wealthy in those

societies, while only 8 per cent of loans went to those who own less than a fifth of what the wealthy do. The wealthy also pay much lower interest rates than do those lower down the wealth ladder.[8] In a 13-country study of the living conditions of those who find themselves on the lower end of the income distribution in developing countries, Banerjee and Duflo find that while many poor rural households have outstanding debts, only a small fraction of these debts are based on loans from a formal lending source or from cooperatives. Most debts are to informal sources, dominated by moneylenders who charge higher interest rates than formal or cooperative credit institutions, but the lending conditions of these moneylenders also favour those who own land more than those who do not. In the Udaipur region in India, interest rates charged by informal lenders decline by 0.40 per cent per month for each additional hectare of land owned by the borrowing household (Banerjee and Duflo, 2007: 155). These results are representative of trends in developing countries and underline the importance of pro-poor lending initiatives of institutions such as the Grameen Bank founded by Muhammad Yunus. One of the consequences that flow from these imperfections of credit markets in developing countries was mentioned in Chapter 2, where we looked at the investment decisions made by households who have inadequate access to credit: They tend to overinvest in children and underinvest in the education of their children. This sets in trail a further turn in the upward spiral of inequality, as large cohorts of relatively poorly educated job-seekers are added to the employment market. Similarly, in highly unequal societies the providers of health and asset insurance have strong incentives to provide exclusively for the wealthy, as the latter group faces lesser health risks than the poor and have large property portfolios that generate high premiums, especially in countries such as South Africa and Brazil where high inequality is closely related with high crime levels. As a result, less than 10 per cent of poor people in one representative sample of developing countries have access to health insurance, and have to rely on intra-household adjustments, such as decisions to withdraw children from school to help in household production, to deal with income risks (Banerjee and Duflo, 2007: 157).

One of the main effects of the stark inequalities of wealth in developing countries thus is to exclude large numbers of children from the opportunity to undergo formal schooling, through the mechanisms traced by imperfect credit and insurance markets in these societies. This exclusionary effect is worsened by the poor performance of state institutions to provide generalized education and social insurance to their citizens. As we saw in Chapter 4, where states still have the capacity to provide public health and education, these services are often concentrated on the urban areas and due to the relative powerlessness of the median voter are often exclusively enjoyed by the same power elite who benefit from the unequal distribution of wealth and income. Using a measure of the degree to which residents of national societies are included in or excluded from formal schooling developed by Thomas, Wang, and Fan (2003), Figure 5.1 illustrates the very powerful social exclusionary effect of household income inequality working through the distribution of education opportunities: Income inequality at $t–1$ is a highly significant predictor of the concentration of educational opportunities in a society at t. The statistical significance of the net effect of income inequality on educational opportunities is confirmed by a random-effects panel data regression that controls

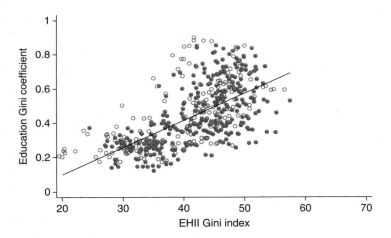

Figure 5.1   Inequality and social exclusion in developing countries: Education, 1960–1999
R-squared = 0.398
$N = 511$
Sources: Estimated Household Income Inequality data from Galbraith and Kum (2005). Education inequality data from Thomas *et al.* (2003).

for state spending on education, for the quality of the institutions maintained by the state, and for the level of political discrimination against subordinate groups.[9] The resulting cost to society as a whole flowing from the concentration of education opportunities is high. Generalized opportunities to receive education are important not only because of education's well-known growth-enhancing effects, but also because the school is the primary institution where social values of reciprocity and cooperation outside of the immediate family or clan culture are inculcated.[10]

Social exclusion resonates also in the political arena. We have already seen in Chapter 4 that under conditions of inconsistent democratization the power-concentration that facilitates high levels of income and wealth inequality in effect shifts the influential (median) voter higher up the income scale. Political influence, we said there, is similar to a consumer good that can be bought by those with the means to do so. The corollary of this is that the concentration of wealth and income can prevent and/or discourage those at the lower end of the distribution from participating in electoral politics. While the institutionalization of democracy in a society entails more than the holding of regular elections, as we showed in Chapter 4, there can be no doubt that the institutions that facilitate competitive elections contribute to social cohesion by providing a peaceful mechanism for the organizing and articulation of interests, and by binding participants into a non-zero sum social scheme of diffuse reciprocity. As Figure 5.2 shows, however, potential-voter participation in parliamentary elections significantly deteriorates as income inequality increases. Again, the net effect of income inequality remains highly significant at the 1 per cent level even when we control for the effect of other relevant explanatory factors.[11]

In unequal societies, those who earn and own the least are systematically excluded, through no fault of their own, from core market and public-forum institutions and hence from the opportunities that can be derived from education and political participation. However, as suggested above, it is also society as a whole that loses: The higher the level of exclusion, the more society is deprived of the benefits, including free collective insurance, generated by social cohesion. Although the privileged obviously gains directly from the skewed distribution of income, wealth, and opportunities, the weakening of the attribute of social cohesion entails fundamental losses for all members of an

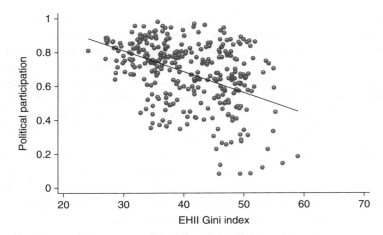

Figure 5.2   Income inequality and social exclusion in developing countries: Political participation, 1960–1999

R-squared = 0.212

$N = 529$

Sources: 'Political participation' = number of votes in parliamentary elections/number of potential voters (voting age population). Data from International Institute for Democracy and Electoral Assistance, available at http://www.idea.int/vt/index.cfm.
Estimated Household Income Inequality data from Galbraith and Kum (2005).

unequal society. Although it is difficult to measure social cohesion directly – individual levels of interpersonal trust is only an imperfect proxy – it is not too difficult to discern the general results of the breakdown of social cohesion in the form of rampant crime, widespread official corruption, and violent social and political conflict. These symptoms of the breakdown of social cohesion turn life 'nasty' and 'brutish' for all in an unequal society and it is to these symptoms that we next turn.

'Nasty' and 'brutish': Inequality, violent civil conflict, crime, and corruption

There can be little doubt that life for many inhabitants of developing countries is extremely 'nasty' and 'brutish'. High incidence rates of crime, including violent crime, widespread corruption, and the destabilization of daily life through violent civil conflict are an all too frequent occurrence in developing countries alike. The most dramatic form that the breakdown of social cohesion can take on in society is the outbreak of violent civil conflict, one of the 'violent trajectories in contentious politics' as Tilly refers to it.[12] Violent civil conflict is not only destructive of life, limb, and property, but also of the incentives that actors face in terms of investing in the future of a society. A recent World Bank study, with good reason, has referred to incidences of violent civil conflict as 'development in reverse' (Collier *et al.*, 2002). Unfortunately, such development in reverse is all too prevalent in poorer countries. The same World Bank study points out that at the end of the twentieth century middle-income countries faced a civil-war risk four times as high as OECD countries (down from five times as high in the 1960s), while the low-income countries have a typical risk 15 times as high as the OECD group of countries.[13] Below, we will see how inequality plays an important part in stimulating such endemic levels of conflict.

While the literature has for a long time recognized the growth- and development-inhibiting effects of crime and corruption (Mauro, 1995), it is only in recent years that the focus has shifted to the possibility of reverse causality between socio-economic factors and deficiencies in the rule of law. One incentive for a more careful look at the determinants of crime has been the perceived cross-national increase of intra-state and international petty and organized crime, although it is not always clear whether the trends for most types of crime are due to *de facto* increases or due simply to idiosyncratic changes in national crime-statistics bookkeeping. As it stands, cross-national crime statistics as collected by the UN Office on Drugs and Crime are problematic, due on the one hand to the resources gaps that prevent many poorer countries to take part in the UN World Crime Surveys. Only eight of 53 African states contributed to the 2005 survey, for instance. On the other hand, there is also evidence that some countries deliberately underreport crime statistics. However, there is considerable anecdotal evidence linking increased violent crime to general patterns of social decline, including rising levels of inequality during recent decades. In addition, a sprinkling of cross-country econometric studies has provided evidence that rising inequality has a statistically significant and robust effect on rates of intentional homicides and other violent crime, net of the effect of economic growth, a range of cultural factors, and the deterrent legal capacity of the states,[14] including the study by Fajnzylber, Lederman, and Loayza (2002). An earlier cross-national study by Francois Bourguignon of the World Bank concluded that

> Simple economic theory shows how property crime and, more generally, all the violence associated with illegal activity may partly be the consequence of excessive inequality and poverty. Limited available evidence in this field suggests that an increase in the degree of relative poverty or income inequality in a country generally leads to a rise in criminality. (1999: 31)

The evidence that inequality is systematically linked with the abuse of political power/office is also pretty convincing, although studies linking official corruption and inequality are only recent phenomena. In the most comprehensive study to date, You and Khagram (2005) find that income inequality is as strong a predictor of official corruption in a cross section of 129 countries as are more conventional economic explanatory variables, such as economic development. With increased inequality, there is a strong incentive for the wealthy and powerful to resist and undermine the rule of law, administrative fairness, and redistributive efficiency in the funding and provision of public services. As we argued before, a high level of economic inequality reflects a deeply skewed distribution of power in a society. This provides the scope for the ruling elite to engage in monopoly rent-seeking by means of the manipulation and abuse of public office at the cost of the weaker sections of society, who have no other recourse than to pay the extortion fees demanded by corrupt officials in order to draw minimally upon public goods. In the minds of actors dealing in or with a society, the fact of high inequality is taken as confirmation that corruption lies at the heart of the distributional unfairness, and birth is thus given to the normative expectation that one cannot do in this society without engaging in corruption, either as a buyer or a seller (You and Khagram, 2005: 140). In their wide-ranging study of equality, corruption and social trust/cohesion, Rothstein and Uslaner (2005) also conclude that many societies face a social trap in which it is increasingly difficult to escape from the socially corrosive effects of inequality and corruption. It is only through the efficient and fair use of redistributive state resources that inequality and its corrosive effects can be addressed. However, the incidence of a skewed distribution of wealth and income compels members of that society to lose trust in the capacity of the state apparatus and in one another, with the result that state institutions have little legitimacy and cannot perform their redistributive tasks. The result is that bribe-taking and bribe-paying, rent-seeking, and state avoidance become self-fulfilling and self-reinforcing norms.

Table 5.1 provides further corroboration of the strong and significant effect that income inequality has on corruption. Making use of

Table 5.1   Household income inequality and control of corruption

Dependent variable	(1) Control of corruption	(2) Control of corruption	(3) Control of corruption	(4) Control of corruption	(5) 'Contract intensive money'
Income	−0.025*	−0.034**	−0.032**	−0.032**	−0.002**
inequality	(0.012)	(0.012)	(0.011)	(0.012)	(0.000)
GDP per capita	0.688**	0.755**	0.672**	0.671**	0.096**
(PPP)	(0.078)	(0.089)	(0.083)	(0.081)	(0.003)
GDP growth	0.043**	0.048**	0.046**	0.045**	0.001
(five-year	(0.017)	(0.016)	(0.017)	(0.016)	(0.001)
moving average)					
Inconsistent	−0.446**	−0.388**	−0.436**	−0.439**	−0.002
regime type	(0.139)	(0.136)	(0.144)	(0.148)	(0.006)
LAC (dummy)	−0.363*				
	(0.118)				
SSA (dummy)		0.467*			
		(0.209)			
SASIA (dummy)			−0.059		
			(0.126)		
Islam (dummy)				0.041	
				(0.141)	
Constant	−4.444**	−4.820**	−4.081**	−4.042**	−0.093*
	(1.047)	(1.134)	(1.044)	(1.067)	(0.042)
Observations	130	130	130	130	2091
Adjusted R^2	0.75	0.75	0.74	0.75	0.44

Notes:
Models 1–4: 73 countries, 1996–1998; dependent variable is World Bank's Governance Indicators 'Control of Corruption' estimate (Kaufmann et al., 2004).
Model 5: 87 countries, 1960–1996; dependent variable is measure of 'contract-intensive money' (Clague et al., 1999).
Ordinary least squares (OLS) regression coefficients.
Robust standard errors in parentheses.
* significant at 5%; ** significant at 1%.

the World Bank Governance Initiative data measuring the *control of corruption* during the latter part of the 1990s (Kaufmann *et al.*, 2004), the first four models are a series of ordinary least squares regressions applied to determine the direction and strength of the net effect of income inequality on corruption, controlling for level of economic development (GDP per capita in PPP), five-year moving averages of economic growth, the presence of inconsistent political regimes (see Chapter 4), and for regional and cultural idiosyncrasies. The coefficient for income inequality is constantly negative and highly significant in all four models, suggesting that the menace of corruption indeed increases with rising inequality in contexts that are typical of developing countries, namely relatively low levels of economic development and growth, and inconsistent political regimes. The coefficients of the regional dummy for Latin America and the Caribbean (LAC) and South Asia (SASIA) are both negative but is significant only in the case of LAC, underlining the challenges posed by corruption in that part of the developing world. In contrast, the coefficient for sub-Saharan Africa is positive and significant, and positive but not significant for countries with Islam as the dominant religion. These results are subject to two important constraints, though. Firstly, the World Bank Governance Initiative data at our disposal cover only a short period of time, namely the second half of the 1990s. Secondly, the data are based on a wide range of sources, but these sources all report only subjective expert perceptions – albeit widely canvassed – of the degree to which the control of corruption is perceived to be operative in a society. In view of what was said above about the normative expectations that build up in unequal societies around corruption, it might well be that the incidence of high levels of inequality stimulates expert opinion to expect more corruption than there really is in a society. To correct for these two problems, Model 5 in Table 5.1 uses data (covering 87 countries between 1960 and 1996) of a measure that captures the extent to which people in the society – in contrast to expert opinion – have faith in the ability of official institutions to protect property rights and uphold the rule of law. This measure is the contract-intensive-money measure devised by Clague *et al.*, which is 'the ratio of non-currency money to the total money supply, or $(M_2 - C)/ M_2$, where M_2 is a broad definition of the money supply and C is currency held outside banks' (1999: 188). The logic behind this measure is that the higher the standards maintained by public officials in a country to enforce contracts, property rights, and the rule of law, the more confidence people will have in financial contracts and the smaller the proportion of money they will hold in currency. This broad measure captures the confidence that ordinary inhabitants have in the rule-of-law standards upheld by public officials, and it is reasonable to expect that the more the inhabitants of a country experience incidents of official corruption, the less confidence they will have in the ability of the state to uphold and back-up contracts. The income inequality coefficient (negative and highly significant) in Model 5 confirms that under conditions of high inequality people encounter or expect more incidents of official corruption and thus have less confidence in the ability of the state to honour and guarantee contracts, and they are thus less inclined to hold money in forms that depend on contract enforcement by the state. There can thus be little doubt that high levels of inequality in a country make the life of the typical inhabitant excessively 'nasty', which translates into a widespread loss of credibility of the organs of public power.

But life for the typical inhabitant of an unequal society in the developing world can also be extremely 'brutish', given the high incidence of violent civil conflict in such societies. Violent civil conflict[15] is a coercive phenomenon, accompanied by attempts 'to destroy, injure, thwart, or otherwise control' (Mack and Snyder, 1957: 218)[16] opponents, their resources, and/or the order on which their position depends. Violence can flow, of course, not only from the action of groups that engage in dissent against the status quo, but also from action taken by the occupiers of the state, especially in autocratic and less-than-democratic societies (Muller, 1985). Physical harm to limb and property, torture, and assassination are all tools of the trade for repressive regimes.

Throughout the history of political thought the incidence of violent civil conflict has theoretically been linked with the prevalence of economic inequality, but empirically the exact nature of the relationship has not emerged clearly (Lichbach, 1989). One reason for this has been the difficulties that analysts have experienced to find consistent inequality data across a wide range of countries (Humphreys, 2003). Another problem relates to the fact that very few studies follow the suggestion made by Lichbach (1989) and Jack Nagel (1974) to explicitly test for the presence of a curvilinear relationship. As explained in Chapter 1, the inequality dataset used here substantively solves the problem of data inconsistency. In what follows, I design an empirical test for the relationship between economic inequality and violent civil conflict that accommodates the persuasive theoretical argument that the incidence of conflict does not linearly increase as inequality levels rise, but rather that the shape of the relationship traces an inverted U-curve.

Here, violent civil conflict refers to actions involving a contested incompatibility between at least two political groups, of which one is the state, involving armed force aimed at challenging, altering, or maintaining a particular distribution of public power and/or control over territory. Data on violent civil conflict are from the Uppsala/PRIO dataset on the onset of violent civil conflict.[17] The onset of at least one incidence of domestic armed conflict per year or the absence of such an onset is recorded as a dichotomous variable. The Uppsala/PRIO dataset focuses only on politically motivated armed conflict, and also records a new onset only after two years of 'inactivity' have passed.[18] Uppsala/PRIO uses a threshold of 25 conflict-related deaths for an incident to be counted as a violent civil conflict.[19] There are 150 observations of the onset of violent civil conflict in the dataset which represent only 3 per cent of the total number of 5126 observations. This means that we are potentially faced with the estimation problem related to what King and Zeng call 'rare events data' (2001). While a logit estimation of the risk that inequality poses for the onset of violent civil conflict is the appropriate estimation technique to use given the dichotomous nature of the dependent variable, the rarity of the onset of violent civil conflict could mean that the estimated event probabilities will be too small. To correct for potentially biased logit estimates of rare events, I employ the procedure suggested by King and Zeng (2001) that generates approximately unbiased and lower-variance estimates of the logit coefficients.[20]

As has been noted elsewhere (Nel and Righarts, 2008; Urdal, 2006), the absence of micro-level data on what inspires people to engage in violent civil conflict means that cross-country studies have to rely on macro-features of social systems to develop a theoretical understanding of the conditions under which violent civil conflict emerges.

The extensive literature on civil conflict suggests that a comparative theoretical analysis must accommodate at least three concepts that link the strategic evaluations made and considerations entertained by actors with macro-societal features, namely *motive*, *incentive*, and *opportunity*. 'Motive' refers to how and when evaluations that an actor is not receiving her due can bring that actor to consider taking drastic action to alter the sources of her discontent. Widespread grievances and other forms of societal frustrations are said to be determined by relative deprivation, that is, the gap between individual expectations related to well-being and actual outcomes (Eckstein, 1980: 144; Gurr, 1970: 24; Thorbecke and Charumilind, 2002). There are many grievances that could possibly induce actors to engage in civil violence to change the situations that gave birth to these grievances in the first place, but socio-economic grievances due to vertical (between individuals) and horizontal (between groups) income and wealth inequality have received considerable attention (Eckstein, 1980; Huntington, 1968; Østby, 2003; Sigelman and Simpson, 1977).[21] Ever since Aristotle in Book V of *The Politics* suggested that inequality is 'generally at the bottom of internal warfare in states' (1974: 191), analysts of conflict have pinned much explanatory value on the distribution of wealth, and in particular on the distribution of income (Sigelman and Simpson, 1977). The argument backing this assumption is well summarized by Lichbach (1989: 436):

> When economic inequality is high, (1) the poor are envious, have nothing to lose, and thus resort to force (e.g. political violence) to achieve redistributive demands; (2) the rich are greedy, have everything to lose, and possess the resources necessary to use force (e.g. governmental repression) to avoid giving in to redistributive demands; and (3) the middle class, which represents property rights, is small. Hence, as economic inequality increases, the pool of conflict participants (both the rich and the poor) increases.

There is a greater likelihood that perceived inequality will become a motive to act if there are structural impediments to mobility under conditions of modernization (Eckstein, 1980; Huntington, 1968; Zimmermann, 1980). Expectations of social mobility will be higher in a society with a rapid rate of urbanization, for instance. If these expectations are thwarted by impediments to mobility related to inequality of opportunities for economic advancement, it is more likely that politically relevant grievances will arise.

All societies have aggrieved citizens who feel that they are getting less than they deserve. However, political violence occurs only in societies in which discontent can be organized and in which violence is an attractive outlet for grievances. The first of these pre-conditions is captured by the term *opportunity*, while the second condition relates to *incentives*. It is with respect to opportunity that it becomes theoretically justified to test for the presence of a curvilinear relationship between inequality and violent civil conflict.[22] High levels of vertical (between households) and horizontal (between societal groups) economic inequality and economic discrimination can induce resentment and grievances, but more inequality does not necessarily translate into more violent resistance. High levels of economic inequality are maintained by powerful elites whose preponderance of power produced the inequality in the first place. These elites can use their established power to suppress expressions of dissent, and it is hence possible that high inequality may be associated with less, not more violence. The disadvantaged have to overcome considerable collective action problems if they wish to express their grievances. Violent political dissent is dependent on access to some resources and mobilization opportunities relative to the power resources controlled by the elite (Besançon, 2005). The concentration of collective action resources in a society could thus be an important determinant of whether violent civil conflict manifests itself. More precisely, 'opportunity' relates to the strategic consideration that a motivated actor makes of the relative distribution of collective action resources in society. The existence of some uncertainty about this distribution can also act as an inducement to action. Secondly, the assessment of opportunities to act made by an aggrieved or otherwise motivated actor in itself can lead to violent resistance, but is probably not a sufficient condition. Strategic evaluations that the actor will be better-off materially when engaging in violent civil conflict than when not could be important inducements to civil violence, as the recent literature that links 'greed' and conflict argues.[23] While *motivation* and *opportunity* can be directly related to the incidence of economic inequality, the link between *incentive* and inequality is at best indirect, probably runs through one or both of the other two, and is therefore not considered separately here.

The first two columns of Table 5.2 contain the results of logit estimations (corrected for rare events) of the effects of economic inequality at $t-1$, measured by our EHII Gini index score, and the risk of the onset of violent civil conflict at t. The concept of risk refers to the likelihood, or odds, that inequality gives rise to violent civil conflict, and should not be read as a prediction that countries with high levels of inequality will necessarily experience violent internal conflict. The estimations control for the effects of a number of variables that have been identified as being important co-determinants of the onset of civil conflict, namely per capita GDP, GDP growth rate, population size, and regime

Table 5.2   Household income inequality and violent civil conflict, 1960–1999

Dependent variable	(1) Violent civil conflict	(2) Violent civil conflict	(3) Adverse regime change
Income inequality	0.697*	0.689*	0.092**
	(0.314)	(0.346)	(0.030)
Income inequality squared	−0.008*	−0.008*	
	(0.004)	(0.004)	
GDP per capita	−0.000		
	(0.000)		
GDP growth (five-year moving average)	−0.034	−0.039	0.043
	(0.034)	(0.035)	(0.053)
Log nat of total population	0.249**	0.274**	
	(0.087)	(0.086)	
Brevity of peace	0.532*	0.517	0.178
	(0.309)	(0.309)	(0.426)
Inconsistent regime type (dummy)	0.515	0.612	2.380**
	(0.307)	(0.315)	(0.789)
Youth-bulge		0.037	−0.008
		(0.029)	(0.041)
Constant	−20.645**	−22.453**	−10.101**
	(6.762)	(7.269)	(1.130)
Observations	2636	2636	2631

Notes:
Relogit estimations of rare-events data.
Standard errors in parentheses.
* significant at 5%; ** significant at 1%.

type (Hegre and Sambanis, 2006; Nel and Righarts, 2008; Sambanis, 2004). Urdal (2006) finds that exceptionally large cohorts of 15–24-year-olds relative to the total adult population of 15 years and older is a strong predictor of violent civil conflict in developing countries, as large concentrations of young people in poorer countries tend to experience high levels of social frustration – low mobility prospects, high levels of unemployment, and overcrowding in urban centres. I include a measure of these so-called 'youth-bulges', based on Urdal (2006). Following Hegre *et al.* (2001), Toset, Gleditsch, and Hegre (2000), and Urdal (2006), I also use a variable called 'Brevity of Peace' to test for the possibility that violent civil conflict is more likely in a political unit that has experienced civil conflict in recent years than it is in a unit where the incidence of violent conflict is few and far between.[24] The results for the income inequality measures in Models 1 and 2 show that household income inequality is indeed a significant and powerful risk factor in the onset of violent civil conflict. As a rule, every point increase in the 100-point Gini index score at *t–1* doubles the risk of the onset of violent civil conflict at *t*. These models also confirm the expectation of a curvilinear relationship between inequality and violent civil conflict. The inequality term and its squared version both have significant coefficients running in opposite directions in both models, suggesting an initial steep upward slope that after a certain point morphs into a downward curve. This implies that the risk of violent civil conflict increases steeply with each increase in the level of inequality, but only up to a point beyond which the risk of violent civil conflict starts to decline with each increase in the inequality score. I calculate this turning point to lie between 45 and 50 on the Gini index score. The explanation for this inverted U-curve relationship between inequality and violent civil conflict, as suggested above, lies in the fact that a high level of inequality reflects not only a disproportional distribution of income, but also a concentration of the collective action resources in a society on the side of those who benefit from economic inequality. There clearly is a threshold in the concentration of wealth, income, and collective action resources beyond which organized armed resistance becomes impossible/too risky/too costly.

The coefficients of the control variables used in the estimation reported in the first two columns of Table 5.2 all have their expected signs, but only the coefficients for population size (in both models) and the coefficient for the 'Brevity of Peace' variable (in Model 1) are highly significant. The risk of violent civil conflict does decline with income level and with economic growth, while the presence of an inconsistent regime type and a large cohort of young people does increase the risk to some degree, but the coefficients of these factors are not statistically significant in Models 1 and 2. Taking everything into consideration, we can conclude that risk of violent civil conflict is highest in populous low- and middle-income countries with medium to high levels of inequality.

Column 3 in Table 5.2 also contains a logit analysis corrected for rare events data, but here the dependent variable is a dichotomous measure indicating the occurrence of an adverse regime change as discussed in Chapter 4. Adverse regime change refers to any regime transition or transformation that leads to a weakening of a country's democracy score in the POLITY IV dataset. The significant and positively signed coefficient for our measure of income inequality shows that inequality not only increases the risk of violent civil conflict, but that it also increases the risk of adverse regime change, specifically if the regime type in place belongs to our category of mixed/inconsistent regime types. One of the well-established empirical findings in the study of comparative politics is that there is a stable positive relationship between the level of socio-economic development and democracy.[25] A contemporary sophisticated formulation of this relationship states that while there are many historical paths on the way to democracy, a democracy, once established for whatever reason, survives in economically developed countries but not necessarily in low-income countries. It is noteworthy that no democracy in the twentieth century fell in a country that had a per capita income higher than that of Argentina in 1975, namely US$6055 (current US dollars; the equivalent in constant international – PPP – dollars in 1975 was $9878), while 47 democracies collapsed in poorer countries since 1946 alone.[26] The evidence presented in Model 3 (Table 5.2) suggests that income inequality, combined with the inconsistency of the regime in place, is one of the reasons for the high incidence of adverse regime change in lower income countries (see also Epstein *et al.*, 2006). Given the close negative association that we have established between income level and inequality, these findings emphasize that high inequality undermines the institutionalization of democracy, and where democracy does get a foothold in unequal societies, it is predominantly weak and inconsistent, thus emasculating the ability of the median voter to make the distribution of economic opportunities and resources more equitable. In the absence of redistribution, such societies face increased risk of violent conflict and the likelihood of an adverse regime change, further weakening the prospects for democracy.

In the preceding pages we have looked at a range of the pathologies that flow from the breakdown of social cohesion in a society and that can be linked theoretically and empirically to economic inequality. The cross section of evidence that we surveyed or generated confirm that the skewed distribution of economic resources condemn whole societies to steady states of sub-optimal social reciprocity and trust, in which social exclusion of the poorer segments of society becomes the norm rather than the exception, standards of public accountability and rectitude crumble under the incentives that the powerful have for rent-seeking, violent crime escalates, and in which whole societies are paralyzed by the repeated breakout of violent civil conflict. Citizens lower down the income and wealth scale face the worst of these adverse affects, and their lives indeed become 'solitary, nasty, and brutish'. However, it would be a mistake to think that the wealthier inhabitants of highly unequal societies are as well of as they possibly could be. Although inequality of wealth and power does create powerful incentives and enticing opportunities for rent-seeking, the wealthy in societies where social cohesion is breaking down can be extremely vulnerable as well. Crime, the collapse of the rule of law and the protection of property rights, and the outbreak of civil conflict increase the insurance and transaction costs of the middle class and wealthy, and they are as much victims of inequalities as are the poor. Excessive inequality harms society as a whole and not only certain segments of it. This general insight is carried over into the next section where we consider the vexed question of the effect of inequality on the rate and quality of economic growth.

'Poor and short': Inequality and the *rate* and *quality* of growth

Extreme deprivation – also known as *absolute poverty* – is the most important factor in developing countries that condemns people to lives that are 'poor' and 'short'. The systematic relief of poverty is appropriately a major focus of attempts to improve human well-being in developing countries, namely the emphasis on poverty relief in the Millennium Development Goals agreed to by the representatives of the world during the 2000 meeting of the United Nations General Assembly. The most commonly used measures of the incidence, depth, and severity of poverty – which are all based on the conception of a minimum income level – have been rightfully criticized for capturing only monetary/resource poverty, while poverty is a multidimensional phenomenon. The resource-based conception of poverty assumes that access to more income or other resources may allow the poor to trade out of poverty, but this ignores the fact that there may be imperfect markets or no markets at all for some of the crucial constituents of a long and fulfilling life, the public goods of health care or education, for example (Bourguignon and Chakravarty, 2003). The anecdotal evidence collected by the World Bank in its 'Voices of the Poor' project testifies to the variety of dimensions of ill-being that poor people themselves emphasize.[27] The search for a more multidimensional measure of absolute deprivation have to be weighed up against the serious data challenges that we face in studying poverty in developing countries, though. By including more dimensions to satisfy the demand for a multidimensional concept, we may be drastically reducing the number of countries about whose poverty levels we can then comment. The infant mortality rate is a readily available measure of the multidimensional nature of absolute deprivation which avoids many of the shortcomings attributed to income-based measures of poverty. The infant mortality rate records the fraction of live-born children who die before the age of one and is an indicator not only of monetary deprivation, but also of the lack of sanitation, clean water, adequate housing and nutrition, and of the failure of publicly provided preventive health care.[28] Infant mortality is at its most pronounced in the lower deciles of the income distribution and also has the benefits of being intuitively clear, being reasonably accurate, and of having the same meaning in every conceivable context: 'A death is a death is a death' as Gerring notes (2007: 69). Long time series and broad cross-sectional data on infant mortality are readily available.[29] It is important to note that infant mortality rates all over the world, including in poor countries, have consistently dropped over the second half of the twentieth century, predominantly because of the widespread diffusion of cheap preventive medicines. In our sample of 147 countries, the mean infant mortality rate per decade declined from 97 deaths per thousand in the 1960s to 77 in the 1970s, 58 in the 1980s, and 46 in the 1990s. To evaluate the performances of countries in relieving absolute deprivation, we thus have to consider not only the absolute rate at which national levels of infant mortality have declined, but also how these national rates shape up relatively to the mean rate of decline for the sample as a whole.

The evidence is pretty overwhelming that sustained economic growth is a necessary, if not sufficient precondition for poverty relief over the longer term (Dollar and Kraay, 2002a; Ravallion, 2001), and in our sample countries with higher levels of GDP growth tend to have better track records with respect to reducing infant mortality rates than do those with stagnant or contracting economies. The crucial question, of course, is what are the prerequisites for sustained growth? While there is much debate about the role that economic openness can play in stimulating growth, as well as the right mixture of state-led versus private-sector initiatives in this regard, a broad cross section of the literature emphasizes the importance of healthy and robust market and public-sector institutions, sustained and quality investment in the improvement of human capital, and a fair degree of social cohesion and generalized trust (Thomas *et al.*, 2000). Looking back at the evidence considered in this chapter so far, it is easy to see why increasing numbers of commentators are turning to economic inequality to explain why some countries find it so difficult to get these prerequisites right. We saw how increasing inequality is closely associated with market failures in the credit and insurance fields, widespread civil violence, and with the breakdown of property rights. In addition, inequality goes with the exclusion of large sections of the population from political participation, thus undermining the legitimacy and responsiveness of public institutions, and from the opportunities to improve their human capital stocks by excluding them from formal schooling and/or by creating strong incentives for households to invest in larger numbers of offspring rather than in the education of smaller numbers of children. This appreciation of the detrimental effects of within-country inequality on the growth potential of nations stands in contrast to the earlier mainstream consensus that there is a trade-off between economic progress and questions of equity, a consensus that relied in part on Kuznets' suggestion that income inequality is bound to increase in societies undergoing economic modernization (see Chapter 2). A further strand was added to this earlier consensus by exogenous growth theories which emphasized the importance of two parameters of growth, namely abstention from current consumption (savings) as the mechanism through which capital is generated and the capital-output ratio which reflects the diminishing marginal productivity of additional increments to the capital stock (Osberg, 1995: 5; Ray, 1998: 51–54). As it is the propensity to save that ultimately drives growth, the channelling of resources and incentives to those with the marginal capacity and disposition to save – the wealthy – enhances the efficiency of an economy. In effect, initial inequalities of wealth and income act as a mechanism (Galor, 2000: 707) that yields higher aggregate savings, capital accumulation, and growth (Nissanke and Thorbecke, 2006: 1342). While there were voices such as Arthur Okun that regretted the tragic nature of trade-off between equity and efficiency and suggested ways of striking a compromise between the two (1975), the core assumption in the exogenous growth literature was that the trade-off was inevitable: One could have growth or equity, but not both.

While this assumption is still stock-in-trade for some undergraduate introductory texts to Economics, a new generation of growth theories has pointed out the potential complementarities between growth and equity (Birdsall, 2001; Landa and Kapstein, 2001; Naschold, 2002). Three themes emerged in these new endogenous-growth theories' explanation of why some countries manage to grow faster than others that are particularly relevant in challenging the notion of a trade-off between equity and growth. Firstly, growth depends on the stock of human capital that an economy can rely upon in an era of rapid technological change. The steady expansion and diffusion of knowledge throughout society is an effective counter to the diminishing returns experienced on physical capital (Ray, 1998: 124), and ensures that societies can benefit from the efficiency creating effects of new technology and the complementarities it makes possible across the economy. Both the production and the intergenerational transfer of human capital are thus important (Thomas *et al.*, 2000: 49–82). While exogenous growth theories used the notion of an intra-generational representative agent to analyze the dynamics of investment, saving, and growth, the newer theories explicitly make provision for heterogeneous actors and for more than one generation which, as Osberg argues, '... immediately raises the issue of inequalities of opportunity in inherited human capital and in access to capital markets' (1995: 6). Secondly, the key to economic growth lies as much in the *quality* of society as it is in the quality and quantity of the factors of production. An economy which is embedded in a society characterized by widespread rent-seeking, by social instability, and by poverty ghettos is bound to be starved of investment and will stagnate. To the extent that inequality is related to these attributes, growth is dependent on the success of public authorities to address inequality and through it the social quality of society. The first and the second theme lead into the third, which emphasizes the importance of having a competent, accountable, and adequately funded public authority to provide the public goods that can optimize human capital and complementarities across the economy, and provide the social cohesion necessary for vibrant growth. Public authorities in unequal societies tend to be caught-up in attempts by the wealthy to use whatever available means to protect and expand their rent-seeking monopoly, which often results in official corruption and patron–client relationships between state leaders and influential groups in society. The bottom-line hypothesis with respect to all these three themes is that initial inequality of income and wealth depresses subsequent growth through a number of mutually reinforcing channels, all of which prevent 'people at the lower end of the wealth or income scale to fully exploit their capabilities', as Ray concludes (1998: 237), which *ipso facto* reduces the aggregate capacity of society to develop optimally.

The availability during the 1990s of new sources of cross-country data on income and land distribution stimulated research to test these hypotheses. By adding measures of asset inequality and income/expenditure distribution to standard growth regressions, a number of authors during the 1990s came to the conclusion that growth is retarded by high levels of income and land inequality (notably Alesina and Rodrik, 1994; Deininger and Squire, 1998; Persson and Tabellini, 1994). As Benabou in his detailed overview of the literature concludes, 'These regressions, run over a variety of data sets and periods with many different measures of income distribution, deliver a consistent message: initial inequality is detrimental to long-run growth' (1996: 13).[30] This conclusion has not gone unchallenged, though, both on conceptual (Quah, 2001) and on empirical grounds (Barro, 1996, 2000; Forbes, 2000; Li and Zou, 1998), with Forbes in particular finding a positive and robust relationship between income inequality and economic growth in the short to medium term in a cross section of 45 countries.

These divergent findings are largely a function of the different estimation methods used and how they influence the selection of data and sample countries (Banerjee and Duflo, 2003). Studies that focus on the variability of data across countries tend to include more cross sections and are more prone to find that initial inequality suppresses subsequent growth than do studies that use country-fixed effects and focus on the time-variability dimension of the available data, such as the study by Forbes (2000). The latter estimation method skews case selection in favour of including more high-income countries than developing countries, because time-series versions of the inequality data used by Forbes are more readily available for high-income than for developing countries.[31] The EHII data used in the current study have, apart from all the other benefits reviewed in Chapter 1, the additional advantage of being available in long time series both for a large number of high-income countries and for many developing countries, and it should thus be possible to weed out the 'disturbances' created by estimation methods that rely on cross-sectional variability versus methods that rely on country fixed-effects and time-variance. A way out of these estimation-dependent results is explored by Pagano (2004), who finds that estimation results are sensitive to the duration of growth observation periods. He uses a broader dataset than Forbes and finds that when he uses annual growth and inequality observations and duplicates her estimation method, there is indeed evidence of a significant negative relationship between income inequality and economic growth in poorer countries (which we know, *pace* Chapter 2, have higher inequality levels as well).

I also find a high negative correlation between the level of inequality and economic growth, but my analysis reveals a further dimension of the data not explored by Pagano. Using all the observations in my dataset, the quadratic regression estimation in Figure 5.3 shows that there is a negative relation between lagged income inequality and economic growth at the two tails of the inequality distribution, but that the relationship is positive at intermediate levels of inequality.[32]

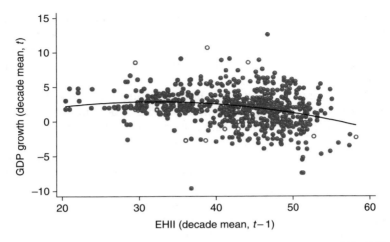

Figure 5.3 High inequality depresses growth: 147 countries, 1960–1999
N = 3941
R-squared = 0.07 (quadratic prediction)
Sources: Decade-country mean EHII data from Galbraith and Kum (2005). Decade-country mean GDP growth calculated from Heston *et al.* (2003).

This finding confirms the results obtained by Cornia *et al.* (2004: 45) who explored UNU-WIDER inequality data for 73 high-, low-, and middle-income countries from the mid-1950s to the 1990s. Cornia and his co-authors also detect an inverted U-curve relationship between inequality and growth. They surmise that low growth performance at lower levels of inequality – which are associated with highly redistributive welfare states – are due to the effect of incentive traps created by high marginal tax rates, the incidence of free-riding and labour shirking, and high supervision costs. Optimal growth is achieved when the Gini index score hovers between 30 and 38, but drops down significantly beyond the 40 index point. The overwhelming majority of developing countries that form the focus of this book have Gini index scores a higher than 40 and rising, and are trapped in the growth-inhibiting effects of high inequality as reviewed in this chapter.[33]

Apart from the fact that inequality is undoubtedly a factor inhibiting growth in poorer countries, there are two important further lessons that we can learn from the debates about inequality and growth. The first is emphasized by Lundberg and Squire (2003), who argue that the search for the causal connection between growth and inequality may be missing the point that both could be determined by the same set of factors over which national decision-makers have some control. Their statistical analysis reveals that the determinants of growth and improved equity are not mutually exclusive and that both equity and growth benefit significantly from increased government expenditure aimed at the redistribution of land and at the provision of universal secondary education, for instance. A second lesson that can be learnt from the debate about growth and inequality is that when considering the effect of inequality it is at least as important to ask questions about the *quality* of growth as it is to consider the *rate* of growth. Given the importance of poverty relief as a goal in and for developing countries, the most important quality dimension of economic growth that should be considered is whether growth is *pro-poor*. Following Ravallion and Chen (2003), I consider growth to be pro-poor if the growth results in an absolute improvement of the well-being of poor people, reflected in one or other agreed-upon meas-ure of well-being. While there is little doubt that rapid economic growth is a pre-condition for poverty relief, evidence is mounting that what matters ultimately is not growth *per se*, but the ability of growth to absolutely increase the range of capabilities accessible to deprived individuals and households. It is in this respect that a focus on inequality has become inescapable when focusing on the quality of growth, as it can be shown that countries that have high levels of initial inequality find it exceedingly difficult to reduce the incidence and depth of material deprivation through economic growth, if meas-ures are not taken to rectify the maldistribution of economic resources and opportunities.[34] On the basis of a careful review of the available evidence, the World Bank's *2006 World Development Report* concludes,

> The balance of evidence does not, therefore, allow much room for doubt that growth elasticities of poverty reduction are stronger in more equal societies. Inequality reduces the effectiveness of eco-nomic growth in reducing poverty. This means that, if all else remain the same, a reduction in income inequality today has a double dividend: it is likely to contribute to a contemporaneous reduction in poverty, and it is likely to make future growth reduce poverty faster. (World Bank, 2005: 87)

Figure 5.4 is a stark illustration of what the authors of the *World Development Report* wanted to convey, and of the terrible toll that odious inequality extracts. As noted, the rate at which the infant mortality rate changes is a useful multidimensional measure of the increase (decrease) of the incidence of poverty. We also noted that the mean infant mortality rate for our sample as a whole declined significantly from decade to decade over the last four decades of the twentieth century. What we have to determine is how sensitive this decline, and hence *poverty relief* was to economic growth[35] across our sample of countries when we control for the distribution of income

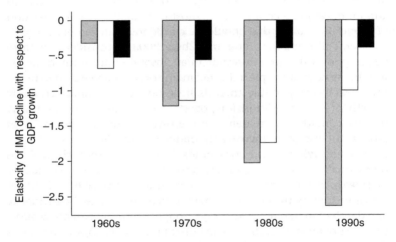

Figure 5.4   Low inequality countries fare better in reducing poverty through economic growth: 147 countries, 1960–1999

Notes: IMR = Infant Mortality Rate. Elasticity of IMR decline with respect to GDP growth is the ratio of proportional change in the decade-mean IMR per inequality country group with respect to proportional change in the decade-mean GDP growth rate per inequality country group.

      Low inequality level (<30 on Gini index).

      Medium inequality level (30–40 on Gini index).

      High inequality level (>40 on Gini index).

Sources: Decade-mean EHII data per country group calculated from Galbraith and Kum (2005). Decade-mean GDP growth rate per country group calculated from GDP growth data in Heston *et al.* (2003). Decade-mean infant mortality rate calculated from infant mortality rate data in Urdal (2006).

in the various countries. The vertical bars indicate how responsive on average the decline in infant mortality rates was to rates of economic growth for each of three groups of states: States with low inequality (<30 on the Gini index); with medium inequality (30–40 on the Gini index); and with high inequality (>40 on the Gini index). The elasticity of poverty relief (captured by the declining infant mortality rate) with respect to economic growth in each of the four decades was much higher in countries with low- and medium-inequality levels, than in high-inequality countries. In the latter case, the growth elasticity of poverty relief actually *declined* during the 1980s and 1990s compared to the 1970s. Thus, despite the wide transnational dissemination of preventative medicines and palliative care during an era of intensified globalization, high-inequality countries failed to translate economic growth into mechanisms that made these medicines and care available to the poor who, as we said, are hardest hit by the incidence of infant mortality. If ever there was proof of the human costs of economic inequality, this surely is it. Faced with evidence such as this, one cannot but agree with Francois Bourguignon when he writes,

A recurring theme in discussions on development is whether the main focus of development strategies should be placed on growth, on poverty, and/or on inequality.... [T]he answer can be simply expressed in two statements: First, the rapid elimination of *absolute* poverty, under all forms, is a meaningful goal for development. Second, to achieve the goal of rapidly reducing absolute poverty requires strong, country-specific *combinations* of growth and distribution policies. (2004: 1; emphasis in the original)

Conclusions

This chapter has reviewed the available evidence concerning a selection of the effects that economic inequality has on the well-being of individuals and the societies that they form, and has also added additional empirical testimony to the indictment against inequality. The adverse consequences of inequality can be summarized under two rubrics: The one has to do with the mostly intangible but crucial attribute of social cohesion, which we showed to be indispensable in the construction and maintenance of societies where the individual has the opportunity to explore her life choices without harming the ability of any other individual to do the same. This can be achieved at best in a society where there is not only guarantees concerning individual liberty, but also a large degree of mutual trust and the institutionalization of reciprocal respect. At the high-inequality levels that are commonly found in low- and middle-income societies, the attribute of social cohesion and the positive externalities that accompany it are fatally compromised. That does not necessarily imply that social capital is totally absent from such societies, but it becomes likely that social capital is constructed only within narrow rent-seeking alliances within the society. A deficiency in the institutionalization of social cohesion manifests itself in a number of social pathologies that are statistically speaking significantly related to income and wealth inequality: Corruption, crime, and conflict in particular.

Contrary to the findings of an economics literature that goes back at least 50 years, there is little evidence of a trade-off between growth and inequality. Recent findings by Forbes (2000) and others that suggest that inequality is positively associated with growth are based on inadequate coverage of developing societies and on data that make cross-sectional comparisons doubtful. Using a set of inequality and related data that uses measures that are consistent across countries, and that allows us to include a large number of developing countries in the sample, we do find persuasive evidence of a *negative* association between economic growth and very low and very high levels of inequality. More substantially, the evidence reviewed here confirms a message that over the past five years has received considerable emphasis from economists at the World Bank. This message is that high levels of initial inequality act as a barrier that insulates the poor from the benefits of economic growth. This negative effect of initial inequality not only on the rate but also on the *quality* of growth has a number of implications. One is that it is too much of a simplification to send slogans such as 'growth is good for the poor' without qualification out into the world. It is only when growth is combined with redistribution that the poor benefit. This is confirmed by a simulation run by Dagdeviren, van der Hoeven, and Weeks (2004) on 50 developing countries. They conclude that for 47 out of 50 developing countries, a strategy of marginal redistribution of wealth from the rich to the poor, or a strategy of equal distribution of growth benefits, are more effective in reducing poverty than increases in economic growth that are distributionally neutral. Growth plus redistribution, it increasingly seems, is what developing countries should pursue.

6
Conclusions: Local Inequalities, Global Responsibilities

The previous chapters have made the case for considering economic inequality as a major scourge on the development and growth potential of developing societies. Having considered the evidence, one cannot but agree with Easterly (2002) who concludes that inequality, independently of other factors, is a large and statistically significant barrier to developing the institutional framework and human capital on which successful human development depends. These pages have also presented evidence that inequality hinders the implementation of sensible macroeconomic strategies, impedes the development of pro-poor policies, limits the growth of human capital stocks, undermines social cohesion, fuels social discontent, narrows political participation, and promotes corruption and crime (Justino *et al.*, 2003).

The consequences and pervasiveness of economic inequality in developing countries justify the use of the adjective *odious* to describe it. But as if that is not already enough, we also found that extreme inequality and its consequences are largely avoidable, in the sense that there are tried and tested policy steps available that can be taken without jeopardizing any other values that we may happen to subscribe to. Repeatedly, I have shown that the rapid and general improvement of human capital through expansive investment in education and health care must be the priority for developing countries, as it has been for the international success stories of development, such as Costa Rica, Uruguay, Singapore, South Korea, Taiwan, and the Indian state of Kerala. This must be coupled with policies that correct the imperfections that have been allowed to develop in the markets for credit and land, and in the political and judicial institutions that determine not only what people have and earn, but also how they are treated. Economic inequality is not only a functional distributional issue but has to do also with fundamental injustices in the basic social institutions of societies, which often have long historical antecedents. These injustices have to do with how power is organized and shared within societies, as the analysis of the effect of democratization on redistribution made clear. The relationship between political regime and economic inequality is not linear and is mediated by a variety of factors, and outcomes do not always match our optimistic expectations. As Chapter 4 argues, the introduction of competitive elections on the basis of universal adult franchise, important though it may be for many reasons, is not a guarantee against the widespread practices of state capture and neo-patrimonial favouritism that bedevil the pursuit of economic equity. These political features, and the ways to counter them, plus ways in which state capacity in developing countries can be increased, deserve at least as much attention as do questions of how they manage free and fair elections.

In addition to emphasizing these 'inside-out' structural determinants of inequality, this study also underlines the determinacy of transnational 'outside-in' factors. We found that the institutional injustices within developing societies and the differential functional returns received by holders of different factors of production are determined also by the fundamental structures of the global division of labour. These structures operate on two levels. One has to do with the conditions under which countries were incorporated into the expanding global mode of production since the emergence of merchant capitalism in the sixteenth century. These conditions determine the place and function of developing countries in the global division of labour. By their very nature, these structures of the global division of labour are not readily amenable to change, and although there are examples of countries who have graduated from playing a 'peripheral' to a more 'core' role in the world capitalist system, these examples are rare.

The structures of the global division of labour operate also on a second level, though, and change can come much more readily on this level. This level has to do with the structural power of ideas, which includes both factual and analytical conceptions about how the world works and normative beliefs about how the world should work. Patterns of beliefs and norms also form determinate structures in the global division of labour, and their effect on outcomes is as powerful as that of any other type of structure (Blyth, 2002; Wendt, 1999). There is no single, simple explanation why within-country inequality increased disastrously in most developing countries during the last decades of the twentieth century and into the third millennium. However, one factor that repeatedly presents itself as unmistakably influential is the macroeconomic ideological context in which decision-makers increasingly had to operate during the second half of the twentieth century. This ideological context has significant similarities with a previous ideological era in the nineteenth century during which international and national inequalities also widened in unison (see Figure 3.1), but the later version has carried its ideological precepts much wider and with more persuasive power than its predecessor. The reigning macroeconomic ideology of the late twentieth century elevated economic openness to being a goal in itself and in whose interest all competing economic and other national values had to be sacrificed. Economic openness in the form of less-constrained trade and the freer flow of investment capital has indeed enhanced world output. However, these results do not match those of the era of embedded liberalism which, as Jeffry Frieden comments, 'oversaw the most rapid rates of economic growth and most enduring economic stability in modern history' (2006: 300). Economic openness during the era of globalization 'Mark II' did assist some countries to narrow the income gap between themselves and the 'old' high-income countries, but these benefits were largely concentrated amongst those countries whose domestic structures and human capital resources had been well-prepared during a preceding era of more inward-oriented national development (Rodrik, 1997, 1999). It is also well known that the most successful developing countries during this era were very selective in their application of the precepts of economic openness. But for many younger, poorer, and less well-prepared countries the ideological hegemony of economic openness robbed them of those very opportunities for inward-focused national development that the more successful 'globalizers' once enjoyed behind the protective walls of tariffs and managed capital accounts. The failure of these poorer and more vulnerable countries to catch-up cannot be attributed solely to the leadership failures that many of them experienced. Leadership failures there indeed were, and still are, but in many cases the rise and prominence of incompetent leaders are the result of a deeper process of national decline, precipitated by the inordinate haste with which the ideology of economic openness was foisted upon unsuspecting and vulnerable countries (Wade, 2007).

Economic openness that came along with the easing of constraints on the flow of goods and services, and on the mobility of capital has had varied distributional consequences in different developing countries (Anderson, 2005; Goldberg and Pavenik, 2007) and it is not possible to generalize with the confidence that ideologues on both sides of the divide often does. What is clear, though, is that the empirical credentials of mainstream economic theory are no longer unassailable. Not enough attention goes into analysing the many ways in which the vulnerabilities faced by developing countries in the global division of labour produce effects that do not square with the expectations of mainstream theory which is still caught-up in the inside-out, national level of analysis that was critiqued in Chapter 2. The promotion of economic openness at all costs, with respect particularly to liberalizing the capital account and promoting capital mobility, had major distributive results within a broad range of low- and middle-income countries, and curtailed the ability of poorer voters to use the ballot as a way of narrowing income and wealth differentials. Economic openness combined with high initial levels of inequality prevented the poor to benefit from economic growth and improve their income share. Both domestically and internationally, one specific class and their allies benefited most from the hegemonic status of this ideology, hence the extraordinary lengths to which their spokespeople go to undermine alternative conceptions of what economic progress can and should mean. This class is transnationally organized and can be referred to as the holders of mobile capital, both in its human and in its financial forms. As happened in the late nineteenth century, when the world also experienced a period of deep economic openness, the ideology justifying the more recent spate also represents a normative revolution of epochal dimensions that have made the world truly a more unequal place.

The preceding brief summary of the conclusions reached in this book implies that responsibility for the prevalence and persistence of odious inequality must be shared more widely than is commonly believed. For sure, blame lies with generations of political leaders in developing countries who not only tolerated economic inequality, but who often deliberately exploited the rent-seeking opportunities that economic inequality and its concomitant imbalance of power creates.

However, responsibility also rests with the idea merchants who indiscriminately extol the value of economic openness as a goal in itself, the decision-makers who turn such indiscriminate notions into policy prescriptions and with all of us who allow the concentration of such inordinate degrees of normative power and influence to take place.

Odious economic inequality within countries can be combated effectively only if we accept global responsibilities. This implies that a negative duty rests on the shoulders of the rule-makers in global regimes to weed out those norms and practices that inadvertently restrain or deliberately discourage redistributive macroeconomic policies in developing countries. Although this point can sometimes be overdone, there is no doubt that open economies lose some control over the setting of prices, that it becomes infeasible to depress the expected after-tax rate of return on mobile capital, and that those in favour of redistribution, such as trade unions, may have their bargaining power undermined in the process (Rudra, 2002a; Rudra and Haggard, 2005). However, it is illusion to think that globalization has totally depleted the redistributive arsenal of the welfare state. Much can still be done to promote equity in wealth and income in poorer countries, also by countries acting on their own, such as land redistribution on a willing-seller, willing-buyer basis and the taxing of absentee landholding, improving imperfections in the credit market so that the poor can gain access to credit and start to build-up human and fixed capital, and the use of progressive taxation to fund general education and primary health care.

We also collectively face the responsibility of living up to a set of positive duties, if we are serious about combating odious inequality within countries. This includes making global market forces work more equitably towards holders of different factors of production within developing countries by opening domestic markets of the North more to imports from the South, by setting trade rules that are fairer to developing countries, and by lifting the draconian constraints imposed by developed countries on international labour flows. It also includes improving development assistance by increasing and targeting aid flows better, and by linking aid more directly to the relieving not only of poverty, but also of income and wealth inequalities in developing countries (through the joint financing of education programmes, the provision of credit to the assetless, and by assisting land redistribution schemes, for instance). Much emphasis is placed on the importance of increased official development assistance to developing countries if we want to achieve the Millennium Development Goals, and rightfully so. But, as Milanovic argues, such assistance can only be beneficial if it respects principles of progressivity. This implies, amongst others, that development assistance must improve and not worsen the distributional imbalances in the recipient countries (Milanovic, 2007). At present, too much development assistance inadvertently aids those who are already better off in developing countries, namely wealthy urbanites and large landholders who are best placed to draw immediate benefit from externally funded improvements in infrastructure and public services (Castro-Leal *et al.*, 1999; Eastwood and Lipton, 2000; IFAD, 2001). Official development assistance that explicitly targets odious inequality, and is thus based on a normative basis that values equity as a goal worth pursuing on a worldwide scale, is ideally suited to meet these requirements (Gugerty and Timmer, 1999). It is also the best way to live up to the injunction that, as the *2006 World Development Report* puts it, 'aid should be targeted where the probability is greatest that it effectively reaches those with the most limited opportunities' (World Bank, 2005: 219). To achieve this, poverty and inequality must be targeted together and simultaneously. Development assistance aimed at reducing odious inequality must focus on the whole of the distributional pattern in recipient countries, thus aiming also to reduce the perverse incentives that those at the top-end of the distribution have to engage in rent-seeking and exploitation of the poor. As Chapter 5 showed, odious inequality affects the whole fabric of a society, not only the poor, and the whole of society therefore should be addressed if we want to deal effectively with the ravages caused by economic inequality. Achieving this will involve a significant reorientation of development thinking away from the current vogue that focuses heavily on poverty relief to the detriment of considerations pertaining to the well-being of societies taken as structured and interdependent social wholes. Poverty relief is indeed important, but poverty is a symptom of odious inequality and without a focus on the latter, attempts to make poverty history are bound to end up on the trash heap of history themselves.

Appendix A: Sample Countries and Summary Statistics on Estimated Household Income Inequality Gini Index Score

Country	Mean EHII	Standard deviation EHII	Observations
Afghanistan	42.43	2.43	15
Albania	41.15	10.57	8
Algeria	38.52	2.48	28
Angola	53.93	3.48	6
Argentina	43.95	1.45	11
Armenia	52.91	4.99	5
Australia	33.06	2.78	35
Austria	34.40	1.27	37
Azerbaijan	40.88	3.29	5
Bahamas	50.00	1.24	3
Bahrain	53.16	–	1
Bangladesh	42.87	2.74	26
Barbados	44.00	1.49	28
Belgium	35.05	1.66	30
Belize	47.24	0.64	2
Benin	49.12	1.18	7
Bhutan	49.86	–	1
Bolivia	47.40	3.03	30
Bosnia and Herzegovina	36.95	2.12	2
Botswana	46.52	1.07	15
Brazil	47.02	1.02	5
Bulgaria	30.75	4.91	36
Burkina Faso	45.09	2.50	10
Cameroon	50.96	4.66	24
Canada	35.65	1.40	37
Cape Verde	35.51	3.33	2
Central African Republic	47.96	2.93	19
Chile	45.28	2.49	37
China	30.99	1.31	10

Colombia	44.02	0.73	37
Republic of Congo	52.05	1.31	14
Costa Rica	41.44	1.80	18
Cote d'Ivoire	47.79	1.27	22
Croatia	33.64	2.36	11
Cyprus	41.45	2.62	37
Czech Republic	21.15	0.90	29
Denmark	30.61	0.52	36
Dominican Republic	46.74	2.02	23
Ecuador	45.31	2.64	37
Egypt	42.23	3.01	36
El Salvador	45.55	2.59	29
Equatorial Guinea	50.34	1.23	2
Ethiopia	44.09	1.60	9
Fiji	43.23	3.22	27
Finland	32.04	1.34	37
France	34.02	0.89	17
Gabon	49.43	4.25	8
Gambia	44.95	1.74	8
Ghana	50.78	2.14	28
Greece	41.96	1.53	37
Guatemala	48.83	3.82	26
Haiti	46.80	1.73	21
Honduras	45.90	2.20	26
Hong Kong	29.41	5.46	27
Hungary	30.49	4.65	37
Iceland	34.14	1.40	29
India	8.40	1.48	37
Indonesia	48.67	2.11	29
Iran	43.09	5.30	30
Iraq	43.18	2.18	27
Ireland	37.85	1.86	36
Israel	39.20	2.81	34
Italy	36.91	1.58	32
Jamaica	49.93	3.58	27
Japan	36.16	1.97	37
Jordan	48.00	1.68	32
Kenya	49.26	1.42	36
Republic of Korea	39.49	2.69	37
Kuwait	52.20	2.41	31
Kyrgyzstan	44.85	1.47	6
Latvia	28.59	7.28	6
Lesotho	50.00	3.63	7
Liberia	50.04	1.37	3
Libya	44.19	4.02	17
Lithuania	39.77	2.31	5

(Continued)

Country	Mean EHII	Standard deviation EHII	Observations
Luxembourg	31.32	1.69	32
Macao	26.19	3.33	20
Macedonia	37.67	2.85	10
Madagascar	45.01	3.21	22
Malawi	49.36	3.31	32
Malaysia	41.23	2.40	32
Malta	35.03	3.00	34
Mauritania	54.85	2.07	2
Mauritius	42.16	4.14	32
Mexico	42.90	1.53	30
Moldova	36.15	7.85	9
Mongolia	57.32	6.06	5
Morocco	48.43	1.20	26
Mozambique	52.25	3.08	14
Myanmar	45.93	3.58	10
Namibia	43.28	–	1
Nepal	47.45	2.58	9
Netherlands	33.52	1.63	37
New Zealand	34.65	3.23	34
Nicaragua	41.81	1.60	21
Nigeria	45.29	2.24	26
Norway	32.28	1.35	36
Oman	50.37	0.69	6
Pakistan	45.76	2.08	30
Panama	46.68	1.69	35
Papua New Guinea	49.79	1.76	27
Paraguay	40.11	–	1
Peru	48.16	2.36	12
Philippines	46.65	1.39	35
Poland	31.32	4.36	30
Portugal	40.04	2.25	27
Puerto Rico	45.11	3.38	15
Qatar	54.53	1.55	8
Romania	30.20	2.17	12
Russia	40.01	1.74	6
Rwanda	48.68	3.56	12
Samoa	48.69	0.21	2
Saudi Arabia	53.67	–	1
Senegal	44.11	4.81	24
Seychelles	36.16	2.39	11
Sierra Leone	53.95	4.91	2

Singapore	39.00	4.19	37
Slovak Republic	33.57	2.64	6
Slovenia	28.98	3.47	12
Somalia	46.52	2.13	14
South Africa	43.35	1.15	33
Spain	39.48	1.35	37
Sri Lanka	45.83	2.20	17
St. Vincent and Grenadines	53.50	0.89	2
Sudan	46.67	–	1
Suriname	45.80	2.36	20
Swaziland	49.19	2.61	26
Sweden	29.19	3.12	37
Syria	45.31	5.16	36
Taiwan	31.60	1.56	25
Tanzania	48.91	2.47	23
Thailand	48.45	2.68	19
Togo	49.32	3.41	14
Tonga	46.46	2.83	15
Trinidad and Tobago	49.07	3.44	23
Tunisia	46.70	2.03	25
Turkey	43.97	2.06	36
Uganda	50.16	4.04	14
Ukraine	36.80	4.75	9
United Arab Emirates	45.70	3.14	4
United Kingdom	32.47	2.55	33
United States	36.56	1.99	37
Uruguay	41.71	2.53	24
Venezuela	44.38	2.63	32
Yugoslavia	42.07	2.20	5
Zambia	47.19	1.57	18
Zimbabwe	45.27	1.71	36

Appendix B: The Relationship between Regime Change and Economic Inequality in Selected Countries, 1960–1999

Country	Year	A to ID	ID to CD	CD to A	CD to ID	ID to A	Inequality at t	Inequality at $t + 5$
Albania	1990	X					30.69	51.23
Albania	1996					X	46.75	47.58
Albania	1997	X					44.77	47.58
Argentina	1973	X						
Argentina	1976					X		
Argentina	1983	X					41.13	44.35
Armenia	1996					X	47.77	
Armenia	1998	X					47.26	54.19
Azerbaijan	1992	X					40.88	
Azerbaijan	1993					X		
Bangladesh	1974					X	40.3	41.23
Bangladesh	1991	X					48.22	
Benin	1963					X		49.71
Benin	1991	X						
Bolivia	1982	X					46.31	48.78
Brazil	1964					X		
Brazil	1985	X						
Bulgaria	1990	X					27.34	39.49
Burkina Faso	1977	X					43.54	43.6
Burkina Faso	1980					X	42.78	43.59
Central African Republic	1993	X					51.98	
Chile	1973					X	39.71	44.01
Chile	1989	X					46.86	45.68
Republic of Congo	1963					X		51.89
Republic of Congo	1992	X					52.38	
Republic of Congo	1997					X		
Croatia	1999	X						36.41

Cyprus	1963			X	47.04	44.43
Cyprus	1968	X			44.43	41.96
Cyprus	1974		X		44.67	40.85
Czech Republic	1990	X			20.58	22.22
Dominican Republic	1962	X				48.08
Dominican Republic	1963			X	43.78	47.58
Dominican Republic	1978	X			47.14	47.37
Ecuador	1961			X		47.1
Ecuador	1968	X			45.45	43.34
Ecuador	1970			X	45.47	41.38
Ecuador	1979	X			42.18	44.43
El Salvador	1982	X			42.49	44.78
Equatorial Guinea	1969			X		
Ethiopia	1993	X			43.3	44.88
Fiji	1987			X	46	47.13
Fiji	1990	X			47.43	48.03
France	1969		X			33.36
Gambia	1994			X		
Ghana	1970	X			51.51	
Ghana	1972			X	53.07	50.88
Ghana	1979	X			51.18	47.74
Ghana	1981			X	50.49	55.16
Ghana	1996	X				53.17
Greece	1967			X	42.15	40.8
Greece	1974	X			40.94	41.44
Greece	1975		X		40.92	41.62
Guatemala	1966	X				47.08
Guatemala	1974			X	47.02	46.26
Guatemala	1986	X			49.01	56.46
Haiti	1990	X			45.58	
Haiti	1991			X		
Haiti	1994	X				
Honduras	1980	X			44.64	46.15
Hungary	1989	X			31.05	38.13
Hungary	1990		X		31.57	39.07
Indonesia	1999	X			45.87	
Iran	1997	X				
Kenya	1966			X	51.41	50.19
Republic of Korea	1961			X		43
Republic of Korea	1963	X			42.9	43.21
Republic of Korea	1972			X	43.99	39.99
Republic of Korea	1987	X			36.55	36.71

(Continued)

Country	Year	A to ID	ID to CD	CD to A	CD to ID	ID to A	Inequality at t	Inequality at $t+5$
Lesotho	1970					X		
Lesotho	1993	X					51.57	51.89
Lesotho	1998					X		
Lesotho	1999	X						
Madagascar	1991	X						
Malawi	1994	X					51.58	53.74
Malaysia	1969				X		45.44	42.09
Mexico	1994	X					45.33	45.2
Mongolia	1990	X					52.97	62.99
Mongolia	1996		X				54.01	
Mozambique	1994	X					53.42	59
Myanmar	1962					X		
Nepal	1990	X					48.53	44.26
Nicaragua	1990	X					41.61	
Nigeria	1966					X		46.26
Nigeria	1979	X					45.75	
Nigeria	1984					X	42.02	43.57
Nigeria	1999	X						47.93
Pakistan	1962	X						42.94
Pakistan	1970					X	42.67	44.43
Pakistan	1972	X					46.79	d
Pakistan	1977					X	45.63	47.2
Pakistan	1988	X					47	48.69
Pakistan	1999					X		
Panama	1968					X	46.18	46.14
Panama	1989	X					47.81	49.06
Paraguay	1989	X						40.11
Peru	1968					X		
Peru	1979	X						47.98
Peru	1992					X		
Peru	1993	X					50.02	
Philippines	1972					X	44.38	47.45
Philippines	1986	X					47.27	48.15
Poland	1989	X					29.24	34.92
Portugal	1975	X					37.37	
Portugal	1982		X				38.18	39.1
Romania	1990	X					24.77	28.98
Sierra Leone	1967					X		
Sierra Leone	1968	X						
Sierra Leone	1971					X		50.48
Sierra Leone	1996	X					57.43	
Sierra Leone	1997					X		
Singapore	1963					X	44.33	45.9
Slovak Republic	1993	X					33.38	36.06
Somalia	1969					X	46.22	45.46
South Africa	1994	X					44.59	45.67

Country	Year	A	CD	ID		
Spain	1976	X			40.34	
Spain	1982		X		37.38	38.94
Sudan	1965	X				
Sudan	1970			X	46.67	
Sudan	1986	X				
Sudan	1989			X		
Taiwan	1992	X			32	31.59
Thailand	1969	X			49.72	50.46
Thailand	1971			X	52.57	50.63
Thailand	1974	X			50.46	49.55
Thailand	1976			X	50.63	48.23
Thailand	1978	X				
Thailand	1991			X	46.83	
Thailand	1992	X				45.52
Turkey	1971			X	42.61	41.33
Turkey	1973	X			41.51	43.22
Turkey	1980			X	44.48	42.44
Turkey	1983	X			42.48	43.17
Uganda	1966			X	47.8	49.26
Uganda	1980	X				57.5
Uganda	1985			X	57.5	52.58
Uruguay	1972			X		38.09
Uruguay	1985	X			41.65	40.8
Uruguay	1989		X		39.81	43.52
Zambia	1968			X	46.25	45.46
Zambia	1991	X			50.04	49.42
Zimbabwe	1987			X	43.57	52.44

Notes: A = Autocracy.
CD = Consistent Democracy.
ID = Inconsistent Democracy.
Selection based on sample of 147 countries for which we have high quality inequality data.
Sources: Regime changes calculated from Polity2 combined regime score, POLITY IV dataset (Marshall and Jaggers, 2002). Inequality data from the EHII dataset (Galbraith and Kum, 2005).

Notes

1 Introduction: developing countries and odious inequality

1. Hereafter, 'developing countries'. See 'A Note on Data Sources and Country Groupings' below for detail on the classification of developing countries.
2. The distribution of income and wealth between individuals/households is sometimes referred to as *vertical* inequality, which can be distinguished from *horizontal* economic inequalities between social groups (gender, ethnic), and between spatial units (regional disparities, urban–rural divide). Frances Stewart justifiably calls horizontal inequality 'a neglected dimension of development' and stresses the importance of group membership as a determinant of well-being (Stewart, 2005). However, there is no need to *contrast* the two types of inequalities. Instead, one should think of inter-group dynamics and spatial differentiation as two of the many factors that determine the relative income and wealth shares accruing to individuals and their households. In this book we focus on the latter, being the 'end-state' of a variety of causal processes, including those related to group dynamics.

3. Money, being the instrument of an important public and private purpose, is rightly regarded as wealth; but everything else which serves any human purpose, and which nature does not afford gratuitously, is wealth also. To be wealthy is to have a large stock of useful articles, or the means of purchasing them. Everything forms therefore a part of wealth, which has a power of purchasing; for which anything useful or agreeable would be given in exchange. Things for which nothing could be obtained in exchange, however useful or necessary they may be, are not wealth in the sense in which the term is used in Political Economy.

    (Mill, 1848/1909: Preliminary remarks, paragraph 14)

    See Schneider (2004) for a discussion of the concept and metrics of the distribution of wealth.
4. Amartya Sen persuasively argues against reducing economic inequality to income inequality, which he believes is more appropriately and comprehensively captured by the notion of a disproportion in the distribution of human capabilities to do the things that people would want to pursue. However, he grants that income (and wealth) is a 'crucially important means ... [that] helps the person to do things that she values doing and to achieve states of being that she has reasons to desire'(1997: 385).

5. See also Atkinson (1999, 2004).
6. For a discussion of the variance in welfare spending among developing countries, and the determinants of that variance, see Rudra and Haggard (2005).
7. Data on income distribution per decile from the World Bank's *World Development Indicators* CD-ROM 2006.
8. The Pearson two-tailed correlation *r* between the income ratio and the headcount poverty measures mentioned in the text is .45, at a significance level of 10 per cent. Data for the income ratio and poverty headcounts are from the World Bank's 2006 *World Development Indicators* CD-ROM.
9. See Somini Sengupta's article 'On India's Farms, A Plague of Suicide', *New York Times*, 19 September 2006.
10. The classic statement is in Rawls (1971: 60–65), but see also Rawls (1982). See Arneson (1990) for a critique.
11. See Smith (1776/1976: 351–352), and Phillips (1999: 79–830).
12. See McGillivray and Shorrocks (2005) and Barry (2005).
13. See Lindert (2004) for the most comprehensive treatment of the emergence and positive effects of social spending in high-income countries.
14. This brief summary of examples of successful redistribution in developing countries is based on Bowles (2006) and World Bank (2006). See also Bourguignon (2000) and Dagdeviren *et al.* (2004).
15. See Robert Wade (2007) and James Galbraith (2002) for summary discussions of the ideological apparatus that underlies the articles of the neo-liberal faith.
16. See the volume edited by Cornia (2004).
17. Young (1990, 2006). See also Forst (2007).
18. On approaches to studying inequality, see Sen (1992, 1997); Champernowne and Cowell (1998); Ray (1998); Fields (2001), and the volume edited by Atkinson and Bourguignon (2000). Significant new data sources are reported and explored in Deininger and Squire (1996, 1998), Cornia (2004), Atkinson and Piketty (2006), Bourguignon and Morrisson (2002), Milanovic (2005), and Galbraith and Kum (2005).
19. The volume by De Ferranti *et al.* (2004) is an important exception, but focuses only on Latin America.
20. See, in particular, Fields (2001), Birdsall and Londono (1997), Birdsall (2001), Ray (1998), Kanbur (2000), and World Bank (2006).
21. Boix (2003) and Acemoglu and Robinson (2006) represent useful recent attempts to explore, from an explicit *political economy* perspective, at least some of the political dimensions of income distribution, both in developing and in high-income countries. However, the narrow methodological individualism and national focus that underlie both these books are not conducive to appreciating the determining role of global social structures and dynamics.
22. The World Bank classification of country groups used here is based on 1994 Gross National Income (GNI) data, using the Atlas conversion method. This conversion method relies on the average of a country's exchange rate in a particular year and the two preceding years, and

adjusts this for the difference between that country's inflation rate and the inflation rate of a basket of benchmark countries.

23. Important to note is that the Republic of Korea, Taiwan, and Singapore in the 1990s were classified as high-income countries, and our analysis for that period treats them as such. However, for analyses of earlier periods they are included in the group of developing countries. There are also other countries in our sample that could, for different purposes, be regarded as developing or transition states, but whose mean income places them in the high-income group. They are Bahamas, Bahrain, Cyprus, Hong Kong, Kuwait, Macao, Malta, Puerto Rico, Qatar, Saudi-Arabia, Slovenia, and the United Arab Emirates. Mexico and Turkey are members of the OECD, but their mean income levels put them in the category of developing countries as defined here.

24. While this convention has served generations of students of inequality well, recent attempts to generate data on and better understandings of the distribution of wealth are to be welcomed. In this regard, see Schneider (2004), and the recently launched 'Personal Assets from a Global Perspective' project of the United Nations University World Institute of Development Economics Research (UNU-WIDER), available at http://www.wider.unu.edu/research/2006-2007/2006-2007-1/2006-2007-1.htm

25. The Deininger and Squire (World Bank) dataset in particular introduced quality criteria and other innovations that contributed much to the upsurge in income inequality research during recent years (Deininger and Squire, 1996, 1998). This dataset, with all its good points but also with all its faults (see below), forms the basis of the refined dataset used by Dollar and Kraay (2002a,b), and the 'UNU/WIDER World Income Inequality Database' (Version 2.0b, May 2007, is available at http://www.wider.unu.edu/wiid/wiid-introduction-2005-1.htm). Data collected by the World Bank on income distribution is also used in the PovCalNet interactive income distribution dataset, available at http://iresearch.worldbank.org/PovcalNet/jsp/index.jsp

26. See Atkinson and Brandolini (2001), Knowles (2005), and Galbraith and Kum (2005).

27. The dataset containing these observations is available at http://utip.gov.utexas.edu/data/UTIP_UNIDO2001rv3.xls

28. Galbraith and Kum use a series of multiple regression estimations to determine the relevance of items of information to include in the eventual estimation of the EHII data. Dummy variables are used to control for the distinctions between income and expenditure measures, between measures of gross and net income/expenditure, and between measures of household and individual income/expenditure (Galbraith and Kum, 2005: 126–133).

29. The most important shortcoming is that due to the methodology used in its construction, it cannot report information about the income shares of different percentiles of the population. This, however, is a small price to pay to enjoy the wide coverage and consistent features of the dataset.

2 Explaining odious inequality

1. The concept of economic vulnerability has been given prominence by United Nations Conference on Trade and Development (UNCTAD), which when applied to less developed countries (LDCs) refers to (a) the instability of agricultural production; (b) the instability of exports of goods and services; (c) the economic importance of non-traditional activities (share of manufacturing and modern services in GDP); (d) merchandise export concentration; and (e) the handicap of economic smallness. See the UNCTAD website dedicated to LDCs, available at http://r0.unctad.org/ldcs/index.html.

2. For discussions of these historical processes, see Engerman and Sokoloff (1997, 2002, 2005); Acemoglu, and Robinson (2006); and De Ferranti *et al.* (2004).

3. As we shall see in Chapter 3, a process of reversed modernization called 'deindustrialization' can also increase inequality. Deindustrialization creates unemployment, driving down the wages of lower skilled labourers and thus widening the income differentials in a society.

4. Kuznets based his notion of the inverted U-curve on a set of cross-sectional data, comparing different countries at different levels of economic development, and not on within-country data. Much of the subsequent empirical research has focused on replicating the cross-sectional effect that Kuznets detected (see Ray, 1998: 199–207). However, the real test of the inverted U-shape hypothesis lies in exploring the history of inequality within countries, and not in comparing the income levels of different countries with one another. Of course, Kuznets had no other choice than to focus on the cross-sectional record, given the absence of reliable intra-country data when he wrote his ground-breaking papers. Recent studies, using more readily available country-specific studies, show that the inverted U-curve is present in the history of some countries – Japan being a prime example – but by no means in all countries (see Tachibanaki, 2005: 71). Also take note of Anand and Kanbur's (1993) suggestion that the validity of Kuznets' proposition concerning the inverted U depends on the nature of the regression specification that he and his followers used. There is also the possibility that the detection of the inverted U in cross-sectional studies is a statistical artefact, driven by the fact that the group of very high inequality countries tends to be dominated by countries from Latin America – countries which as a rule have progressed some way along the path of modernization.

5. See the volume edited by Cornia (2004).

6. In Chapter 4, we shall have the opportunity to discuss the question concerning the connection between the dynamic process of democratization and economic equity in detail.

7. Useful discussions concerning the biased and complex nature of the term 'political instability' can be found in Przeworski *et al.* (2000: Chapter 4), and Sanders (1981).

8. The inequality measure used here and in the rest of the book is the Estimated Household Income Inequality Gini index score (0–100) as explained in Chapter 1. The scaled additive Polity2 regime measure developed in the POLITY IV dataset (Marshall and Jaggers, 2002) runs from –10 for 'consistent' autocracies to +10 for 'consistent' democracies.

9. The Polity2 regime measure provides us with the means to operationalize the distinctions between consistent and inconsistent regime types. It is of course problematic to use what is intended as a continuous scale of regime scores to arrive at a categorical distinction between types of regimes. Nevertheless, the POLITY IV dataset has so many advantages in terms of clarity of conceptualization and operationalization that researchers interested in the categorization of types of democracy prefer to use it instead of less transparent categorizations such as Reich (2002). The important question is where exactly to draw the line on this continuous scale between a consistent and an inconsistent democracy. The opinions differ: Epstein *et al.* (2006) arbitrarily count only polities that score +8 and higher as consistent democracies, while Lee (2005) bases his decision to count only polities that score +9 and +10 as 'full' democracies on sensitivity analysis of various options, but what this sensitivity analysis entails is left unspecified. To avoid the element of arbitrariness, I treat only polities with a Polity2 score of +10 as consistent democracies, that is, regimes that have all the attributes of democracy as specified in Marshall and Jaggers (2002) and Diamond (1999). I discuss these attributes in more detail in Chapter 4.

10. The POLITY IV regime durability measure simply counts the years that a regime has been in place.

11. The Pearson two-tailed correlation between the indicator of an inconsistent regime and the POLITY IV regime durability measure is –0.36 (significant at the 1 per cent level), while the same correlation between our income inequality measure and regime durability is –0.35 (again significant at the 1 per cent level). $N = 2721$.

12. See Chapter 5 for discussion of concepts, data, and methodology used to determine this likelihood.

13. Ordinary least squares regression with robust standard errors. Data on violent civil conflict are derived from the Uppsala/PRIO dataset on the *onset of domestic armed conflict*, defined as a contested incompatibility involving armed force and concerning regime and/or territory between at least two parties, of which one is the occupier of the state apparatus and which leads to the loss of at least 25 lives in the current year of conflict (Gleditsch *et al.*, 2002). The onset of at least one incidence of domestic armed conflict per year or the absence of such an onset is recorded as a dichotomous variable. The Uppsala/PRIO dataset focuses only on politically motivated armed conflict, and also records a new onset only after two years of 'inactivity' have passed. To control for the potential effect of regime type, we use the 21 value Polity2 combined regime indicator from the POLITY IV dataset (Marshall and Jaggers, 2002). The unit of analysis is the country-year

($N = 2876$). Coefficient for violent civil conflict is statistically significant at the 1 per cent level.

14. Ordinary least squares regression with robust standard errors. Not restricted by the availability of income inequality data, this result is based on country-year data that we have for 187 countries, covering the period 1950–2000. I use five-year averages of the Penn World Tables measure of growth in per capita GDP, weighted for purchasing power, as calculated by Urdal (2006) from Heston, Summers and Aten (2003). Coefficient for violent civil conflict is statistically significant at the 1 per cent level.

15. The Pearson two-tailed correlation between a measure estimating public sector effectiveness and the indicator of an inconsistent regime is –0.56, and between the same measure of public sector effectiveness and our income inequality measure is –0.62. The estimates of government effectiveness are from Kaufmann *et al.* (2004), but are only available for a limited period of time, beginning in the 1990s. $N = 120$.

16. Data on estimates of state capacity to control corruption during the 1980s from Easterly and Levine (1997), and for 1990s from Kaufmann *et al.* (2004). The relevant Pearson two-tailed correlations are –0.44 in the case of the Easterly and Levine data ($N = 931$), and –0.6 in the case of the 1990s data from Kaufmann *et al.* ($N = 241$). Both correlations are highly significant at the 1 per cent level.

17. Pearson two-tailed correlation between inconsistent regime type and revenue generated (as per cent of GDP) is –0.4, significant at the 1 per cent level ($N = 2349$). Revenue data from *World Development Indicators*, 2006 CD-ROM.

18. Figures on central government expenditure as percentage of GDP from *World Development Indicators, 2006* CD-ROM. Estimations, from 1970 onwards, on the size of government consumption for selected states are available in the Fraser Institute publication, *Economic Freedom in the World, 2004* (Gwartney and Lawson, 2004).

3   The evolution of economic inequality in the periphery, 1500–1999

1. See Engerman and Sokoloff (1997, 2000, 2002, 2005) and De Ferranti *et al.* (2004).

2. See Williamson, 2006: Chapter 5 for a discussion also of the 'supply-side' domestic problems associated with this process of deindustrialization in India.

3. See Chapter 1 for a discussion of the features and relative merits of this dataset.

4. Composition of the regions is listed in Table 3.4; p. 79.

5. Note that the group of countries classified as Latin America in Table 3.1 does not include the Caribbean countries, which are included here as part of the LAC region. Caribbean countries tend to have lower inequality levels than the Latin American countries and their inclusion in the LAC

region thus lowers the mean inequality figure for this group. Taken on their own, without the Caribbean included, the Latin American countries have the highest mean inequality of all regions over the period under review, though.

6. SEASIA's share of mean 'world' inequality (that is, the mean for our 147 sample states) continued to decline in the 1980s and 1990s. The moderate increase in the second half of the 1990s probably does not fully capture the worsening of inequality experienced by SEASIA developing countries subsequent to the financial crisis of 1997, though. There are only a few countries in the Oceania region for which we have data, and generalizations concerning this region should be approached with care.

7. For a careful and comprehensive review of the available evidence concerning the effects of economic openness on poverty and inequality in developing countries, see Goldberg and Pavenik (2007).

8. As we shall see in Chapter 4, the targeting of education spending in particular is a crucial factor in explaining why educational opportunities remain concentrated in many developing societies even though they have undergone democratic transitions, which are supposed to make government more receptive to the needs of the general population.

9. These experiments in democratization were often accompanied by high levels of political instability and civil conflict. In some cases, the instability produced by the regime changes spilled over into the eruption of violent civil conflict (Schatzman, 2005). The most immediate effect of these forms of political instability was to worsen the economic vulnerability of the poorer sectors of the population and their earning potential, with the rural areas in Africa particularly hit hard (Mkandawire, 2002).

4 Democratization to the rescue?

1. See, amongst others, Acemoglu and Robinson (2006: 63–65), Lindert (2004: *passim*), Boix (2003: 171–203), and Ziblatt (2006: 311–338).

2. See Doorenspleet (2000) for an analysis of this phase of global democratization.

3. One exception is the quasi-experimental study by Chan (1997). Chan looks at the effect of democratization in Taiwan, South Korea, and Singapore on public policies that have redistributive effects. His results for Taiwan and South Korea indicate that public spending on education and social security did increase after the introduction of democracy. However, apart from being limited to three case studies, Chan's study also has two other shortcomings: first, it focuses on public expenditure *per se* and not on the distributive effects that public spending has on various income groups. Second, his study is not based on an explicit theory that sets out the causal mechanism through which democratization can lead to redistribution.

4. This chapter thus can also be seen as a study of the conditions under which democratization can enable the 'rabble to redistribute', to paraphrase

Putterman (1997). Some of the arguments used here are also developed in Nel (2005a and 2007).

5. See Reich (2002), Lee (2005), Merkel (2005), Epstein *et al.* (2006), and Gates *et al.* (2006). See also the discussion in Chapter 2.

6. See Marshall and Jaggers (2002), O'Donnell (1996, 1999), and Diamond (1999).

7. Based on Diamond (1999) and Marshall and Jaggers (2002).

8. As explained in Chapter 2, this inconsistency can be operationalized as any score between +1 and +9 inclusive on the Polity2 combined regime score (Marshall and Jaggers, 2002).

9. This heading is a play on the title of Putterman's well-known chapter (1997).

10. For students of comparative politics, the MVH also explains why it is not easy to democratize a highly unequal society in which wealth is not mobile. Regime choice and redistributive struggles go together, as Boix (2003) reminds us. See also Burkhart (1997: 148).

11. For contemporary discussions, applications, and tests of the MVH see Alesina and Rodrik (1994), Alesina and Perotti (1996), Persson and Tabellini (1994), Evans (2004), Mueller (2003), Congleton (2002), Borck (2003), Milanovic (2000), and De Mello and Tiongson (2003).

12. The discussion here is based on the very useful summary of the MVH that can be found in an unpublished paper by John Roemer (2001).

13. See Chapter 2.

14. See Lipset (1959) for an initial statement of the association between democracy and education. Acemoglu *et al.* (2005) have challenged the view that higher average levels of education lead to democracy. However, there is general agreement that within democracies, the more educated a citizen the more he/she is likely to become involved in electoral politics.

15. It was pointed out in Chapter 1 that the differences between income and expenditure measures of household income can be a confounding factor. Not in this case, though, as we are not comparing countries, but are rather looking at what happens within countries over time. The important thing is to make sure that all the data for a specific country comes from surveys that use the same measure and same methodology. The 'Global Poverty Monitoring Database' has been incorporated into the World Bank POVCAL Network, available at http://iresearch.worldbank.org/PovcalNet/jsp/index.jsp. For more information on the methodology used by the GPM, see Chen and Ravallion (2000).

16. The countries are Algeria, Bangladesh, Brazil, Chile, PRC, Colombia, Costa Rica, Cote d'Ivoire, Dominican Republic, Ecuador, Egypt, El Salvador, Ethiopia, Ghana, Guatemala, Honduras, India, Indonesia, Jamaica, Jordan, Lesotho, Madagascar, Mauritania, Mexico, Morocco, Nepal, Pakistan, Paraguay, Peru, Philippines, Sri Lanka, Thailand, Tunisia, Turkey, Uganda, and Zambia.

17. For extensive and very useful overviews of the reasons why the median voter may not necessarily prefer a tax rate of unity, or may not be able to

secure it even if she prefers it, see Shapiro (2003: Chapter 5), Putterman (1997), Borck (2003), Lee (2003), and Roemer (1998).

18. In many developing countries, this ideological hegemony was institutionalized in the 1980s and 1990s in the form of structural adjustment programmes promoted by the international financial institutions. Although these programmes did not reduce government spending *in toto*, certain sectors with distributive potential did suffer significantly: Education, infrastructure and agriculture in Africa; agriculture and health in Asia; education and infrastructure in Latin America (Fan and Rao, 2003).

19. See Weyland (1996) for a detailed analysis of the institutional supply-side problems that prevented Brazil to marry democratization and redistribution in the post-authoritarian era to 1994.

20. RPC is calculated using this regression equation: Tax/GDP = ß0 + ß1 (time) + ß2 (Mining/GDP) + ß3 (Agriculture/GDP) + ß4 (Exports/GDP) + error term (Feng, Kugler, and Zak, 2000).

21. Stasavage (2005) relates how African states increased education spending in the 1990s, while De Ferranti *et al.*, present evidence that social spending on average increased by almost 50 per cent between 1990 and 1991 and 1998 and 1999 in 17 Latin American countries (2004: 259).

22. As discussed earlier in this chapter, the 'relative political capacity' measure of the ratio between revenue raised and potential revenue can also be used to capture elements of state capacity (Feng, Kugler, and Zak, 2000), but as the relevant data are relatively scarce, the introduction of this measure would reduce the sample size drastically. Data on revenue raised by states are from the World Bank's *World Development Indicators* 2006 CD-ROM. Although there is a positive correlation between level of GDP per capita and the relative size of the revenue that a state can generate, the latter depends on institutional features that are not fully captured by the former alone.

5 The consequences of inequality

1. It is striking how close Hobbes' description of the state of nature reflects the breakdown of commerce, politics, and culture in many high-inequality societies of our day:

> Whatsoever therefore is consequent to a time of Warre, where every man is Enemy to every man; the same is consequent to the time, wherein men live without other security, than what their own strength, and their own invention shall furnish them with all. In such condition, there is no place for Industry; because the fruit thereof is uncertain; and consequently no Culture of the Earth; no Navigation, nor use of the commodities that may be imported by Sea; no commodious Building; no Instruments of moving, and removing such things as require much force; no Knowledge of the face of the Earth; no account

of Time; no Arts; no Letters; no Society; and which is worst of all, continuall feare, and danger of violent death; And the life of man, solitary, poore, nasty, brutish, and short. (Hobbes, 1651/2003: 102)

2. Bueno De Mesquita *et al.* (2003) develop a Hobbes index composed of similar dimensions of human-development focused upon in this chapter, but they conceptualize and measure the dimension differently.
3. See the special edition of the journal *Review of Income and Wealth*, Series 51, No. 2, 2005, devoted to the question of measuring well-being. See also Alkire (2002) and Dasgupta (2001).
4. Bourdieu and Wacquant, 1986: 119, cited in Sabatini, 2005: 159–160.
5. See the UK Department for International Development policy paper *Reducing Poverty by Tackling Social Exclusion* (DFID, 2005), and Chapter 2 of the 2006 World Bank *World Development Report* (World Bank, 2005).
6. See Nissanke and Thorbecke (2006: 1342–1344).
7. Cited in Narayan *et al.* (2000: 58).
8. These and comparable findings for other parts of the developing world are reported in World Bank's *Equity and Development: World Development Report* (2005: 89–91).
9. The dependent variable is the Gini coefficient of educational opportunities, as in Figure 5.1. The regression coefficient for income inequality is positive and has statistical significance at the 1 per cent level. Education spending as percentage of GDP is from the World Bank (2006) *World Development Indicators* (CD-ROM). Data on political discrimination is the 'Poldis' measure from the 'Minorities at Risk' dataset, available at http://www.cidcm.umd.edu/mar/data.asp. The 'quality of institutions' measure is the ratio of non-currency money to the total money supply, or $(M_2 - C)/M_2$. M_2 is a broad measure of money supply and C is currency held outside banks. See Clague *et al.* (1999) for a justification of using this 'contract-intensive-money' measure as an indicator of the trust that people have in the institutions upheld by state power.
10. See Gradstein and Justman (2002).
11. Panel data random-effects regression model as above (Endnote 9), except that education spending is replaced by mean school years achieved by cohort 15 years and older, from Barro and Lee (2000). Voter participation rates and potential voter data (= voting age population) from the International Institute for Democracy and Electoral Assistance (IDEA), available at http://www.idea.int/vt/index.cfm.
12. See Tilly (2002) for a discussion of the various forms that violent behaviour in 'contentious politics' can take.
13. See Collier *et al.* (2002).
14. Sample consisted of 45 states for intentional homicides, and 34 states for other violent crime.
15. This discussion of violent civil conflict summarizes insights that are developed in Nel and Righarts (2008) and Nel (2006a).

16. See also Gurr (1980: 2).
17. PRIO = Peace Research Institute Oslo. For discussions and evaluations of this dataset, see Gleditsch *et al.* (2002), Harbom and Wallensteen (2005), and Urdal (2006).
18. The major shortcoming that the Uppsala/PRIO dataset shares with other cross-country violent civil conflict datasets is the absence of conflict information on the sub-national level, on the date and duration (in days/months) of conflicts, and on the exact number of conflict deaths (Miguel *et al.*, 2004). The Uppsala/PRIO dataset also does not make provision, in the time period that we are looking at, for cross-border contagion of violent civil conflict. These shortcomings set limits to the exactness of the following empirical analyses. Despite these shortcomings, this dataset is preferred because of its clarity of conception and consistency, and because of its lower conflict threshold.
19. See Nel and Righats (2008).
20. I use their Relogit software to generate the corrected estimations. Available at http://gking.harvard.edu/stats.shtml.
21. This literature is well-surveyed in Zimmermann (1980), and Lichbach (1989).
22. The concept of 'opportunity' stems from the work of Tilly and others (Gamson, 1975; Oberschall, 1973; Tilly, 1978).
23. For example, it is suggested that resource-rich countries in the developing world tend to have more violent and more protracted extreme political conflicts than do resource-poor countries. See Collier and Hoeffler (2004), but also Fearon (2005) for a critical perspective. Rebels and other political opponents of the reigning elite may resort to extra-constitutional and violent means if (a) other avenues of gaining a stake in the riches of a country are systematically blocked (through a winner-takes-all political regime, for instance), and (b) if the political opponents calculate that their material gain will offset whatever personal or communal sacrifices they have to make in the process. A preponderance of exploitable resources could also affect the actor's strategic calculations of the relative availability of the means to pursue and sustain violent dissent.
24. Hegre *et al.* (2001) and Urdal (2006) assume that the effect of a previous conflict declines geometrically at a rate which halves the risk of conflict every three years. The 'Brevity of Peace' variable has a value of one while a political unit is experiencing a conflict, and a value of close to one immediately after a unit-conflict has ceased. Over time, the value decreases to close to zero, provided there is no onset of a new armed civil conflict.
25. While there continues to be difference of opinion about the factors that determine this stable positive relationship, and about the direction of the casual arrows, the available evidence confirms Seymour Martin Lipset's breakthrough contribution of 1959 that first linked the institutionalization of democracy and economic development statistically. See especially Epstein *et al.* (2006) for a recent confirmation of this 'modernization thesis'.

26. See Przeworski *et al.* (2000: 98) for detail on methodology and data.
27. The World Bank's 'Voices of the Poor' report underlines the multidimensionality of the experiences of ill-being that poor people themselves associate with being poor. See Narayan *et al.* (2000: 21–43).
28. For other praises of the merits of infant (and child) mortality as an indicator of the lack of human development, see Sen (1998), Urdal (2006), and Gerring (2007).
29. Urdal (2006) uses the UN's *World Population Prospects* (1999) and the UN's annual *Demographic Yearbook* to compile infant mortality rate data for the period 1950 to 2000, covering more than 200 states and territories.
30. See Aghion and Garcia-Penalosa (1999), Thorbecke and Charumilind (2002), and Nissanke and Thorbecke (2005) for reviews of this literature.
31. Forbes relies, as do many inequality researchers, on the data compiled from World Bank sources by Deininger and Squire (1996, 1998). As we saw in Chapter 1, there are many remaining problems with these data. More than half of Forbes' *N* consists of observations from OECD countries, and there are no observations from African states at all in her study.
32. This finding is robust also to using the alternative inequality dataset used by Pagano (2004), although the inverted U-curve is less pronounced.
33. See also Nissanke and Thorbecke (2006) for an overview discussion of the various causal mechanisms that link high inequality with lower economic growth.
34. See the collection of papers published in the UNU-WIDER volume edited by Anthony Shorrocks and Rolph van der Hoeven (2004).
35. Which is what economists mean when they speak about the elasticity of infant mortality (here = poverty) with respect to growth. This elasticity is calculated by dividing the percentage rate of change in infant mortality by the percentage rate of economic growth.

Bibliography

Acemoglu, D. and J. A. Robinson (2000) 'Why Did the West Extend the Franchise? Democracy, Inequality and Growth in Historical Perspective', *Quarterly Journal of Economics* 115(4): 1167–99.

Acemoglu, D. and J. A. Robinson (2006) *Economic Origins of Dictatorship and Democracy*, Cambridge: Cambridge University Press.

Acemoglu, D., S. Johnson, J. Robinson, and P. Yared (2005) 'From Education to Democracy?' *American Economic Association Papers and Proceedings* 95: 44–9.

Addison, T. and G. A. Cornia (2001) 'Income Distribution Policies for Faster Poverty Reduction', *UNU-WIDER Discussion Paper* No. 2001/93.

Aghion, P. E. C. and C. Garcia-Penalosa (1999) 'Inequality and Economic Growth: The Perspective of the New Growth Theories', *Journal of Economic Literature* 37(4): 1615–60.

Alderson, A. S. and F. Nielsen (1999) 'Income Inequality, Development, and Dependence: A Reconsideration', *American Sociological Review* 64(4): 606–28.

Alesina, A. and R. Perotti (1996) 'Income Distribution, Political Instability and Investment', *European Economic Review* 81(5): 1170–89.

Alesina, A. and D. Rodrik (1994) 'Distributive Politics and Economic Growth', *Quarterly Journal of Economics* 109(2): 465–90.

Alkire, S. (2002) 'Dimensions of Human Development', *World Development* 30(2): 181–205.

Anand, S. and R. Kanbur (1993) 'The Kuznets Process and the Inequality-Development Relationship', *Journal of Development Economics* 40(1): 25–52.

Anderson, E. (2005) 'Openness and Inequality in Developing Countries: A Review of Theory and Recent Evidence', *World Development* 33(7): 1045–63.

Aristotle (1974) *The Politics*, translated and introduced by T. A. Sinclair, Penguin Books, Harmondsworth.

Arneson, R. J. (1990) 'Primary Goods Reconsidered', *Nous* 24(3): 429–54.

Atkinson, A. B. (1983) *The Economics of Inequality*, Oxford: Clarendon Press.

Atkinson, A. B. (1999) 'Equity Issues in a Globalizing World: The Experience of OECD Countries', in V. Tanzi, K.-Y. Chu, and S. Gupta (eds) *Economic Policy and Equity*, Washington, DC: International Monetary Fund.

Atkinson, A. B. (2004) 'Increased Income Inequality in OECD Countries and the Redistributive Impact of the Government Budget', in G. A. Cornia (ed.) *Inequality, Growth, and Poverty in an Era of Liberalization and Globalization*, Oxford: Oxford University Press: 220–48.

Atkinson, A. B. and F. Bourguignon (eds) (2000) *Handbook of Income Distribution, Vol. 1*, Amsterdam: Elsevier.

Atkinson, A. B. and A. Brandolini (2001) 'Promise and Pitfalls in the Use of Secondary Data-sets; Income Inequality in OECD Countries as a Case Study', *Journal of Economic Literature* 39(3): 771–99.

Atkinson, A. B. and T. Piketty (eds) (2006) *Top Incomes over the Twentieth Century*, Oxford: Oxford University Press.

Azam, J.-P. (2001) 'The Redistributive State and Conflicts in Africa', *Journal of Peace Research* 38(4): 429–44.

Bairoch, P. (1995) *Economics and World History: Myths and Paradoxes*, Chicago: University of Chicago Press.

Banerjee, A. and E. Duflo (2000) 'Inequality and Growth: What Can the Data Say?' *NBER Working Paper Series* No. 7793, Cambridge, MA: National Bureau of Economic Research.

Banerjee, A. V. and E. Duflo (2003) 'Inequality and Growth: What Can the Data Say?' *Journal of Economic Growth* 8(3): 267–99.

Banerjee, A. V. and E. Duflo (2007) 'The Economic Lives of the Poor', *Journal of Economic Perspectives* 21(1): 141–67.

Barro, R. (1991) 'Economic Growth in a Cross Section of Countries', *Quarterly Journal of Economics* 106: 407–44.

Barro, R. (1996) 'Democracy and Growth', *Journal of Economic Growth* 1(1): 1–27.

Barro, R. (2000) 'Inequality and Growth in a Panel of Countries', *Journal of Economic Growth* 5(1): 5–32.

Barro, R. and J.-W. Lee (2000) 'International Data on Educational Attainment: Updates and Implications', *CID Working Paper* No. 42, April 2000.

Barry, B. (1998) 'International Society From a Cosmopolitan Perspective', in D. Mapel and T. Nardin (eds) *International Society: Diverse Ethical Perspectives*, Princeton: University Press: 144–63.

Barry, B. (2002) 'Social Exclusion, Social Isolation, and the Distribution of Income', in J. Hills, J. Le Grand, and D. Piachaud (eds) *Understanding Social Exclusion*, Oxford: Oxford University Press: 13–29.

Barry, B. (2005) *Why Social Justice Matters*, Cambridge: Polity Press.

Bassett, W. F., J. P. Burkett, and L. Putterman (1999) 'Income Distribution, Government Transfers, and the Problem of Unequal Influence', *European Journal of Political Economy* 15: 207–28.

Basu, P. and A. Guarigli (2004) 'FDI, Inequality and Growth', *Working Paper in Economics and Finance* No. 04/01, School of Economics, Finance and Business, University of Durham.

Bearse, P., G. Glomm, and E. Janeba (2000) 'Why Poor Countries Rely Mostly on Redistribution In-kind', *Journal of Public Economics* 75: 463–81.

Beck, T., A. Clarke, A. Groff, P. Keefer, and P. Walsh (2001) 'New Tools in Comparative Political Economy: The Database of Political Institutions', *World Bank Economic Review* 15(1): 165–76. Database and documentation available at: http://www.worldbank.org/research/bios/keefer/DPI2000_documentation_changes.doc

Becker, G. S. and K. M. Murphy (2005) 'The Equilibrium Distribution of Income and The Market for Status', *Journal of Political Economy* 113(2): 282–310.

Beer, L. (1999) 'Income Inequality and Transnational Corporate Penetration', *Journal of World-Systems Research* 5(1): 1–25.

Beer, L. and T. Boswell (2002) 'The Resilience of Dependency Effects in Explaining Income Inequality in the Global Economy: A Cross-National Analysis, 1975–1995', *Journal of World Systems Research* VIII(1): 30–59.

Benabou, R. (1996) 'Inequality and Growth', *Discussion Paper* 1450, London: Centre for Economic Policy Research.

Benabou, R. (2000) 'Unequal Societies: Income Distribution and the Social Contract', *American Economic Review* 90(1): 96–129.

Benhabib, J. and A. Przeworski (2003) 'The Political Economy of Redistribution Under Democracy', unpublished paper, available at, http://www.econ.nyu.edu/user/benhabib/dg98.PDF.

Bergesen, A. J. and M. Bata (2002) 'Global and National Inequality: Are They Connected?' *Journal of Word-Systems Research* 8(1): 130–44.

Besançon, M. L. (2005) 'Relative Resources: Inequality in Ethnic Wars, Revolutions, and Genocides', *Journal of Peace Research* 42(4): 393–415.

Birdsall, N. (1998) 'Life is Unfair: Inequality in the World', *Foreign Policy* 112: 76–83.

Birdsall, N. (2001) 'Why Inequality Matters: Some Economic Issues', *Ethics and International Affairs* 15(2): 3–28.

Birdsall, N. and J. Londono (1997) 'Asset Inequality Matters: An Assessment of the World Bank's Approach to Poverty Reduction', *The American Economic Review* 87(2): 32–7.

Blecher, M. (2005) 'Inequality and Capitalism in China', unpublished report prepared for the American Political Science Association Task Force Conference on Inequality and Difference in Developing Societies, available at: http://www.apsanet.org/content_13916.cfm

Blyth, M. (2002) *Great Transformations: Economic Ideas and Institutional Change in the 20th Century*, New York: Cambridge University Press.

Boix, C. (2003) *Democracy and Redistribution*, Cambridge: Cambridge University Press.

Boix, C. (2004) *Political Violence*, Paper prepared for the Yale Conference on Order, Conflict and Violence.

Bollen, K. A. and R. W. Jackman (1985) 'Political Democracy and the Size Distribution of Income', *American Sociological Review* 50: 438–57.

Borck, R. (2003) 'Voting, Inequality, and Redistribution', DIW Working Paper, available at: http://www.polecon.de/Redistribution.pdf

Bornschier, V. and C. Chase-Dunn (1985) *Transnational Corporations and Underdevelopment*, New York: Praeger.

Bourdieu, P and L. Wacquant (1986) *An Invitation to Reflective Sociology*, Cambridge: Polity Press.

Bourguignon, F. (1999) 'Crime, Violence and Inequitable Development', Paper delivered at Annual World Bank Conference on Development Economics, Washington, DC, April: 28–30.

Bourguignon, F. (2000) 'Can Redistribution Accelerate Growth and Development?' Unpublished paper prepared for the Annual Bank Conference on Development Economics/Europe, Paris 26–28 June 2000. Available at: http://www.worldbank.org/research/abcde/eu_2000/papers_eu2.html

Bourguignon, F. (2004) 'The Poverty-Growth-Inequality Triangle', Paper presented at the Indian Council for Research on International Economic

Relations, available at http://siteresources.worldbank.org/DEC/Resources/84797-1104785060319/598886-1104852366603/33634_PovertyInequality GrowthTriangleFeb24_ICRIER.pdf

Bourguignon, F. and S. Chakravarty (2003) 'The Measurement of Multidimensional Poverty', *Journal of Economic Inequality* 1: 25–49.

Bourguignon, F. and C. Morrisson (2002) 'Inequality Among World Citizens: 1820–1992', *The American Economic Review* 92(4): 727–44.

Bourguignon, F. and T. Verdier (2005) 'The Political Economy of Education and Development in an Open Economy', *Review of International Economics* 13(3): 529–48.

Bowles, S. (2000) 'Globalization and Redistribution: Feasible Egalitarianism in a Competitive World', *Working Paper* No. 34, Political Economy Research Institute, University of Massachusetts at Amherst. Available at http://www.umass.edu/peri/pdfs/WP34.pdf

Bowles, S. (2006) 'Egalitarian Redistribution in Globally Integrated Economies', in P. Bardhan, S. Bowles, and M. Wallerstein (eds) *Globalization and Egalitarian Redistribution*, Princeton NJ: Princeton University Press: 120–47.

Bradshaw, Y., R. Noonan, L. Gash, and C. Buchmann Sershen (1993) 'Borrowing Against the Future: Children and Third World Indebtedness', *Social Forces* 71: 629–56.

Bratton, M. and N. van de Walle (1997) *Democratic Experiments in Africa: Regime Transitions in Comparative Perspective*, Cambridge: Cambridge University Press.

Bruno, M., M. Ravallion, and L. Squire (1998) 'Equity and Growth in Developing Countries: Old and New Perspectives on the Policy Issues', in V. Tanzi and K.-Y. Chu (eds) *Income Distribution and High-quality Growth*, Cambridge MA: MIT Press: 117–46.

Bueno De Mesquita, B., A. Smith, R. M. Siverson, and J. D. Morrow (2003) *The Logic of Political Survival*, Cambridge, MA: MIT Press.

Burchardt, T., J. Le Grand, and D. Piachaud (2002) 'Introduction', in J. Hills, J. Le Grand, and D. Piachaud (eds) *Understanding Social Exclusion*, Oxford: Oxford University Press: 1–12.

Burkhart, R. E. (1997) 'Comparative Democracy and Income Distribution: Shape and Direction of the Causal Arrow', *Journal of Politics* 59(1): 149–64.

Byrne, D. (2005) *Social Exclusion* (2nd edition), Maidenhead: Open University Press.

Campano, F. and D. Salvatore (2006) *Income Distribution*, Oxford: Oxford University Press.

Campante, F. R., D. Chor, and Q.-A. Do (2005) 'Instability and the Incentives for Corruption', *CID Working Paper* No. 6.

Castro-Leal, F., J. Dayton, L. Demery, and K. Mehra (1999) 'Public Social Spending in Africa: Do the Poor Benefit?' *The World Bank Research Observer* 14(1): 49–72.

Chakravorty, S. (2006) *Fragments of Inequality: Social, Spatial, and Evolutionary Analyses of Income Distribution*, London: Routledge.

Champernowne, D. and F. Cowell (1998) *Economic Inequality and Income Distribution*, Cambridge: Cambridge University Press.

Chan, S. (1997) 'Democracy and Inequality: Tracking Welfare Spending in Singapore, Taiwan, and South Korea', in M. Midlarsky (ed.) *Inequality, Democracy, and Economic Development*, Cambridge: Cambridge University Press: 227–43.

Checci, D. (2004) 'Does Educational Achievement Help Explain Income Inequality?' in G.A. Cornia (eds) *Inequality, Growth, and Poverty in an Era of Liberalization and Globalization*, Oxford: Oxford University Press: 81–111.

Chen, S. and M. Ravallion (2000) 'How Did The World's Poorest Fare In the 1990s?' *World Bank Policy Research Working Paper* No. 2409, August, available at: http://www.worldbank.org/research/povmonitor/method.htm

Chu, K.-Y., H. Davoodi, and S. Gupta (2004) 'Income Distribution, Tax, and Government Social Spending Policies in Developing Countries', in G. A. Cornia (ed.) *Inequality, Growth, and Poverty in an Era of Liberalization and Globalization*, Oxford: Oxford University Press: 249–70.

Clague, C., P. Keefer, S. Knack, and M. Olson (1996) 'Property and Contract Rights in Autocracies and Democracies', *Journal of Economic Growth* 1: 243–76.

Clague, C., P. Keefer, S. Knack, and M. Olson (1999) 'Contract-Intensive Money: Contract Enforcement, Property Rights, and Economic Performance', *Journal of Economic Growth* 4(2): 185–211.

Clingingsmith, D. and J. G. Williamson (2005) 'Mughal Decline, Climate Change, and Britain's Industrial Ascent: An Integrated Perspective on India's 18th and 19th Century Deindustrialization', *NBER Working Paper* No. 11730, available at http://www.economics.harvard.edu/faculty/jwilliam/papers/w11730.pdf

Collier, P. and J. Gunning (1999) 'Why Has Africa Grown So Slowly?' *Journal of Economic Perspectives* 13(3): 3–22.

Collier, P. and A. Hoeffler (2004) 'Greed and Grievance in Civil War', *Oxford Economic Papers* 56: 563–95.

Collier, P. and A. Hoeffler (2005) 'Resource Rents, Governance, and Conflict', *Journal of Conflict Resolution* 49(4): 625–33.

Collier, P., L. Elliott, H. Hegre, A. Hoeffler, M. Reynal-Querol, and N. Sambanis (2002) *Breaking the Conflict Trap: Civil War and Development Policy*, New York: World Bank and Oxford University Press, available at: http://econ.world bank.org/prr/CivilWarPRR/text-26671/

Congleton, R. (2002) 'The Median–Voter Model', Contribution prepared for the *Encyclopedia of Public Choice*. Available at http://rdc1.net/forthcoming/medianvt.pdf

Conteh-Morgan, E. (2004) *Collective Political Violence: An Introduction to the Theories and Cases of Violent Conflicts*, London: Routledge.

Cornia, G. (ed.) (2004) *Inequality, Growth, and Poverty in an Era of Liberalization and Globalization*, Oxford: Oxford University Press.

Cornia, G. A. (2004) 'Inequality, Growth, and Poverty: An Overview of Changes Over the Last Two Decades', in G. A. Cornia (ed.) *Inequality, Growth, and Poverty in an Era of Liberalization and Globalization*, Oxford: Oxford University Press: 3–25.

Cornia, G. A. and J. Court (2001) 'Inequality, Growth and Poverty in the Era of Liberalization and Globalization', Policy Brief 4, Helsinki: United Nations University – World Institute for Development Economics Research. Available at: http://www.wider.unu.edu/publications/policy-biref.htm

Cornia, G. A., T. Addison, and S. Kiiski (2004) 'Income Distribution Changes and Their Impact In the Post-Second World War Period', in G. A. Cornia (ed.) *Inequality, Growth, and Poverty in an Era of Liberalization and Globalization*, Oxford: Oxford University Press: 26–54.

Dagdeviren, H., R. van der Hoeven, and J. Weeks (2004) 'Redistribution Does Matter: Growth and Redistribution for Poverty Reduction', in A. Shorocks and R. van der Hoeven (eds) *Growth, Inequality, and Poverty: Prospects for Pro-Poor Economic Development*, Oxford: Oxford University Press: 125–53.

Dahl, R. (1971) *Polyarchy: Participation and Opposition*, New Haven: Yale University Press.

Dasgupta, P. (2001) *Human Well-Being and the Natural Environment*, Oxford: Oxford University Press.

De Ferranti, D. *et al.* (2004) *Inequality in Latin America and the Caribbean: Breaking with History?* Washington, DC: World Bank Latin American and Caribbean Studies, The World Bank.

De Mello, L. and E. R. Tiongson (2003) 'Income Inequality and Redistributive Government Spending', *IMF Working Paper* WP/03/14. Available at: http://www. imf.org/external/pubs/ft/wp/2003/wp0314.pdf

Deininger, K. and L. Squire (1996) 'Measuring Income Inequality: A New Data Base', *World Bank Economic Review* 10(3): 565–91.

Deininger, K. and L. Squire (1998) 'New Ways of Looking at Old Issues: Inequality and Growth', *Journal of Development Economics* 57: 259–87.

DFID (Department for International Development, UK) (2005) *Reducing Poverty by Tackling Social Exclusion*, London: DFID Policy Paper.

Diamond, L. (1999) *Developing Democracy: Towards Consolidation*, Baltimore: Johns Hopkins Press.

Diamond, L., J. Linz, and S. M. Lipset (1989) *Democracy in Developing Countries: Asia, Africa, and Latin America*, Boulder Co: Lynne Rienner Publishers.

Dollar, D. and A. Kraay (2002a) 'Growth is Good for the Poor', *Journal of Economic Growth* 7: 195–225.

Dollar, D. and A. Kraay (2002b) 'Spreading the Wealth', *Foreign Affairs*, January–February: 120–33.

Doorenspleet, R. (2000) 'Reassessing the Three Waves of Democratization', *World Politics* 52: 384–406.

Downs, A. (1957) *An Economic Theory of Democracy*, New York: Harper and Row.

Easterly, W. (1997) 'Life During Growth', *Journal of Economic Growth* 4(3): 239–75.

Easterly, W. (2002) 'Inequality *Does* Cause Underdevelopment: New Evidence', *Center for Global Development Working Paper* No. 1, June. Available at: http://www.cgdev.org/wp/cgd_wp001_rev.pdf

Easterly, W. and R. Levine (1997) 'Africa's Growth Tragedy: Policies and Ethnic Divisions', *Quarterly Journal of Economics* 112(4): 1203–50.

Eastwood, R. and M. Lipton (2000) 'Rural-urban Dimensions of Inequality Change', World Institute for Development Economics Research, *Working Paper* No. 2003.

Eckstein, H. (1980) 'Theoretical Approaches to Explaining Collective Political Violence', in T. Gurr (ed.) *Handbook of Political Conflict: Theory and Research*, New York: The Free Press: 135–66.

Engerman, S. and K. Sokoloff (1997) 'Factor Endowments, Institutions, and Differential Paths of Growth Among New World Economies', in S. Haber (ed.) *How Latin America Fell Behind*, Stanford, CA: Stanford University Press.

Engerman, S. and K. Sokoloff (2000) 'Institutions, Factor Endowments, and Paths of Development in the New World', *Journal of Economic Perspectives* 3: 217–32.

Engerman, S. and K. Sokoloff (2002) 'Factor Endowments, Inequality, and Paths of Development Among New World Economies', *Economia* 3: 41–109.

Engerman, S. and K. Sokoloff (2005) 'Colonialism, Inequality, and Long-run Paths of Development', *NBER Working Paper* 11057, January.

Epstein, D. L., R. Bates, J. Goldstone, I. Kristensen, and S. O'Halloran (2006) 'Democratic Transitions', *American Journal of Political Science* 50: 551–69.

Estevadeordal, A., B. Frantz, and A. Taylor (2002) 'The Rise and Fall of World Trade, 1870–1939', *NBER Working Paper* No. 9318, available at: http://www.nber.org/papers/w9318

Evans, J. A. J. (2004) *Voters & Voting: An Introduction*, London: Sage.

Everingham, C. (2003) *Social Justice and the Politics of Community*, Aldershot: Ashgate.

Fajnzylber, P., D. Lederman, and N. Loayza (2002) 'What Causes Violent Crime?' *European Economic Review* 46: 1323–57.

Fan, S. and N. Rao (2003) 'Public Spending in Developing Countries: Trends, Determination, and Impact', *Environment and Production Technology Division Discussion Paper* No. 99, International Food Policy Research Institute, Washington, DC, available at: http://www.ifpri.org/divs/eptd/dp/papers/eptdp99.pdf

Fearon, J. D. (2005) 'Primary Commodity Exports and Civil War', *The Journal of Conflict Resolution* 49(4): 483–507.

Feng, Y., Y. Kugler, and P. J. Zak (2000) 'The Politics of Fertility and Economic Development', *International Studies Quarterly* 44(1): 667–93.

Fields, G. S. (2001) *Distribution and Development: A New Look at the Developing World*, Cambridge, MA: MIT Press.

Fischer, S. (2003) 'Globalization and its Challenges', *American Economic Review* 93(2): 1–30.

Forbes, K. (2000) 'A Reassessment of The Relationship Between Inequality and Growth', *The American Economic Review* 90(4): 869–87.

Forst, R. (2007) 'Radical Justice: On Iris Marion Young's Critique of the "Distributive Paradigm" ', *Constellations* 14(2): 260–65.

Frieden, J. A. (2006) *Global Capitalism: Its Fall and Rise in the Twentieth Century*, New York: W.W. Norton.

Frieden, J. A. and R. Rogowski (1996) 'The Impact of the International Political Economy on National Policies: An Analytical Overview', in R. Keohane and H. Milner (eds) *Internationalization and Domestic Politics*, New York: Cambridge University Press: 25–47.

Friedman, J. (ed.) (2003) *Globalization, the State, and Violence*, New York: Altamira Press.

Galbraith, J. K. (2002) 'A Perfect Crime: Inequality In The Age of Globalization', *Daedalus* Winter: 11–25.

Galbraith, J. K. and H. Kum (2005) 'Estimating the Inequality of Household Income: A Statistical Approach to the Creation of A Dense And Consistent Data Set', *Review of Income and Wealth* 51(1): 115–43.

Galor, O. (2000) 'Income Distribution and the Process of Development', *European Economic Review* 44: 706–12.

Galor, O. and J. Zeira (1993) 'Income Distribution and Macroeconomics', *Review of Economic Studies* 60: 35–52.

Gamson, W. A. (1975) *The Strategy of Social Protest*, Homewood, IL: Dorsey.

Garrett, G. (2000) 'The Causes of Globalization', *Comparative Political Studies* 33: 941–91.

Gasiorowski, M. (1995) 'Economic Crisis and Political Regime Change: An Event History Analysis', *American Political Science Review* 89(4): 882–97.

Gates, S., H. Hegre, M. P. Jones, and H. Strand (2006) 'Institutional Inconsistency and Political Instability: Polity Duration, 1800–2000', *American Journal of Political Science* 50(4): 893–908.

Gerring, J. (2007) 'Global Justice as an Empirical Question', *PS: Political Science and Politics* 40(1): 67–77.

Gissinger, R. and N. P. Gleditsch (1999) 'Globalization and Conflict: Welfare, Distribution, and Political Unrest', *Journal of World-Systems Research* 5(2): 327–65.

Glaeser, E. (2005) 'Inequality' in B. R. Weingast and D. A. Wittman (eds) *The Oxford Handbook of Political Economy*, Oxford: Oxford University Press: 625–41.

Glaeser, E., J. Scheinkman, and A. Shleifer (2003) 'The Injustice of Inequality', *Journal of Monetary Economics* 50: 199–222.

Gleditsch, N. P., P. Wallensteen, M. Eriksson, M. Sollenberg, and H. Strand (2002) 'Armed Conflict 1946–2001: A New Dataset', *Journal of Peace Research* 39: 615–37.

Goldberg, P. K. and N. Pavenik (2007) 'Distributional Effects of Globalization in Developing Countries', *Journal of Economic Literature* 65(1): 39–82.

Gradstein, M. and M. Justman (2002) 'Education, Social Cohesion, and Economic Growth', *American Economic Review* 92(4): 1192–204.

Gradstein, M., B. Milanovic, and Y. Ying (2001) 'Democracy and Income Inequality: An Empirical Analysis', *World Bank Research Department*. Available at: http://www.worldbank.org/research/inequality/inequalityandpolitics/dem,ineq.pdf

Gramsci, A. (1971) *Selections from the Prison Notebooks*, London: Lawrence and Wishart.

Gugerty, M. K. and C. P. Timmer (1999) 'Growth, Inequality, and Poverty Alleviation: Implications for Development Assistance', *Consulting Assistance on Economic Reform II Discussion Paper* No. 50, Harvard Institute for International Development, December. Available at: http://www.cid.harvard.edu/caer2/htm/content/papers/confpubs/paper50/paper50.pdf

Gupta, D. (1990) *The Economics of Political Violence: The Effect of Political Instability on Economic Growth*, New York: Praeger.

Gurr, T. R. (1970) *Why Men Rebel*, Princeton: Princeton University Press.

Gurr, T. R. (1980) 'Introduction', in T. Gurr (ed.) *Handbook of Political Conflict: Theory and Research*, New York: The Free Press: 1–18.

Gwartney, J. and R. Lawson (2004) *Economic Freedom of the World: 2004 Annual Report*, Vancouver: The Fraser Institute. Data retrieved from http://www.freetheworld.com

Gylfason, T. (2001) 'Natural Resources, Education, and Economic Development', *European Economic Review* 45(4–6): 847–59.

Haggard, S. (1990) *Pathways from the Periphery: The Politics of Growth in the Newly Industrializing Countries*, Ithaca, NY: Cornell University Press.

Haggard, S. and R. Kaufman (eds) (1992) *The Politics of Economic Adjustment: International Constraints, Distributive Conflicts and the State*, Princeton: Princeton University Press.

Harberger, A. C. (1998) 'Monetary and Fiscal Policy for Equitable Economic Growth', in V. Tanzi and K.-Y. Chu (eds) *Income Distribution and High Quality Growth*, Cambridge, MA: MIT Press.

Harbom, L. and P. Wallensteen (2005) 'Armed Conflict and its International Dimensions', 1946–2004. *Journal of Peace Research* 42(5): 623–625.

Hegre, H. and N. Sambanis (2006) 'Sensitivity Analysis of Empirical Results on Civil War Onset', *Journal of Conflict Resolution* 50: 508–35.

Hegre, H., T. Ellingen, S. Gates, and N. P. Gleditsch (2001) 'Toward a Democratic Civil Peace? Democracy, Political Change, and Civil War, 1816–1992', *American Political Science Review* 95(1): 33–48.

Hegre, H., R. Gissinger, and N. P. Gleditsch (2003) 'Globalization and Internal Conflict', in G. Schneider, K. Barbieri, and N. P. Gleditsch (eds) *Globalization and Armed Conflict*, New York: Rowman & Littlefield: 251–76.

Held, D. and A. Kaya (eds) (2007) *Global Inequality*, Cambridge, MA: Polity Press.

Held, D., A. McGrew, D. Goldblatt, and J. Perraton (1999) *Global Transformations*, Stanford, CA: Stanford University Press.

Hellman, J., G. Jones, and D. Kaufmann (2003) 'Seize the State, Seize the Day: State Capture and Influence in Transition Economies', *Journal of Comparative Economies* 31: 751–73.

Heston, A., R. Summers, and B. Aten (2003) 'Penn World Table Version 6.1', Center for International Comparisons at the University of Pennsylvania

(CICUP). Available at: http://datacentre2.cass.utoronto.ca/pwt/docs/pwt61. html

Hobbes, T. (1651/2003) *Leviathan, or the Matter, Forme, & Power of a Commonwealth Ecclesiastical and Civil*, critical edition by G. A. J. Rogers and K. Schuhmann, London: Continuum International Publishing.

Huber, E., J. Pribble, F. Nielsen, and J. D. Stevens (2006) 'Politics and Inequality in Latin America and the Caribbean', *American Sociological Review* 71: 943–63.

Humphreys, M. (2003) 'Economics and Violent Conflict', available at: http://www.preventconflict.org/portal/economics

Huntington, S. P. (1968) *Political Order in Changing Societies*, New Haven: Yale University Press.

IDEA (2004) 'Voter Turnout from 1945 to Date', International Institute for Democracy and Electoral Assistance, accessed on 19 Feb 2004 you did not mention the date beforehand. available at: http://www.idea.int/vt/country_view.cfm

International Fund for Agricultural Development (IFAD) (2001) *Rural Poverty Report 2001: The Challenge of Ending Rural Poverty*, available at: http://www.ifad.org/poverty/

Jong-sung, Y. and S. Khagram (2005) 'A Comparative Study of Inequality and Corruption', *American Sociological Review* 70(1): 136–57.

Jordan, B. (2003) 'Welfare and Social Exclusion', in R. Bellamy and A. Mason (eds) *Political Concepts*, Manchester: Manchester University Press: 77–92.

Justino, P., J. Litchfield, and L. Whitehead (2003) 'The Impact of Inequality in Latin America', *Poverty Research Unit at Sussex Working Paper* No. 21, available at: http://www.sussex.ac.uk/Users/PRU

Kanbur, R. (2000) 'Income Distribution and Development', in A. Atkinson and F. Bourguignon (eds) *Handbook on Income Distribution*, Amsterdam: Elsevier: 791–841.

Kanbur, S. M. (1979) 'Of Risk Taking and the Personal Distribution of Income', *Journal of Political Economy* 87(4): 769–97.

Kannyo, E. (2004) 'A New Opening?' *Journal of Democracy* 15(2): 125–39.

Kaufman, R. and B. Stallings (1994) 'The Political Economy of Latin American Populism', in R. Dornbusch and S. Edwards (eds) *The Macroeconomics of Populism in Latin America*, Chicago: University of Chicago Press: 15–43.

Kaufmann, D., A. Kraay, and M. Mastruzzi (2004) 'Governance Matters III: Governance Indicators for 1996–2002', *World Bank Policy Research Working Paper* No. 3106, available at: http://www.worldbank.org/wbi/governance/pubs/govmatters3.html

Kentor, J. (2001) 'The Long-term Effects of Globalization on Income Inequality, Population Growth, and Economic Development', *Social Problems* 48(4): 435–55.

King, G. and L. Zeng (2001) 'Explaining Rare Events in International Relations', *International Organization* 55(3): 693–715.

Knack, S. (2004) 'Does Foreign Aid Promote Democracy?' *International Studies Quarterly* 48(1): 251–66.

Knowles, S. (2005) 'Inequality and Economic Growth: The Empirical Relationship Reconsidered in the Light of Comparable Data', *Journal of Development Studies* 41: 135–59.

Kremer, M. and S. Jayachandran (2003) 'Odious Debt: When Dictators Borrow, Who Repays the Loan?' *The Brookings Review* 21(2): 32–5.

Kuznets, S. (1955) 'Economic Growth and Income Inequality', *American Economic Review* 45: 1–48.

Kuznets, S. (1963) 'Quantitative Aspects of the Economic Growth of Nations: VIII. Distribution of Income by Size', *Economic Development & Cultural Change* 11(2): 1–80.

Landa, D. and E. Kapstein (2001) 'Inequality, Growth, and Democracy' (Review Article), *World Politics* 53: 264–96.

Lane, J. and S. Ersson (2003) *Democracy: A Comparative Approach*, London: Routledge.

Lee, C.-S. (2005) 'Income Inequality, Democracy, and Public Sector Size', *American Sociological Review* 70(1): 158–81.

Lee, W. (2003) 'Is Democracy More Expropriative than Dictatorship? Tocquevillian Wisdom Revisited', *Journal of Development Economics* 71: 155–98.

Lee, W. and J. E. Roemer (1998) 'Income Distribution, Redistributive Politics, and Economic Growth', *Journal of Economic Growth* 3(3): 217–40.

Li, H. and H.-F. Zou (1998) 'Income Inequality is Not Harmful for Growth: Theory and Evidence', *Review of Development Economics* 2: 318–34.

Lichbach, M. I. (1989) 'An Evaluation of "Does Economic Inequality Breed Political Conflict" Studies', *World Politics* 41(4): 431–70.

Lindert, P. H. (2000) 'Three Centuries of Inequality in Britain and America', in A. Atkinson and F. Bourguignon (eds) *Handbook of Income Distribution, Vol. 1*, Amsterdam: Elsevier: 167–216.

Lindert, P. H. (2004) *Growing Public: Social Spending and Economic Growth Since The Eighteenth Century, Vol. 1*, Cambridge, MA: Cambridge University Press.

Lindert, P. H. and J. G. Williamson (2003) 'Does Globalization Make the World More Unequal?' in M. Bordo, A. Taylor, and J. Williamson (eds) *Globalization in Historical Perspective*, Chicago: University of Chicago Press: 227–76.

Lipset, S. M. (1959) 'Some Social Requisites of Democracy: Economic Development and Political Legitimacy', *American Political Science Review* 53: 69–105.

Liu, Z. (2005) 'Institution and Inequality: The *Hukou* System in China', *Journal of Comparative Economics* 33: 133–57.

Ljungqvist, L. (1993) 'Economic Underdevelopment: The Case of a Missing Market for Human Capital', *Journal of Development Economics* 40: 219–39.

Lundberg, M. and L. Squire (2003) 'The Simultaneous Evolution of Growth and Inequality', *The Economic Journal* 113(87): 326–44.

Mack, R. W. and R. C. Snyder (1957) 'The Analysis of Social Conflict: Towards an Overview and Synthesis', *Journal of Conflict Resolution* 1: 212–48.

Maddison, A. (2003) *The World Economy: Historical Statistics*, Paris: Development Centre Studies, OECD.

Maddison, A. (2005) 'Measuring and Interpreting World Economic Performance 1500–2001', *Review of Income and Wealth* 51(1): 1–35.

Marshall, M. G. and K. Jaggers (2002) *Polity IV Project: Political Regime Characteristics and Transitions, 1800–2002*, University of Maryland, Centre for International Development and Conflict Management. <http://www.bsos. umd.edu/ cidcm/inscr/polity> (2004 June 12).

Mauro, P. (1995) 'Corruption and Growth', *Quarterly Journal of Economics* 110: 681–712.

McGillivray, M. (2005) 'Measuring Non-economic Well-Being Achievement', *Review of Income and Wealth* 51(2): 337–64.

McGillivray, M. and A. Shorrocks (2005) 'Inequality and Multidimensional Well-Being', *Review of Income and Wealth* 51(2): 193–99.

Meltzer, A. H. and S. F. Richard (1981) 'A Rational Theory of the Size of Government', *The Journal of Political Economy* 89(5): 914–27.

Merkel, W. (2005) 'Embedded and Defective Democracies', *Democratization* 11(5): 33–58.

Miguel, E., S. Satyanath, and E. Sergenti (2004) 'Economic shocks and civil conflict: an instrumental variables approach', *Journal of Political Economy* 112(4): 725–753.

Milanovic, B. (2000) 'The Median-voter Hypothesis, Income Inequality, and Income Redistribution: An Empirical Test with the Required Data', *European Journal of Political Economy* 16: 367–410.

Milanovic, B. (2002) 'Can We Discern the Effect of Globalisation on Income Distribution? Evidence from Household Budget Surveys', *World Bank Policy Research Working Paper* 2876.

Milanovic, B. (2005) *Worlds Apart: Measuring International and Global Inequality*, Princeton: Princeton University Press.

Milanovic, B. (2007) 'Globalization and Inequality', in D. Held and A. Kaya (eds) *Global Inequality*, Cambridge: Polity Press.

Mill, J. S. (1848/1909) *Principles of Political Economy with Some of Their Applications to Social Philosophy*, London: Longmans, Green and Co., edited by William J. Ashley, 1909, Seventh edition.

Mkandawire, T. (2002) 'The Terrible Toll of Post-colonial Rebel Movements in Africa: Towards and Explanation of Violence against the Peasantry', *Journal of Modern African Studies* 40(2): 181–215.

Mueller, D. C. (2003) *Public Choice III*, Cambridge, MA: Cambridge University Press.

Muller, E. N. (1980) 'The Psychology of Political Protest and Violence', in T. Gurr (ed.) *Handbook of Political Conflict: Theory and Research*, New York: The Free Press: 69–99.

Muller, E. N. (1985) 'Income Inequality, Regime Repressiveness, and Political Violence', *American Sociological Review* 50(1): 47–61.

Muller, E. N. (1988) 'Democracy, Economic Development, and Income Inequality', *American Sociological Review* 53: 50–68.

Munro, J. F. (1976) *Africa and the International Economy 1800–1960*, London: J.M. Dent & Sons.

Murphy, C. (1994) *International Organization and Industrial Change: Global Governance Since 1850*, Oxford: Oxford University Press.

Nafziger, E. W. (1988) *Inequality in Africa: Political Elites, Proletariat, Peasants and the Poor*, Cambridge, MA: Cambridge University Press.

Nagel, J. (1974) 'Inequality and Discontent: A Nonlinear Hypothesis', *World Politics* 26(4): 453–72.

Nagel, T. (1977) 'Poverty and Food: Why Charity is Not Enough', in P. Brown and H. Shue (eds) *Food Policy: The Responsibility of the United States in Life and Death Choices*, New York: Free Press.

Narayan, D., R. Chambers, K. S. Meera, and P. Petesch (2000) *Voices of the Poor: Crying out for Change*, New York: Oxford University Press.

Naschold, F. (2002) 'Why Inequality Matters for Poverty', *Inequality Briefing Paper* No. 2, UK Department for International Development, March.

Nel, P. (2003) 'Income Inequality, Economic Growth, and Political Instability in Sub-Saharan Africa', *Journal of Modern African Studies* 41(4): 611–39.

Nel, P. (2005a) 'Democratisation and the Dynamics of Income Distribution in Low and Middle-income Countries', *Politikon* 32(1): 17–43.

Nel, P. (2005b) 'Global Inequality Revisited: A Review Article', *Global Society* 19(3): 317–27.

Nel, P. (2006a) 'Globalization and Violent Political Dissent in Developing Countries', in R. G. Patman (ed.) *Globalization and Conflict: National Security in a 'New' Strategic Era*, London: Routledge: 56–76.

Nel, P. (2006b) 'The Return of Inequality', *Third World Quarterly*, 27(4): 689–706.

Nel, P. (2007) 'When can the Rabble Redistribute? Democratization and Income Distribution in Low and Middle-Income Countries', in R. Garside (ed.) *Institutions and Market Economies: The Political Economy of Growth and Development*, Basingstoke: Palgrave Macmillan, 222–49.

Nel, P. and M. Righarts (2008) 'Natural Disasters and the Risk of Violent Civil Conflict', *International Studies Quarterly*, 52(2): 159–184.

Nelson, P. (1999) 'Redistribution and the Income of the Median Voter', *Public Choice* 98: 187–94.

Neumayer, E. (2005) 'Inequality and Violent Crime: Evidence from Data on Robbery and Violent Theft', *Journal of Peace Research* 42(1): 101–12.

Nissanke, M. and E. Thorbecke (2005) 'The Impact of Globalization on the World's Poor: Transmission Mechanisms', Paper prepared for the WIDER Jubilee Conference in Helsinki, June 17–8, 2005.

Nissanke, M. and E. Thorbecke (2006) 'Channels and Policy Debate in the Globalization-Inequality-Poverty Nexus', *World Development* 34(8): 1338–60.

Nooruddin, I. and J. W. Simmons (2006) 'The Politics of Hard Choices: IMF Programs and Government Spending', *International Organization* 60: 1001–33.

Nussbaum, M. (2000) *Women and Human Development: The Capabilities Approach*, Cambridge, MA: Cambridge University Press.

Oberschall, A. (1973) *Social Conflict and Social Movements*, Englewood Cliffs, NJ: Prentice-Hall.

O'Brien, P. (2006) 'The Global Economic History of European Expansion Overseas', in V. Bulmer-Thomas, J. Coatsworth, and R. Cortes Conde (eds) *The Cambridge Economic History of Latin America Vol. 1*, Cambridge: Cambridge University Press: 7–42.

O'Donnell, G. (1996) 'Illusions about Consolidation', *Journal of Democracy* 7(2): 34–51.

O'Donnell, G. (1999) 'Polyarchies and the (Un)Rule of Law in Latin America', in J. Mendez, G. O'Donnell, and P. S. Pinheiro (eds) *The Rule of Law and the Underprivileged in Latin America*, Notre Dame: University of Notre Dame Press: 303–38.

Okun, A. M. (1975) *Equality and Efficiency: The Big Trade-Off*, Washington, DC: The Brookings Institution.

Olson, M. (1965) *The Logic of Collective Action*, Cambridge, MA: Harvard University Press.

O'Rourke, K and J. Williamson (1999) *Globalization and History: The Evolution of a Nineteenth-Century Atlantic Economy*, Cambridge, MA: The MIT Press.

Osberg, L. (1995) 'The Equity/Efficiency Trade-off in Retrospect', *Canadian Business Economics* 3(3): 5–20.

Osberg, L. and A. Sharpe (2005) 'How Should We Measure the "Economic" Aspects of Well-Being?' *Review of Income and Wealth* 51(2): 311–36.

Østby, G. (2003) *Horizontal Inequalities and Civil War: Do Ethnic Group Inequalities Influence the Risk of Domestic Armed Conflict?*, Canadian Political Thesis in Political Science, Centre for the Study of Civil War, International Peace Research Institute, Oslo (PRIO).

Pagano, P. (2004) 'An Empirical Investigation of the Relationship Between Inequality and Growth' *(Economic Working Papers)* 536, Bank of Italy, Economic Research Department, available at: http://www.bancaditalia.it/ricerca/consultazioni/temidi/td04/td536_04/td536/tema_536.pdf

Perotti, R. (1996) 'Growth, Income Distribution, and Democracy: What the Data Say', *Journal of Economic Growth* 1(2): 149–88.

Persson, T. and G. Tabellini (1994) 'Is Inequality Harmful for Growth?' *American Economic Review* 84(3): 600–21.

Petersen, T. (2004) 'Analyzing Panel Data: Fixed- and Random-effects Models', in M. Hardy and A. Bryman (eds) *Handbook of Data Analysis*, London: Sage: 331–45.

Phillips, A. (1999) *Which Inequalities Matter?*, Cambridge, MA: Cambridge University Press.

Piketty, T. and E. Saez (2006) 'The Evolution of Top Incomes: A Historical and International Perspective', *Working Paper* 11955, National Bureau of Economic Research, available at: http://www.nber.org/papers/w11955

Pogge, T. (2001) 'Priorities of Global Justice', *Metaphilosophy* 32(1 and 2), January: 6–24.

Pogge, T. (2002) *World Poverty and Human Rights: Cosmopolitan Responsibilities and Reforms*, Cambridge, MA: Polity Press.

Pogge, T. (2007) 'Why Inequality Matters', in D. Held and A. Kaya (eds) *Global Inequality*, Cambridge: Polity Press; 132–47.

Polanyi, K. (1945) *Origins of Our Time: The Great Transformation*, London: Gollanz.

Prados de la Escosura, L. (2006) 'The Economic Consequences of Independence', in V. Bulmer-Thomas, J. Coatsworth, and R. Cortes Conde (eds) *The Cambridge Economic History of Latin America Vol. 1*, Cambridge, MA: Cambridge University Press: 463–504.

Pritchett, L. (1997) 'Divergence, Big Time', *Journal of Economic Perspectives* 11: 3–17.

Przeworski, A. (1991) *Democracy and the Market: Political and Economic Reforms in Eastern Europe and Latin America*, Cambridge, MA: Cambridge University Press.

Przeworski, A., M. Alvarez, J. Cheibub, and F. Limongi (2000) *Democracy and Development: Political Institutions and Well-Being in the World, 1950–1990*, Cambridge, MA: Cambridge University Press.

Putterman, L. (1997) 'Why Have the Rabble not Redistributed the Wealth? On the Stability of Democracy and Unequal Property', in J. E. Roemer (ed.) *Property Relations, Incentives, and Welfare*, London: Macmillan: 359–89.

Quah, D. (2001) 'Some Simple Arithmetic on How Income Inequality and Economic Growth Matters', Unpublished paper from the LSE Economics Department, available at: http://econ.lse.ac.uk/~dquah/

Ranis, G., F. Stewart, and E. Samman (2006) 'Human Development: Beyond the Human Development Index', *Journal of Human Development* 7(3): 323–58.

Ravallion, M. (2001) 'Growth, Inequality and Poverty: Looking beyond Averages', *World Development* 29: 1803–15.

Ravallion, M. and S. Chen (1997) 'What Can New Survey Data Tell Us About Recent Changes in Distribution and Poverty?' *World Bank Economic Review* 11: 357–82.

Ravallion, M. and S. Chen (2003) 'Measuring Pro-Poor Growth', *Economics Letters* 78: 93–9.

Rawls, J. (1971) *A Theory of Justice*, Oxford: Oxford University Press.

Rawls, J. (1982) 'Social Unity and Primary Goods', in A. Sen and B. Williams (eds) *Utilitarianism and Beyond*, Cambridge, MA: Cambridge University Press: 159–86.

Rawls, J. (1999) *The Law of Peoples*, Cambridge, MA: Harvard University Press.

Ray, D. (1998) *Development Economics*, Princeton, NJ: Princeton University Press.

Reich, G. (2002) 'Categorizing Political Regimes: New Data for Old Problems', *Democratization* 19(4): 1–24.

Renner, K. L. (1985) 'Exclusionary Democracy', *Studies in Comparative International Development* 20(6): 64–85.

Reuveny, R. and Q. Li (2003) 'Economic Openness, Democracy and Income Inequality: An Empirical Analysis', *Comparative Political Studies* 36(5): 575–601.

Robbins, D. (1996) 'HOS Hits Facts: Facts Win; Evidence on Trade and Wages in the Developing Countries', Development Discussion Paper 557, Harvard Institute for International Development, Cambridge, MA.

Robinson, W. (1996) *Promoting Polyarchy: Globalization, US Intervention ad Hegemony*, Cambridge, MA: Cambridge University Press.

Rodrik, D. (1997) *Has Globalization Gone Too Far?* Washington, DC: Institute for International Economics.

Rodrik, D. (1999) *The New Global Economy and Developing Countries: Making Openness Work*, Washington DC: Overseas Development Council and the Johns Hopkins Press.

Roemer, J. E. (1998) 'Why the Poor do not Expropriate the Rich: An Old Argument in New Garb', *Journal of Public Economics* 70: 399–424.

Roemer, J. E. (2001) 'Democracy, Educational Finance, and the Distribution of Human Capital: A Dynamic Analysis', Unpublished paper, available at: http://mora.rente.nhh.no/projects/EqualityExchange/Portals/0/articles/roemer3.pdf.

Roemer, J. E. (2003) 'Defending Equality of Opportunity', *The Monist* 86(April): 261–82.

Ross, M. (2006) 'Is Democracy Good for the Poor?' *American Journal of Political Science*, 50(4): 860–74.

Rothstein, B. and E. Uslaner (2005) 'All for All: Equality, Corruption, and Social Trust', *World Politics* 50: 41–72.

Rudra, N. (2002a) 'Globalization and the Decline of the Welfare State in Less-developed Countries', *International Organization* 56(2): 411–45.

Rudra, N. (2002b) 'Openness, Welfare Spending, and Inequality in the Developing World', Paper delivered at the Conference on Globalisation, Growth and Inequality, Centre for the Study of Globalisation and Regionalisation, Warwick University.

Rudra, N. (2005) 'Globalization and the Strengthening of Democracy in the Developing World', *American Journal of Political Science* 49(4): 704–30.

Rudra, N. and S. Haggard (2005) 'Globalization, Democracy, and Effective Welfare Spending in the Developing World', *Comparative Political Studies* 38(9): 1015–49.

Rueschemeyer, D., E. H. Stephens, and J. D. Stephens (1992) *Capitalist Development and Democracy*, Chicago: University of Chicago Press.

Ruggie, J. G. (1983) 'Introduction: International Interdependence and National Welfare', in J. G. Ruggie (ed.) *The Antinomies of Interdependence: National Welfare and the Division of Labour*, New York: Columbia University Press: 1–42.

Sabatini, F. (2005) 'The Empirics of Social Capital and Economic Development: A Critical Perspective', *Munich Personal RePEc Archive Paper* No. 2366, available at: http://mpra.ub.uni-muenchen.de/2366

Sachs, J. and A. Warner (2001) 'The Curse of Natural Resources', *European Economic Review* 45(4–6): 827–38.

Sambanis, N. (2004) 'What is Civil War?' *Journal of Conflict Resolution* 48(6): 818–58.

Sanders, D. (1981) *Patterns of Political Instability*, New York: St Martin's Press.

Schatzman, C. (2005) 'Political Challenge in Latin America: Rebellion and Collective Protest in an Era of Democratization', *Journal of Peace Research* 42(3): 291–310.

Schneider, M. (2004) *The Distribution of Wealth*, Cheltenham: Edward Elgar.

Sen, A. (1992) *Inequality Re-examined*, Oxford: Oxford University Press.

Sen, A. (1997) 'From Income Inequality to Economic Inequality', *Southern Economic Journal* 64(2): 384–401.

Sen, A. (1998) 'Mortality as an Indicator of Economic Success and Failure', *Economic Journal* 108(446): 1–25.

Sen, A. (2000a) *Development as Freedom*, New York: Anchor Books.

Sen, A. (200b) 'Social Exclusion: Concept, Application, and Scrutiny', *Social Development Papers* No. 1, Asian Development Bank.

Shafter, J. (2007) 'The Due Diligence Model: A New Approach to the Problem of Odious Debts', *Ethics and International Affairs* 21(1): 49–67.

Shambaugh, G. (2004) 'The Power of Money: Global Capital and Policy Choices in Developing Countries', *American Journal of Political Science* 48(2): 281–95.

Shapiro, I. (2003) *The State of Democratic Theory*, Princeton: Princeton University Press.

Shorrocks, A. and R. van der Hoeven (eds) (2004) *Growth, Inequality, and Poverty: Prospects for Pro-Poor Economic Development*, UNU-WIDER Studies in Development Economics, Oxford: Oxford University Press.

Sigelman, L. and M. Simpson (1977) 'A Cross-national Test of the Linkage Between Economic Inequality and Political Violence', *Journal of Conflict Resolution* 21(1): 105–28.

Simpson, M. (1990) 'Political Rights and Income Inequality: A Cross-national Test', *American Sociological Review* 55: 682–93.

Smith A. (1776/1976) *An Inquiry into the Nature and Causes of the Wealth of Nations*, republished, edited by R. H. Campbell and A. S. Skinner, Oxford: Clarendon Press.

Solimano, A. (ed.) (1998) *Social Inequality: Values, Growth, and the State*, Ann Arbor: University of Michigan Press.

Solimano, A., E. Aninat, and N. Birdsall (eds) (2000) *Distributive Justice and Economic Development: The Case of Chile and Developing Countries*, Ann Arbor: University of Michigan Press.

Spilimbergo, A., J. L. Londono, and M. Szekely (1999) 'Income Distribution, Factor Endowments, and Trade Openness', *Journal of Development Economics* 59: 77–101.

Stallings, B. (1992) 'International Influence on Economic Policy: Debt, Stabilization, and Structural Reform', in S. Haggard and R. Kaufman (eds) *The Politics of Economic Adjustment: International Constraints, Distributive Conflicts and the State*, Princeton: Princeton University Press: 41–88.

Stanley, D. (2003) 'What Do We Know About Social Cohesion: The Research Perspective of the Federal Government's Social Cohesion Research Network', *Canadian Journal of Sociology* 28(1): 5–17.

Stasavage, D. (2005) 'Democracy and Education Spending in Africa', *American Journal of Political Science* 29(2): 343–58.

Stewart, F. (2005) 'Horizontal Inequalities: A Neglected Dimension of Development', in A. Atkinson *et al. WIDER Perspectives on Global Development*, New York: Palgrave Macmillan: 101–35.

Stolper, W. and P. Samuelson (1941) 'Protection and Real Wages', *Review of Economic Studies* 9: 58–73.

Sutcliffe, B. (2004) 'World Inequality and Globalization', *Oxford Review of Economic Policy* 20(1): 15–37.

Sutcliffe, B. (2007) 'The Unequalled and Unequal Twentieth Century', in D. Held and A. Kaya (eds) *Global Inequality*, Cambridge, MA: Polity Press: 50–72.

Tachibanaki, T. (2005) *Confronting Income Inequality in Japan: A Comparative Analysis of Causes, Consequences, and Reform*, Cambridge, MA: MIT Press.

Taylor, A. (1996) 'International Capital Mobility in History: The Savings-Investment Relationship', *NBER Working Paper* No. 5743, available at: http://www.nber.org/papers/w5743

Taylor, I. (2001) *Stuck in Middle Gear: South Africa's Post-Apartheid Foreign Relations*, Westport, CT: Praeger publishers.

Taylor, L. (2004) 'External Liberalization, Economic Performance, and Distribution in Latin America and Elsewhere', in G. Cornia (ed.) *Inequality, Growth, and Poverty in an Era of Liberalization and Globalization*, Oxford: Oxford University Press: 166–96.

Temple, J. R. W. and P. A. Johnson (1998) 'Social Capability and Economic Growth', *Quarterly Journal of Economics* 113: 965–90.

Terreblanche, S. (2002) *A History of Inequality in South Africa, 1652–2002*, Pietermaritzburg: University of Natal Press.

Thomas, V. *et al.* (2000) *The Quality of Growth*, New York: The Word Bank and Oxford University Press.

Thomas, V., Y. Wang, and X. Fan (2003) 'Measuring Education Inequality: Gini Coefficients of Education for 140 Countries, 1960–2000', *Journal of Education, Planning and Administration* 17(1): 5–33.

Thorbecke, E. and C. Charumilind (2002) 'Economic Inequality and Its Socioeconomic Impact', *World Development* 30(9): 1477–95.

Tilly, C. (1978) *From Mobilization to Revolution*, Reading, MA: Addison-Wesley.

Tilly, C. (2002) 'Violent and Nonviolent Trajectories in Contentious Politics', in K. Worcester, S. A. Bermanzohn, and M. Ungar (eds) *Violence and Politics: Globalization's Paradox*, London: Routledge: 13–31.

Toset, H., N. Gleditsch, and H. Hegre (2000) 'Shared Rivers and Interstate Conflict', *Political Geography* 19(8): 971–996.

Tsai, P.-L. (1995) 'Foreign Direct Investment and Income Inequality: Further Evidence', *World Development* 23: 469–83.

UNCTAD (1994) *World Investment Report*, United Nations, Geneva.

UNCTAD (1996) *World Investment Report*, United Nations, Geneva.

UNCTAD (2002) 'FDI Inflows As Percentage of GDP', available at: <http://stats.unctad.org/fdi/eng/TableViewer/wdsview>

UNCTAD (2004) 'Global FDI Flows Continue to Fall: UNCTAD Now Forecasts 2004 Rebound', UNCTAD/PRESS/PR/2003/85.

UNDP (1999) *Human Development Report 1999*, New York: Oxford University Press.

Urdal, H. (2006) 'A Clash of Generations? Youth Bulges and Political Violence', *International Studies Quarterly* 50: 607–29.

Van Rossem, R. (1996) 'The World-system Paradigm as a General Theory of Development: A Cross-national Test', *American Sociological Review* 61(3): 508–27.

Wade, R. H. (1990) *Governing the Market: Economic Theory and the Role of Government in East-Asian Industrialization*, Princeton, NJ: Princeton University Press.

Wade, R. H. (2004) 'Is Globalization Reducing Poverty and Inequality?' *World Development*, 32(4): 567–89.

Wade, R. H. (2005a) 'Failing States and Cumulative Causation in the World System', *International Political Science Review* 26(1): 17–36.

Wade, R. H. (2005b) 'Global Inequalities: What Is All the Fuss About?' *For American Political Science Association Task Force on Inequalities*, Charlottesville: University of Virginia.

Wade, R. H. (2007) 'Should We Worry about Income Inequality?' in D. Held and A. Kaya (eds) *Global Inequality*, Cambridge: Polity Press: 104–31.

Wallerstein, I. (1979) *The Capitalist World-Economy*, Cambridge: Cambridge University Press.

Walzer, M. (1983) *Spheres of Justice: A Defense of Pluralism and Equality*, New York: Basic Books.

Wendt, A. (1999) *Social Theory of International Politics*, Cambridge: Cambridge University Press.

Weyland, K. (1996) *Democracy without Equity: Failures of Reform in Brazil*, Pittsburgh: University of Pittsburgh Press.

Williamson, J. G. (1997) 'Globalization and Inequality: Past and Present', *World Bank Research Observer* 12: 117–35.

Williamson, J. G. (1998) 'Real Wages and Relative Factor Prices in the Third World before 1940: What Do They Tell Us About The Sources of Growth?' Unpublished paper, available at: http://www.economics.harvard.edu/faculty/ jwilliam/papers.html

Williamson, J. G. (2002) 'Land, Labour, and Globalization in the Third World, 1870–1940', *Journal of Economic History* 62: 55–85.

Williamson, J. G. (2006) *Globalization and the Poor Periphery before 1950*, Cambridge, MA: MIT Press.

Wintrobe, R. (1998) *The Political Economy of Dictatorship*, New York: Cambridge University Press.

Wood, A. (1997) 'Openness and Wage Inequality in Developing Countries: The Latin American Challenge to East Asian Conventional Wisdom', *World Bank Economic Review* 11: 33–57.

World Bank (2001) *Attacking Poverty – World Development Report 2000–2001*, Washington, DC: The World Bank.

World Bank (2004) 'Global Poverty Monitoring Database', accessed on 22 January 2004. Available at: http://www.worldbank.org/research/povmonitor/

World Bank (2005) *Equity and Development: World Development Report 2006*, New York: The World Bank and Oxford University Press.

World Bank (2006) *World Development Indicators, CD-Rom*. Washington, DC: World Bank.

You, J.-S. and S. Khagram (2005) 'A Comparative Study of Inequality and Corruption', *American Sociological Review* 70(1): 136–57.

Young, I. M. (1990) *Justice and the Politics of Difference*, Princeton: Princeton University Press.

Young, I. M. (2006) 'Taking the Basic Structure Seriously', *Perspectives on Politics*, 4(1): 91–7.

Young, C. M. and T. Turner (1988) *The Rise and Decline of the Zairian State*, Madison: University of Wisconsin Press.

Ziblatt, D. (2006) 'Review Article: How Did Europe Democratize?' *World Politics* 58(2): 311–38.

Zimmermann, E. (1980) *Political Violence, Crises, and Revolutions*, Cambridge: Schenkman.

Index

In this index tables; figures; appendices and notes are indicated in italics, enclosed in parenthesis, following the page number. E.g. income, ratio of, 56(*tab.3.1*)

Notes are indicated by *n*. Tables by *tab*. Figures by *fig*. Appendices by *app*.